Piano • Vocal • Guitar

W9-AAD-759

Karaoke FAVORITES

ISBN 978-1-4584-1876-0

HAL•LEONARD®
CORPORATION
7777 W. BLUEMOUND RD. P.O. BOX 13819 MILWAUKEE, WI 53213

Visit Hal Leonard Online at
www.halleonard.com

APOLOGIZE

Words and Music by
RYAN TEDDER

Moderately slow

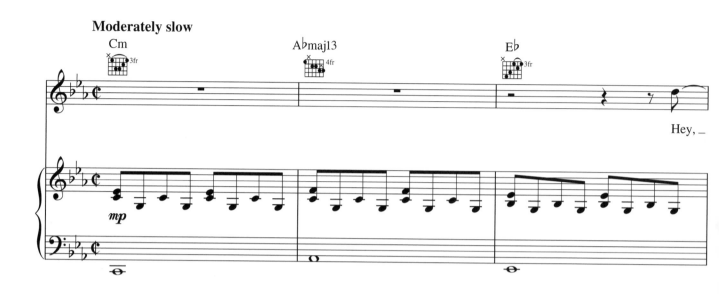

Hey, —

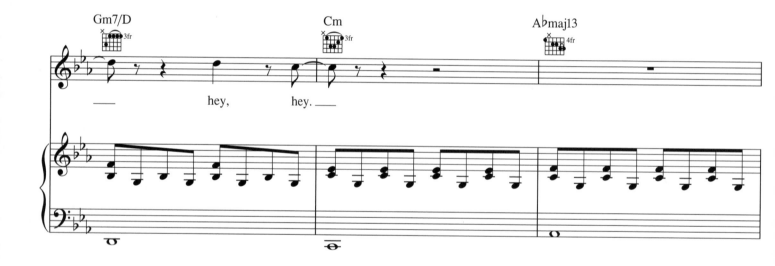

— hey, hey. — Hey, — hey, I'm hold-in' on your rope, got me

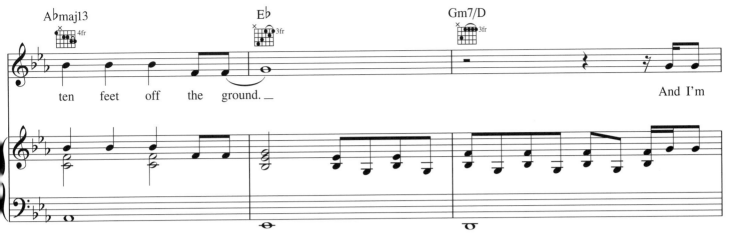

ten feet off the ground. ___ And I'm

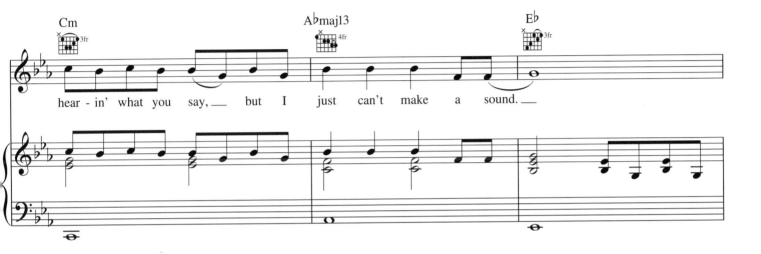

hear - in' what you say, ___ but I just can't make a sound. ___

You tell me that you need me, then you go and cut me down, ___

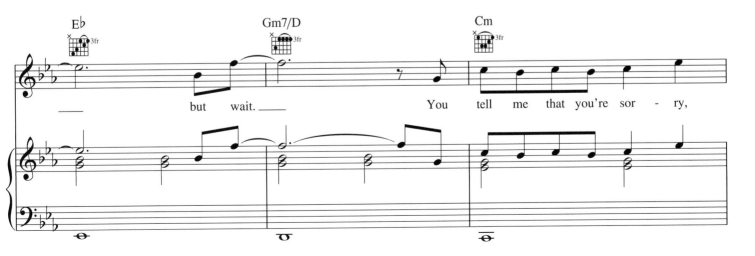

___ but wait. ___ You tell me that you're sor - ry,

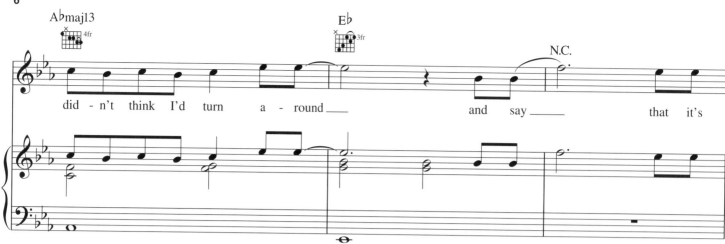

did - n't think I'd turn a - round ____ and say ____ that it's

too late to 'pol - o - gize. ____ It's too late. _____

____ I said it's too late to 'pol - o - gize. _____ It's

too late, __ hey, ___ hey, hey. ___

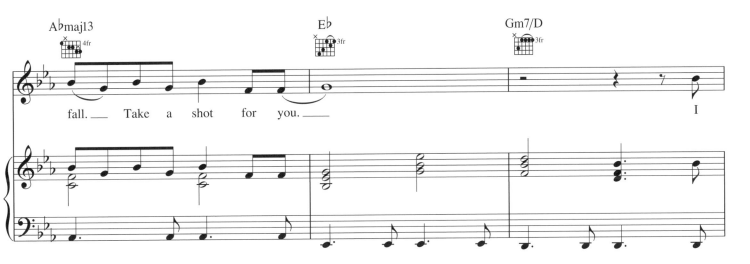

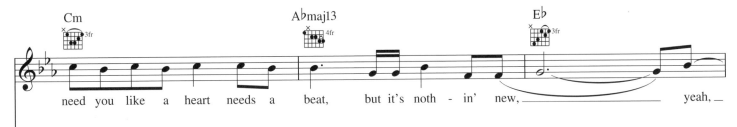

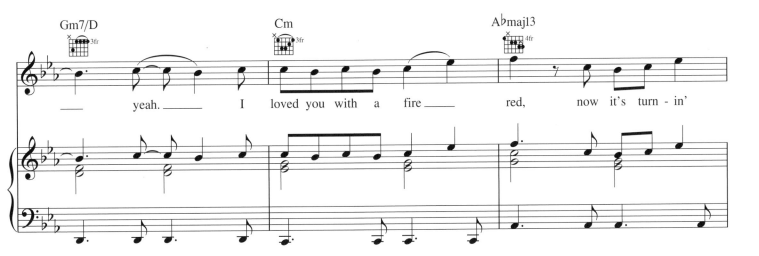

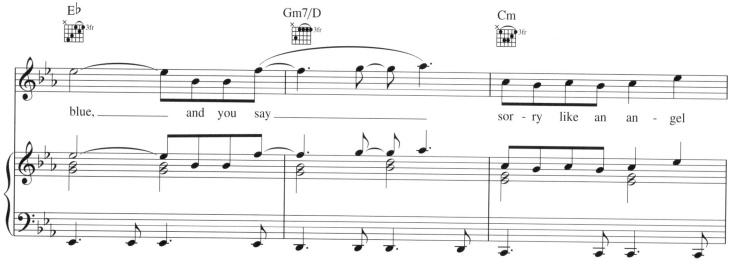

blue, _____ and you say _____ sor-ry like an an-gel

heav-en let me think was you. ____ But, I'm ____ a-fraid _____ it's

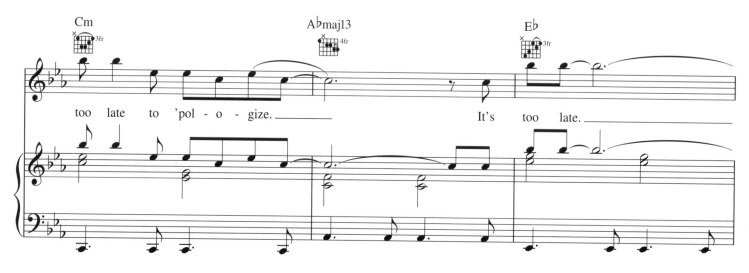

too late to 'pol-o-gize. _____ It's too late. _____

_____ I said it's too late to 'pol-o-gize. _____ It's

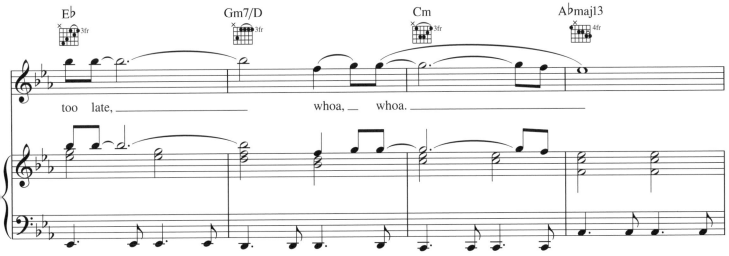

too late, _____ whoa, _ whoa. _____

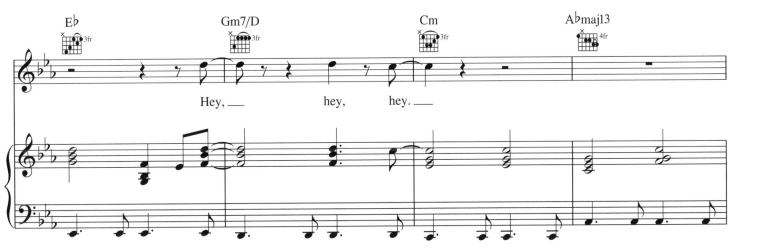

Hey, ___ hey, hey. ___

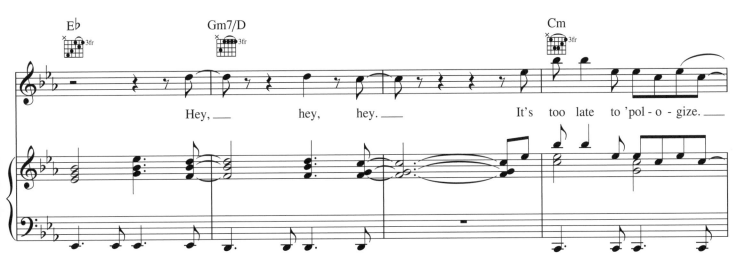

Hey, ___ hey, hey. ___ It's too late to 'pol - o - gize. ___

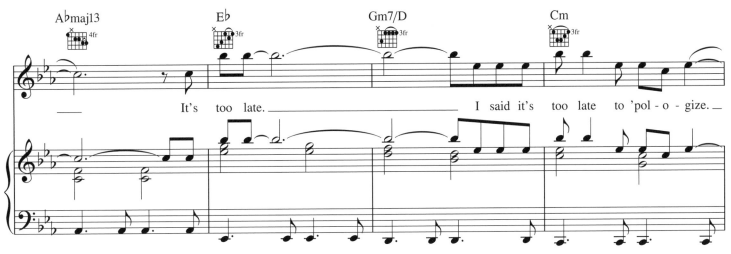

___ It's too late. _____ I said it's too late to 'pol - o - gize. ___

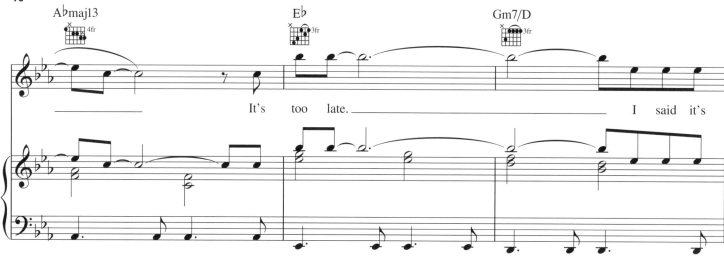

It's too late. _____ I said it's

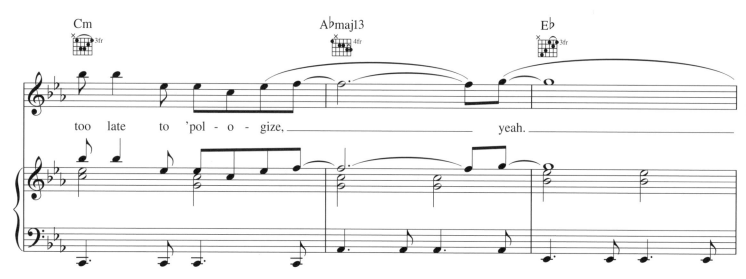

too late to 'pol - o - gize, _____ yeah. _____

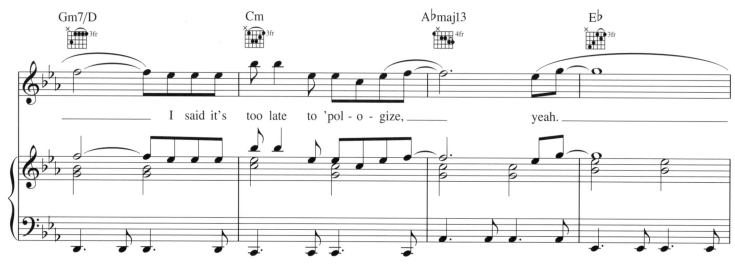

_____ I said it's too late to 'pol - o - gize, _____ yeah. _____

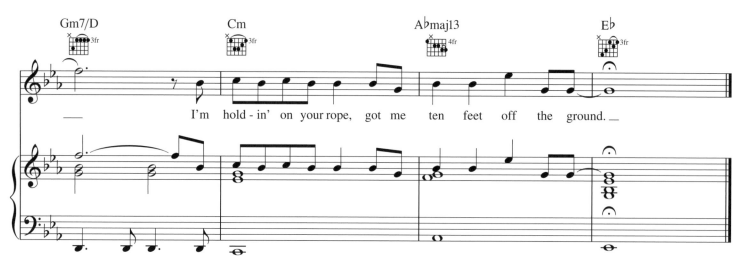

I'm hold - in' on your rope, got me ten feet off the ground. __

BROWN EYED GIRL

Words and Music by
VAN MORRISON

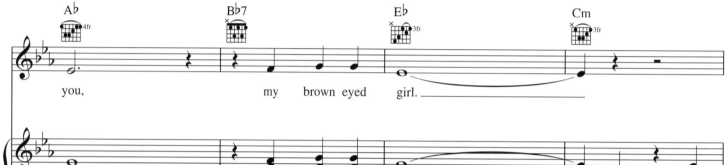

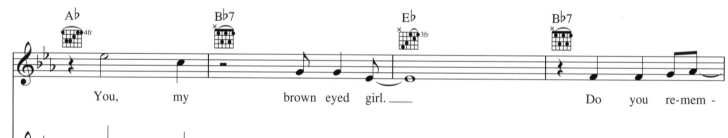

la la la la la la la te da? ___ Sha la __ la la __

__ la la __ la la __ la la la te da __ la te da. __

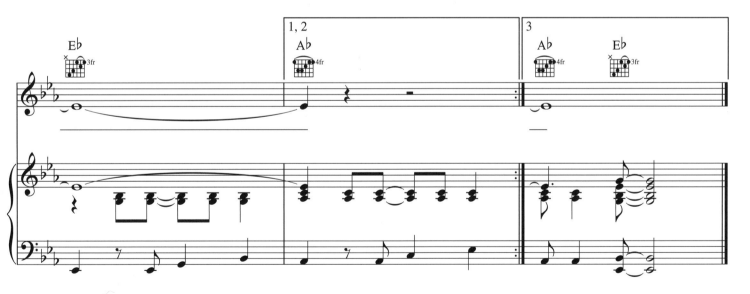

Additional Lyrics

2. Whatever happened to Tuesday and so slow
   Going down the old mine with a transistor radio
   Standing in the sunlight laughing
   Hiding behind a rainbow's wall
   Slipping and a-sliding
   All along the waterfall
   With you, my brown eyed girl
   You, my brown eyed girl.
   Do you remember when we used to sing:
   Chorus

3. So hard to find my way, now that I'm all on my own
   I saw you just the other day, my, how you have grown
   Cast my memory back there, Lord
   Sometime I'm overcome thinking 'bout
   Making love in the green grass
   Behind the stadium
   With you, my brown eyed girl
   With you, my brown eyed girl.
   Do you remember when we used to sing:
   Chorus

BABY

Words and Music by JUSTIN BIEBER,
CHRISTOPHER STEWART, CHRISTINE FLORES,
CHRISTOPHER BRIDGES and TERIUS NASH

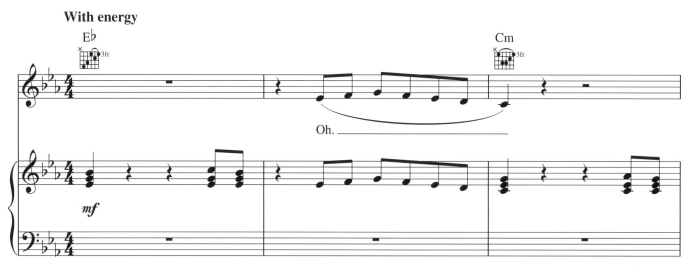

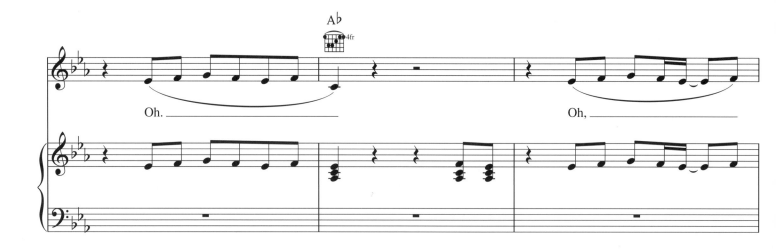

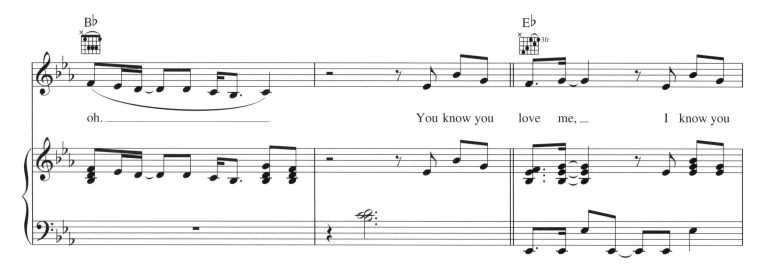

care. Just shout when - ev - er, ___ and I'll be there. ___ You are my

love, ___ you are my heart, and we will nev - er ev - er ev - er be a -

part. Are we an i - tem? ___ Girl, quit play - in'. ___ We're

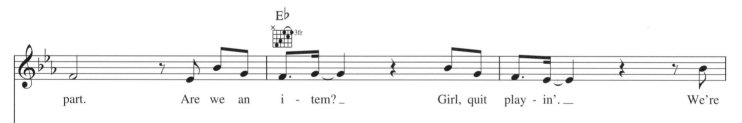

just friends, what are you say - in'? Said there's an - oth - er ___ and looked right in my

eyes. My first love broke my heart for the first _____ time. And I was like,

"Ba - by, ba - by, ba - by, oh, _____ like ba - by, ba - by, ba -

- by, no, _____ like ba - by, ba - by, ba - by, oh,

thought you'd al - ways be _____ mine, _____ mine. _____ Ba - by, ba - by, ba -

los - in' you. I'll buy you an - y - thing,__ I'll buy you an - y ring.__ And I'm in

piec - es;_____ ba - by, fix me. And you shake me 'til you wake me from this

bad dream._____ I'm go - ing down,_____ down, down, down, and I just

D.S. al Coda

can't be - lieve ____ my first love ____ won't be a - round. And I'm like,

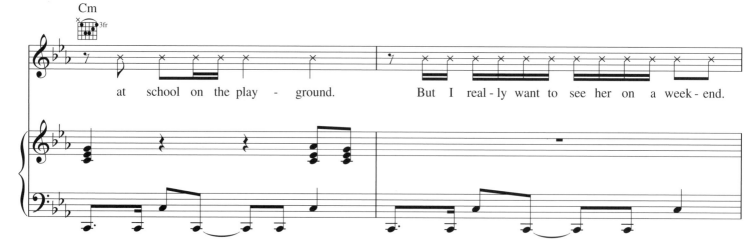

at school on the play - ground. But I real - ly want to see her on a week - end.

She knows she got me daz - ing, 'cause she was so a - maz - ing, and now my heart is break - ing.

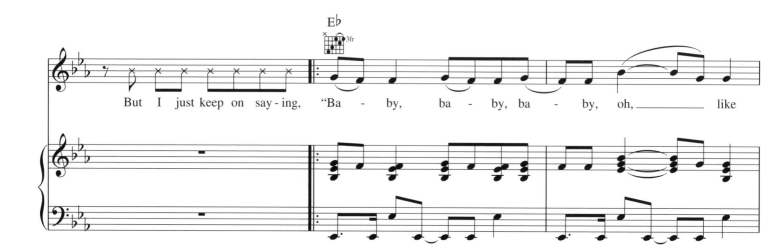

But I just keep on say - ing, "Ba - by, ba - by, ba - by, oh, _____ like

ba - by, ba - by, ba - by, no, _____ like ba - by, ba - by, ba -

BAD MOON RISING

Words and Music by
JOHN FOGERTY

Moderately

I see the bad moon a-ris - ing.
I hear hur-ri-canes a-blow - ing.
Hope you got your things to-geth - er.

I see trou-ble on the way.
I know the end is com-ing soon.
Hope you are quite pre-pared to die.

I see earth - quakes and light - nin'.
I fear riv-ers o-ver-flow - ing.
Looks like we're in for nas-ty weath - er.

I see bad _____ times to - day. _____
I hear the voice of rage and ruin. _____
One eye is tak - en for an eye. _____

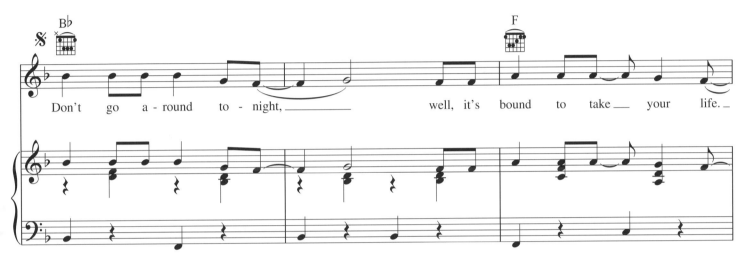

Don't go a - round to - night, _____ well, it's bound to take _____ your life. _____

There's a bad _____ moon on the rise. _____

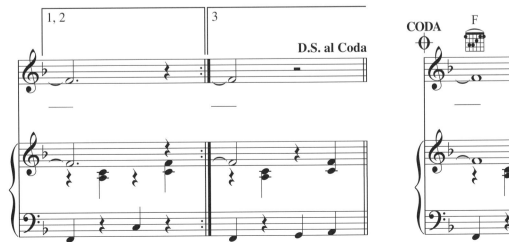

D.S. al Coda

CODA

BLACK VELVET

Words and Music by DAVID TYSON
and CHRISTOPHER WARD

Mis - sis - sip - pi in the mid - dle of a dry ___ spell.
Up in Mem - phis the mu - sic's like a heat wave.

Jim - mie Rod - gers on the Vic - trola up high. _____
"White Light - nin'" bound to drive you wild. _____

Ma - ma's danc - in' with ba - by _____ on her shoul - der.
Ma - ma's ba - by _____ is in the heart of _____ ev -'ry school- girl.

The sun is set - tin' like _____ mo - las - ses _____ in the sky. _____
"Love Me Ten - der" leaves 'em cry - in' _____ in the aisle. _____

B7sus   B7   A7sus   A7

The boy could sing; ___ knew ___ how to move ev -'ry - thing. _____
The way he moved ___ it _____ was a sin so sweet ___ and true.

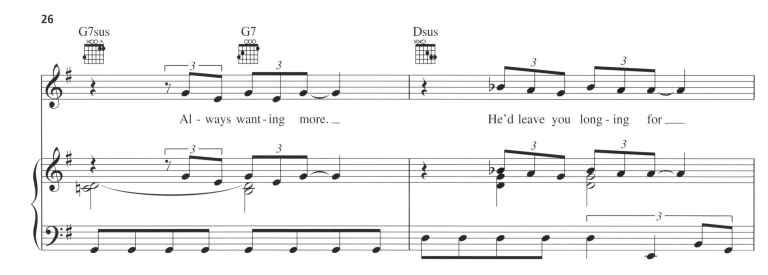

Al - ways want - ing more. __ He'd leave you long - ing for __

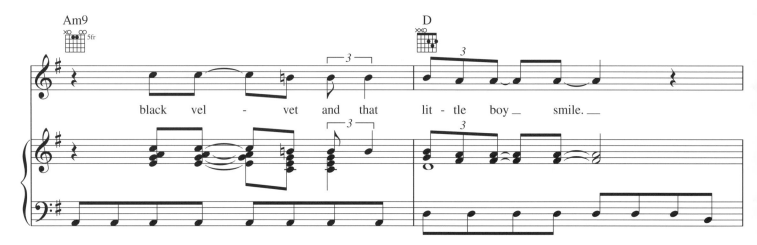

black vel - vet and that lit - tle boy __ smile. __

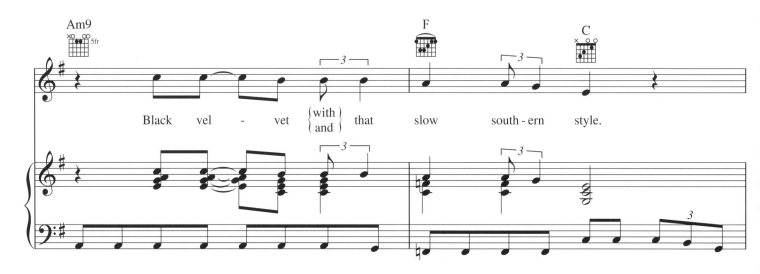

Black vel - vet {with / and} that slow south - ern style.

A new re - li - gion __ that -'ll bring you __ to your knees.

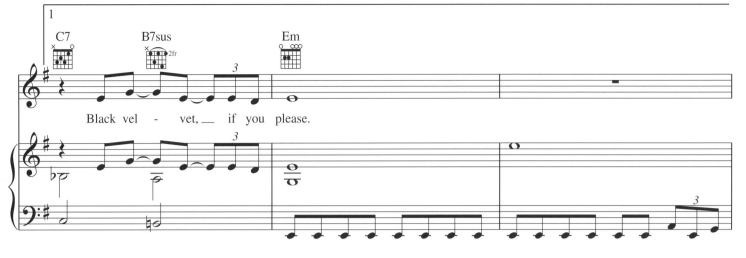

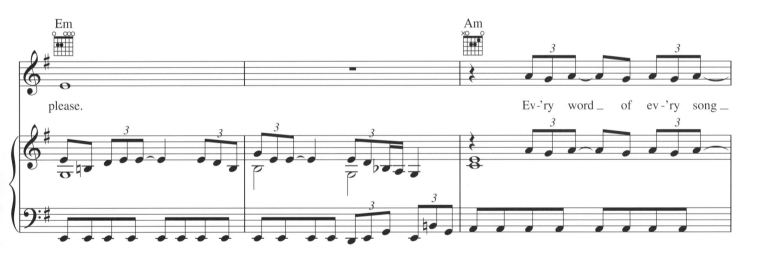

In a flash ___ he was gone; ___ it hap - pened so

soon. ___ What could you ___ do? ___

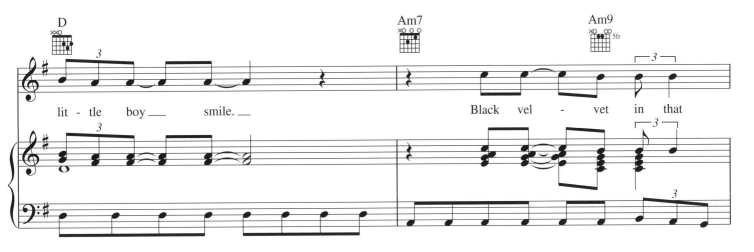

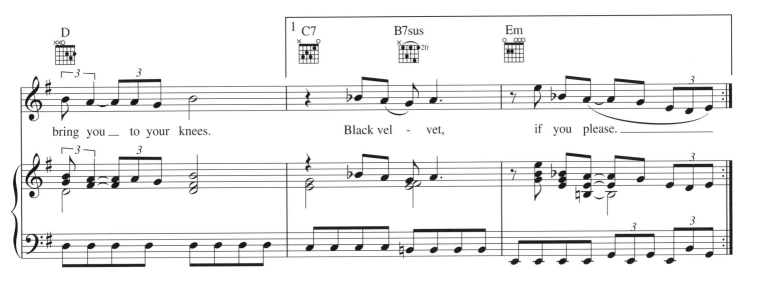

Black vel - vet, if ____ you ____ please. _____

If you

please. _____

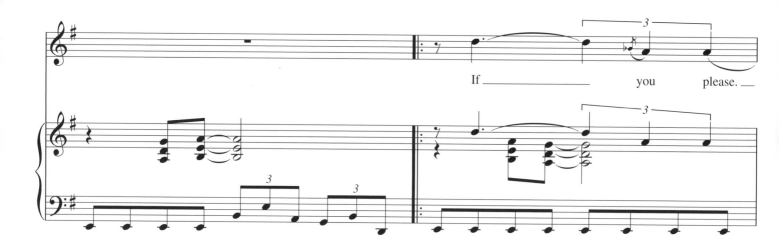

If _____ you please. ___

If you please.

Mm.   Mm.

Optional Ending

Repeat and Fade

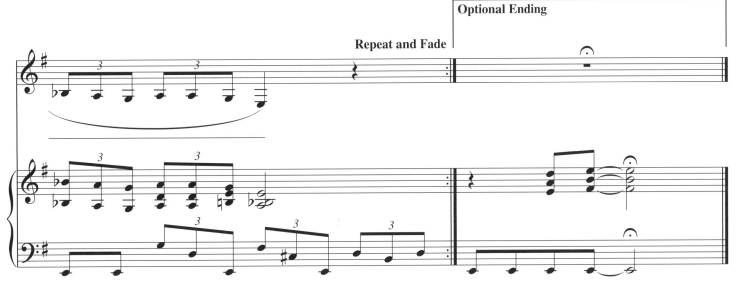

BLEEDING LOVE

Words and Music by JESSE McCARTNEY
and RYAN TEDDER

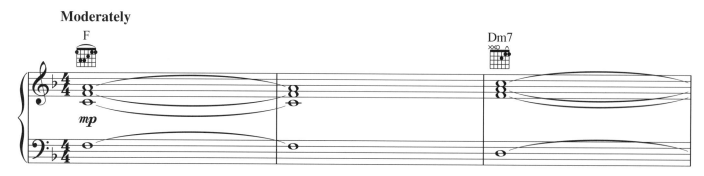

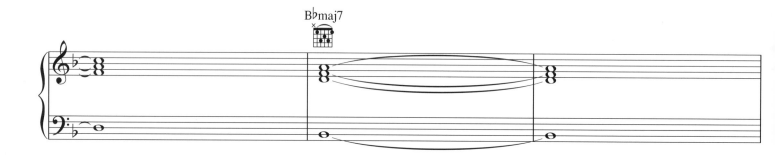

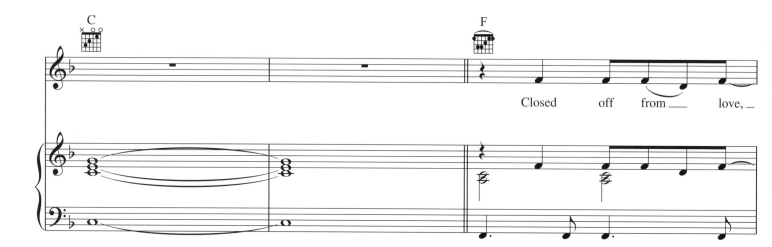

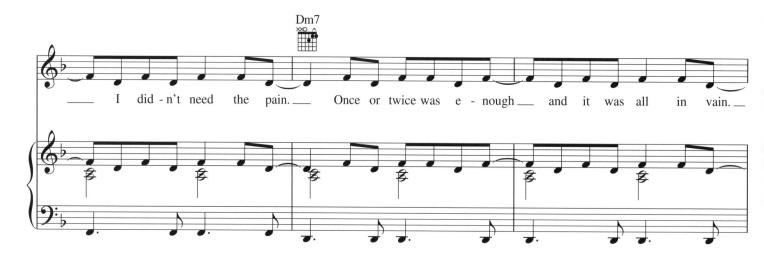

Time starts to pass; __ be - fore you know it you're fro - zen,

oh. __ But some - thin' hap - pened for the ver - y first time with you. __

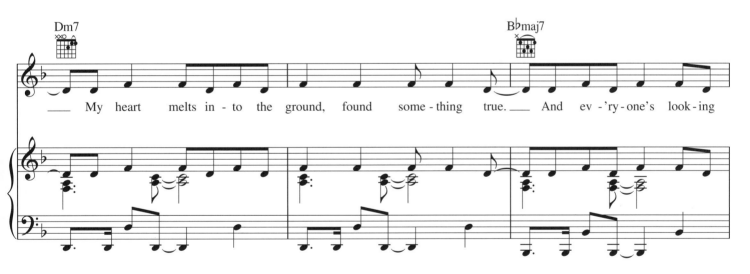

__ My heart melts in - to the ground, found some - thing true. __ And ev - 'ry - one's look - ing

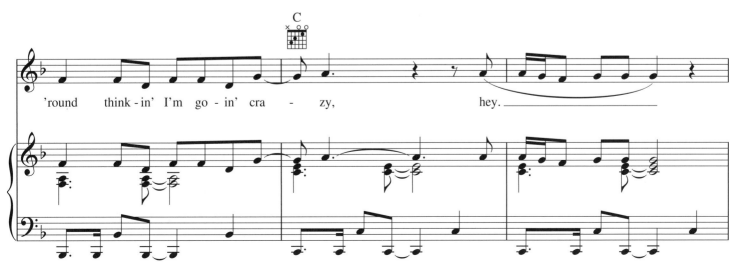

'round think - in' I'm go - in' cra - zy, hey. __

But I don't care what they say, ___ I'm in love ___ with you. ___ They try to pull me a - way, ___

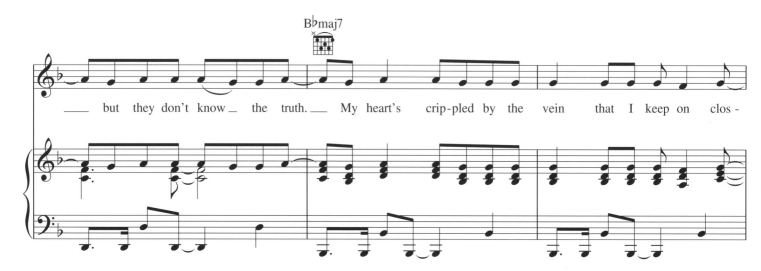

___ but they don't know ___ the truth. ___ My heart's crip-pled by the vein that I keep on clos-

- in'. You cut me o - pen and I ___ keep bleed-in', keep, ___

___ keep bleed-in' love. ___ I keep bleed-in', I keep, ___ keep bleed-in' love.

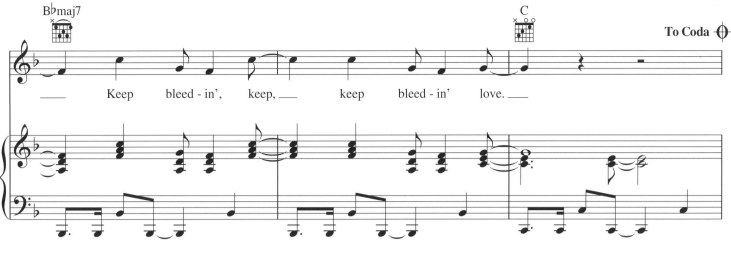

Keep bleed - in', keep, __ keep bleed - in' love. __

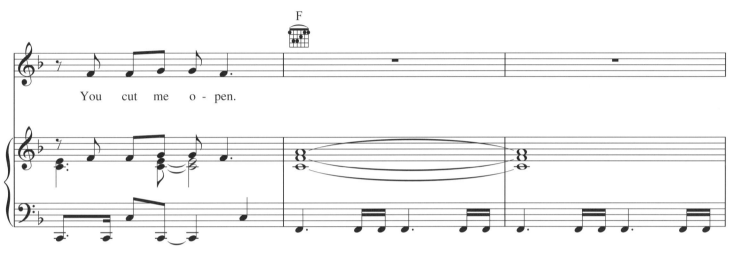

You cut me o - pen.

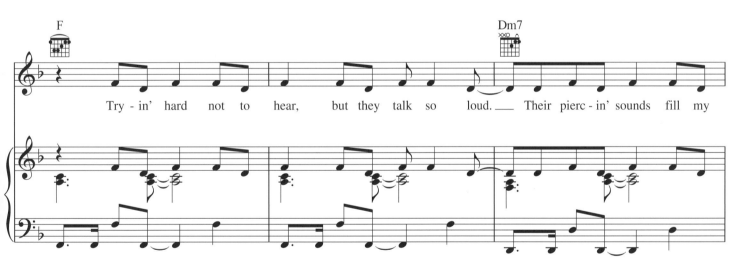

Try - in' hard not to hear, but they talk so loud. __ Their pierc - in' sounds fill my

ears, try to fill me with doubt. __ Yet, I know that the goal is to keep me from fall -

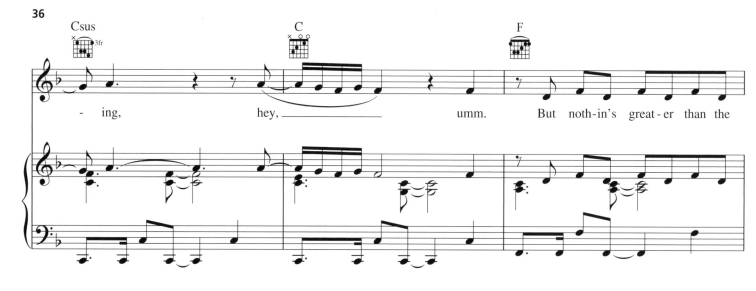

-ing, hey, _____ umm. But noth-in's great-er than the

rush that comes from your em - brace.___ And in this world of lone - li -ness, I see___ your face.

___ Yet, ev -'ry -one a - round___ me thinks that I'm go - in' cra - zy, may-

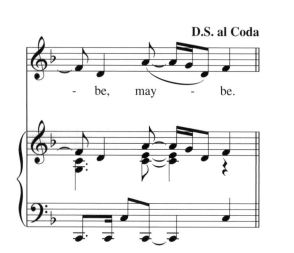

D.S. al Coda

- be, may - be.

CODA

You cut me o - pen.___ And it's

drain - in' all _____ of _____ me. Oh, they find it hard _____ to be - lieve. _____

_____ I'll be wear - in' these scars _____ for ev - 'ry - one _____ to see. _____

I don't care what they say, _____ I'm in love _____ with you. _____

_____ They try to pull me a - way, _____ but they don't know _____ the truth. _____ My heart's crip - pled by the

vein that I keep on clos - in'. Ooh, ___ you cut me o - pen and I ___

___ keep bleed - in', keep, ___ keep bleed - in' love. ___ I keep bleed - in', I keep, ___

___ keep bleed - in' love. ___ Keep bleed - in', keep, ___ keep bleed - in' love. ___

___ Oh, ___ you cut me o - pen and I ___ keep bleed - in', keep, ___

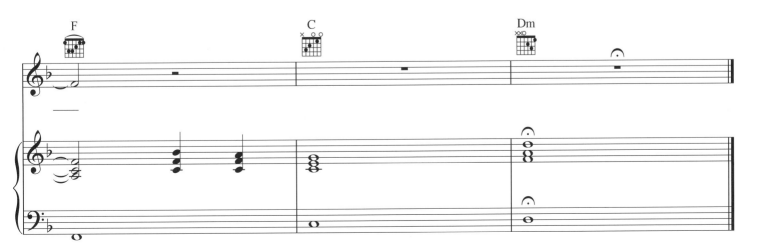

BRIDGE OVER TROUBLED WATER

Words and Music by
PAUL SIMON

Moderately, like a Spiritual

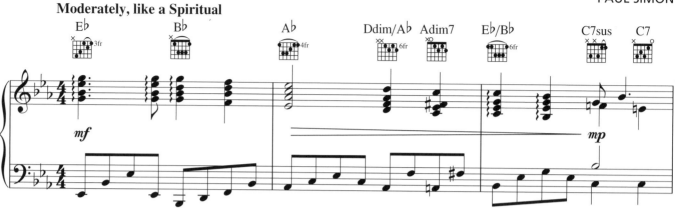

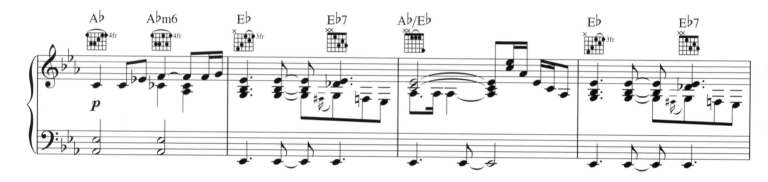

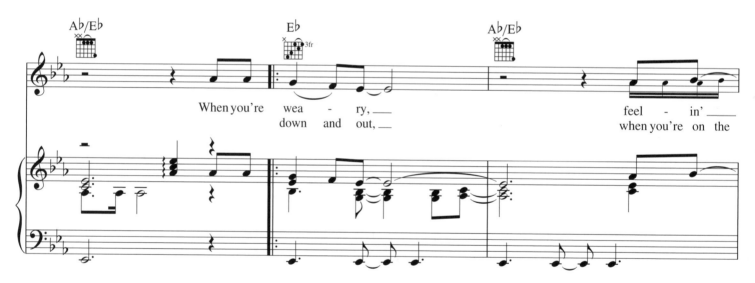

When you're wea - ry, ___
down and out, ___
feel - in' ___
when you're on the

___ small,
street,
when tears are in
when eve - ning falls
your eyes, ___
so hard, ___

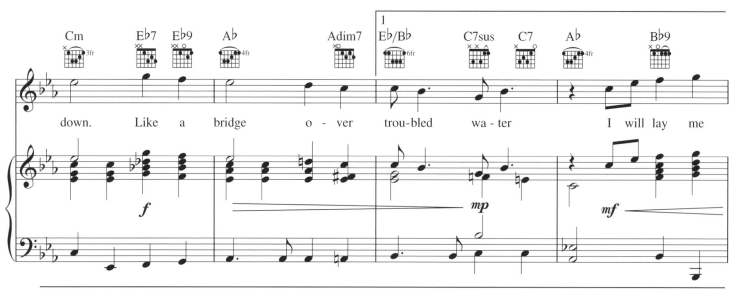

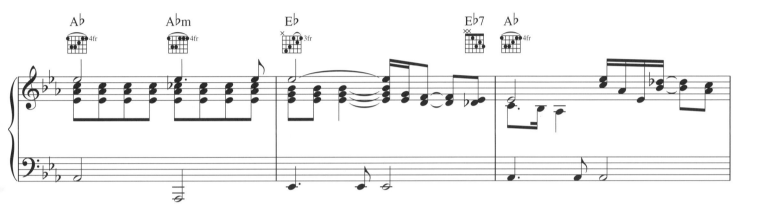

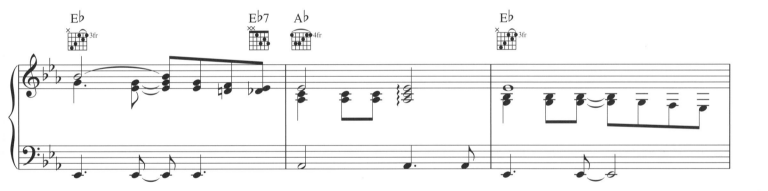

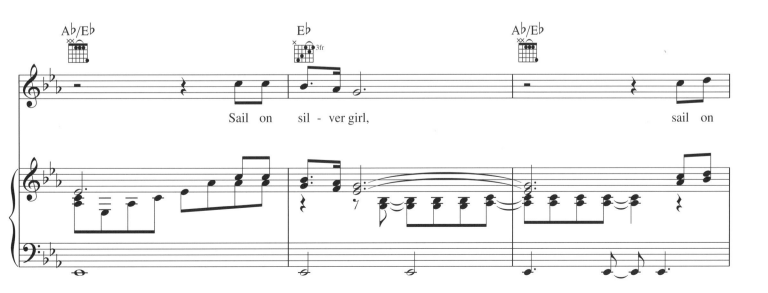

Sail on sil - ver girl,   sail on

44

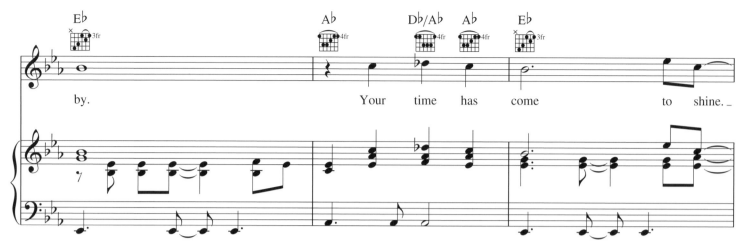

CALIFORNIA GURLS

Words and Music by MAX MARTIN,
LUKASZ GOTTWALD, BENJAMIN LEVIN,
CALVIN BROADUS, BONNIE McKEE,
MIKE LOVE and BRIAN WILSON

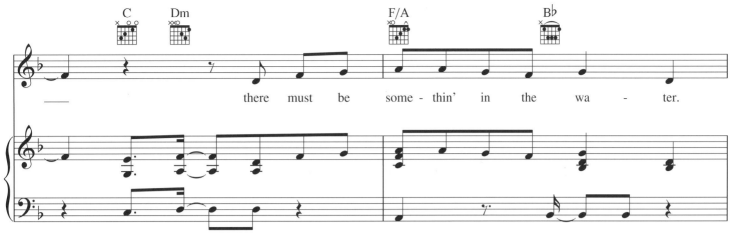

there must be some - thin' in the wa - ter.

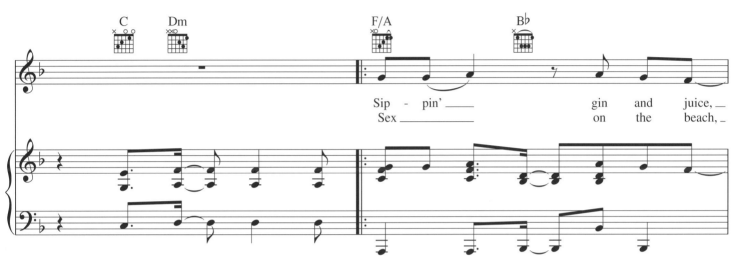

Sip - pin' _____ gin and juice, _
Sex _____ on the beach, _

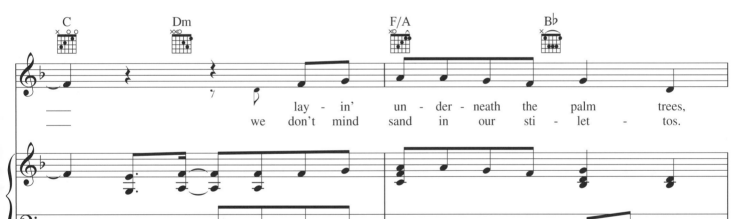

_____ lay - in' un - der - neath the palm trees,
_____ we don't mind sand in our sti - let - tos.

un - done. _ The boys break their necks _
We freak in my jeep, _

try'n' to creep a lit - tle sneak peek
Snoop Dog - gy Dogg ___ on the ster - e - o.

at us. ___
Oh, oh. ___

You could trav - el the w -

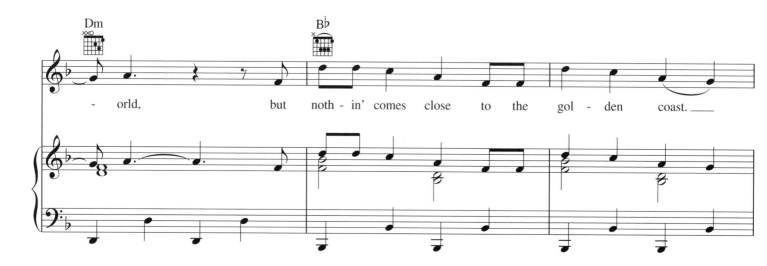

- orld, but noth - in' comes close to the gol - den coast. ___

Once you par - ty with u - us, you'll be

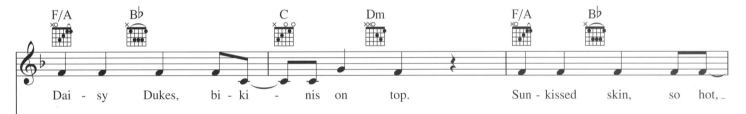

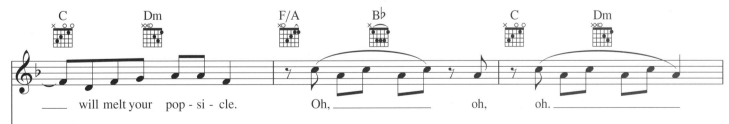

Cal - i - for - nia gurls, __ we're un-de-ni-a-ble. Fine, fresh, fierce, we got __

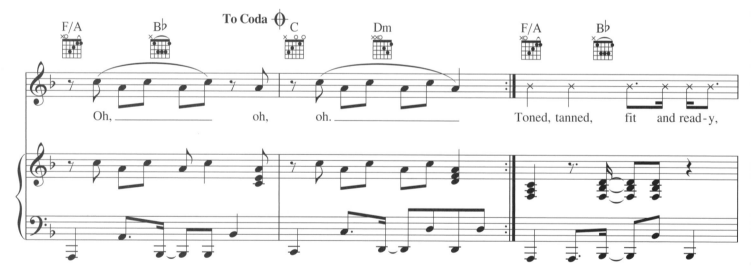

__ it on lock. West Coast, rep - re - sent, __ now put your hands up.

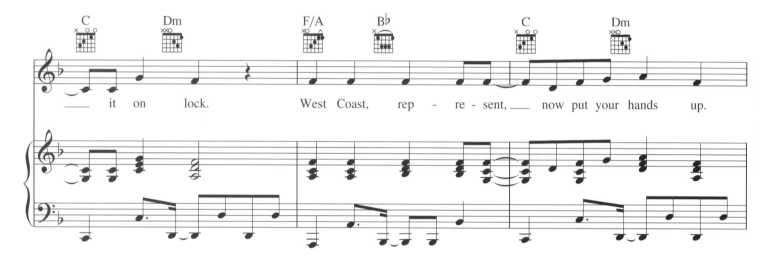

Oh, _____ oh, oh. _____ Toned, tanned, fit and read - y,

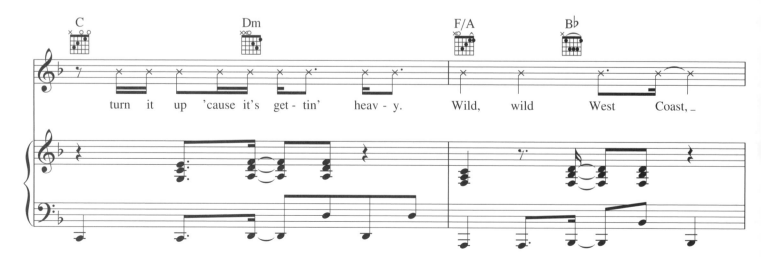

turn it up 'cause it's get - tin' heav - y. Wild, wild West Coast, _

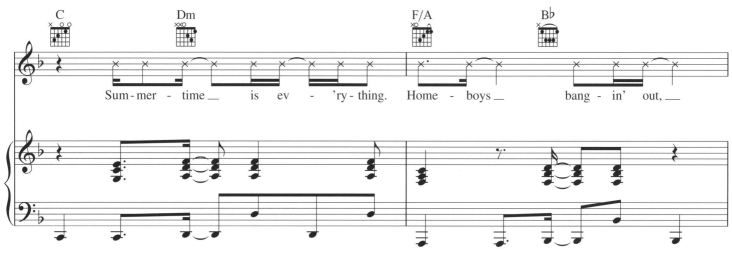

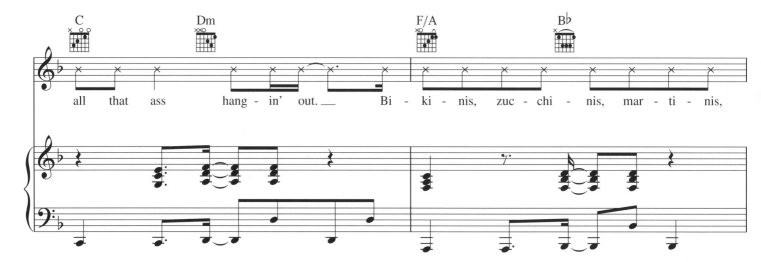

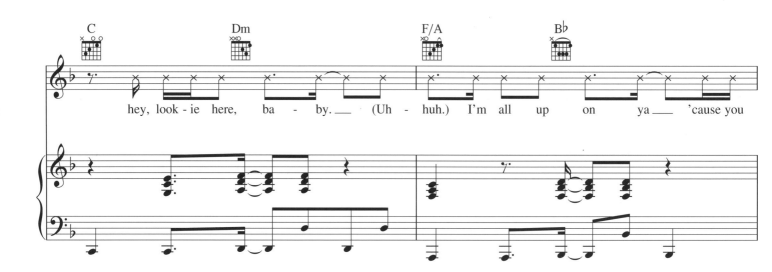

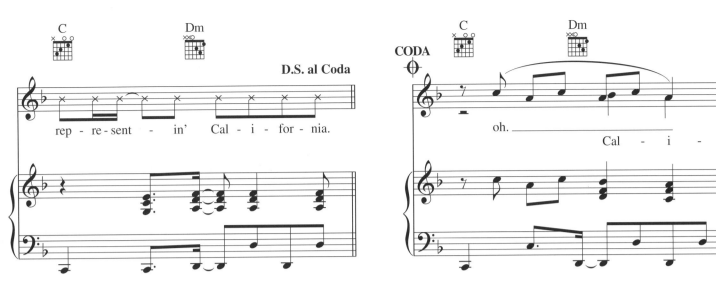

D.S. al Coda

rep - re - sent - in' Cal - i - for - nia.

CODA

oh. _____ Cal - i -

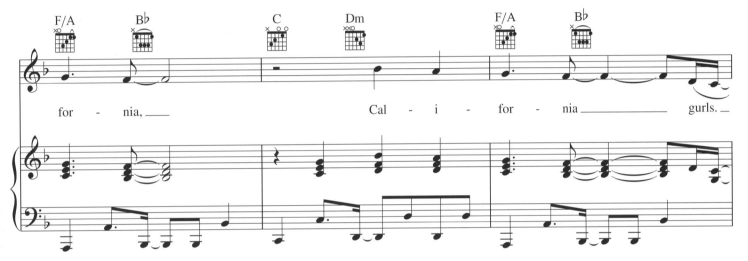

for - nia, _____ Cal - i - for - nia _____ gurls. _____

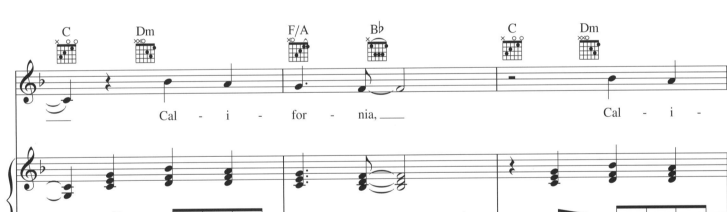

Cal - i - for - nia, _____ Cal - i -

for - nia _____ gurls. _____

CALL ME
from the Paramount Motion Picture AMERICAN GIGOLO

Words by DEBORAH HARRY
Music by GIORGIO MORODER

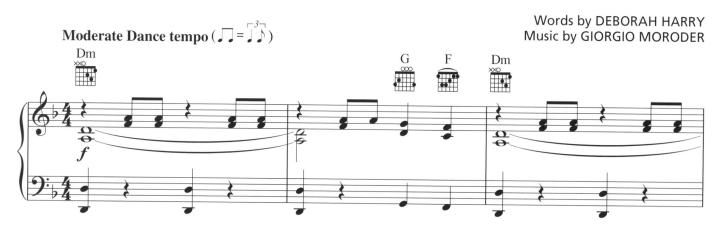

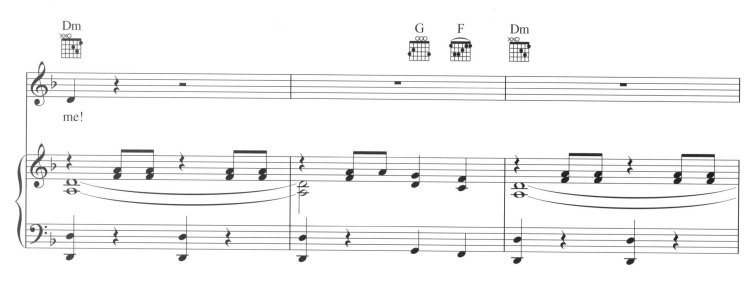

Cov - er me ___ with kiss - es, ba - by,

cov - er me ___ with love. ___ Roll me in de - sign -

- er sheets, ___ I'll nev - er get ___ e - nough. ___ E - mo -

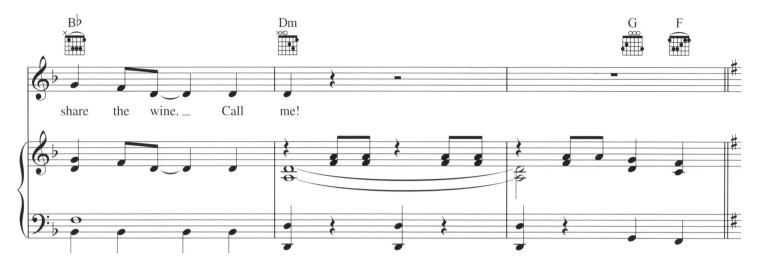

share the wine.__ Call me!

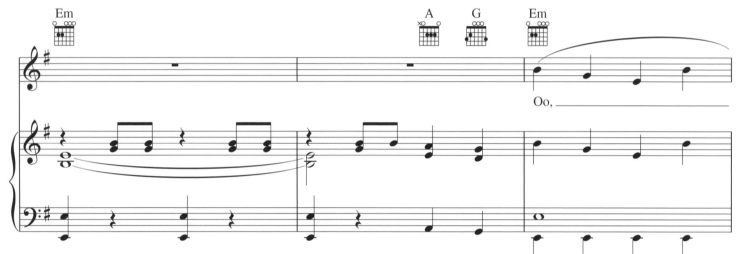

Oo,_____

__ he speaks __ the lan - guag - es __ of love.

Oo,_____ a - mo - ré, chia - ma mi,___

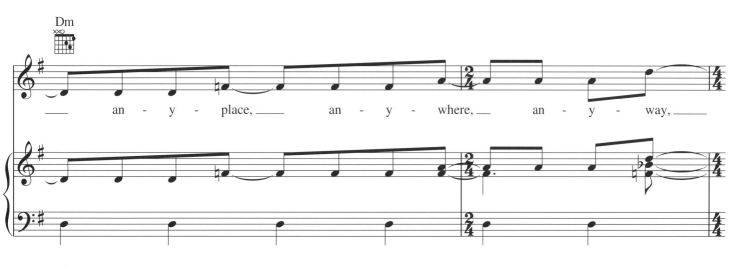

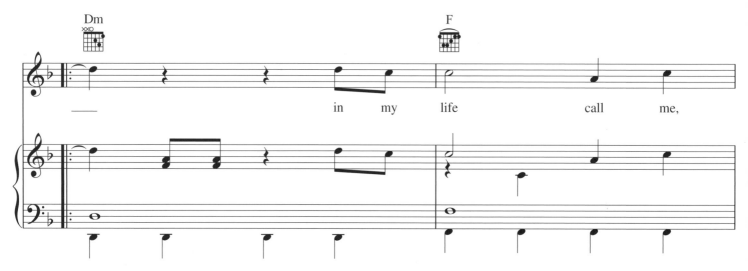

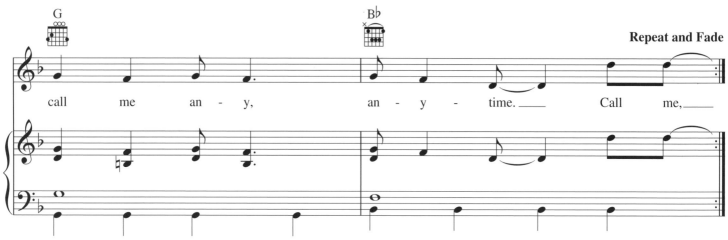

CAN'T HELP FALLING IN LOVE

Words and Music by GEORGE DAVID WEISS,
HUGO PERETTI and LUIGI CREATORE

Moderately slow

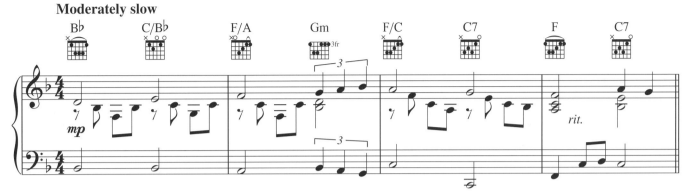

Wise men say only fools rush

in, but I can't help fall-ing in

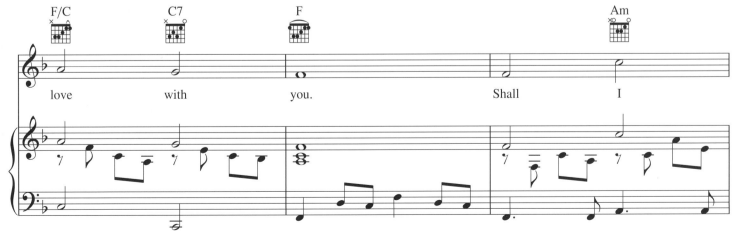

love with you. Shall I

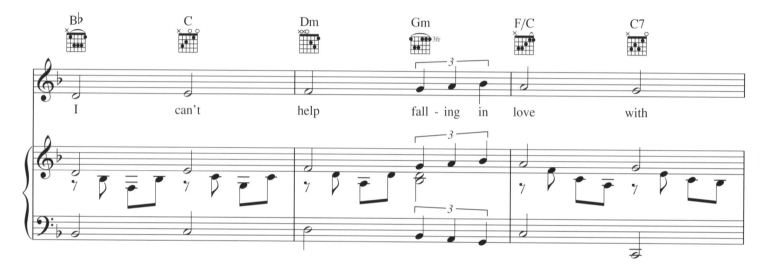

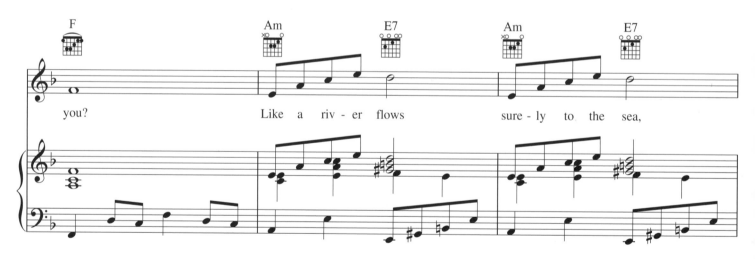

Take my hand, take my whole life

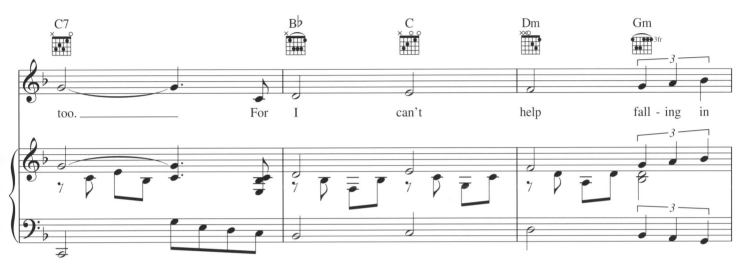

too. For I can't help fall-ing in

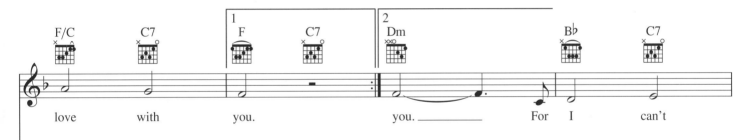

love with you. you. For I can't

help fall-ing in love with you.

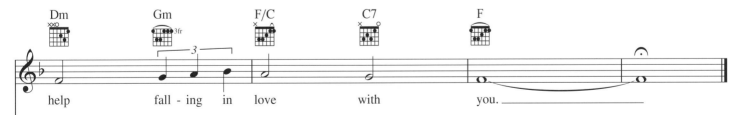

THE CLIMB

Words and Music by JESSI ALEXANDER
and JON MABE

lost with no __ di - rec - tion; my faith is shak - en. But
I'm gon - na re - mem - ber most, yeah. Just got - ta keep go - ing. And

I, I got - ta keep try'n'; got - ta keep _ my _ head _ held _ high.
I, I got - ta be strong, just _ keep _ push - ing _ on. _

_ There's al - ways gon - na be an - oth - er moun - tain; _
_ 'Cause, there's al - ways gon - na be an - oth - er moun - tain; _

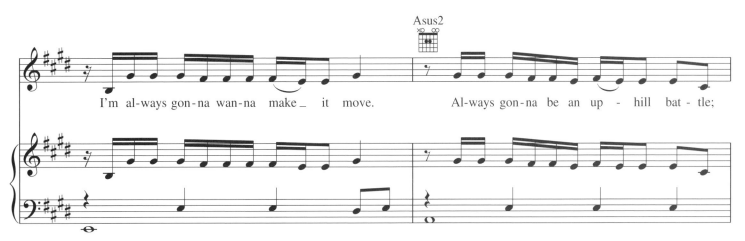

I'm al - ways gon - na wan - na make _ it move. Al - ways gon - na be an up - hill bat - tle;

some-times, I'm gon-na have to lose. Ain't a-bout how fast I get there;

ain't a-bout what's wait-ing on the oth - er side;

it's the climb.

side; it's the climb.

There's al-ways gon-na be an-oth - er moun-tain; I'm al-ways gon-na wan-na make it move.

-ing, keep climb-ing; keep the faith, ba - by.

It's all a-bout, it's all a-bout the climb.

Keep the faith, keep your faith.

COME FLY WITH ME

Words by SAMMY CAHN
Music by JAMES VAN HEUSEN

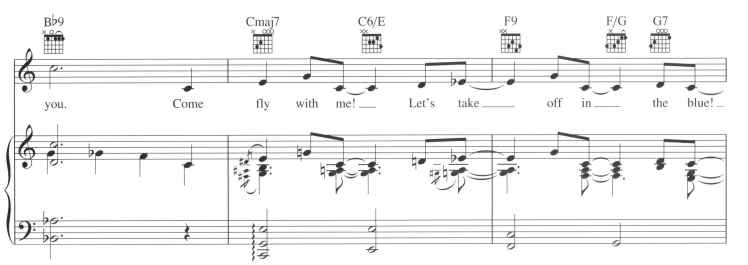

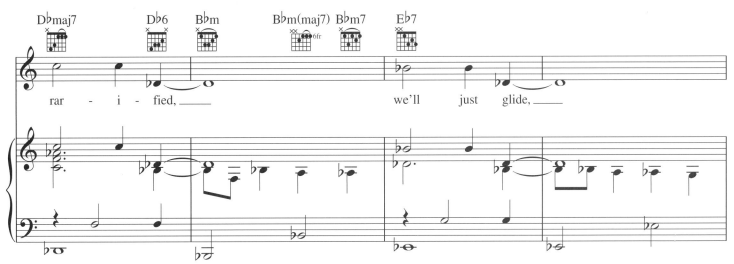

star - ry - eyed.___ Once I get you up there, _ I'll be hold - ing

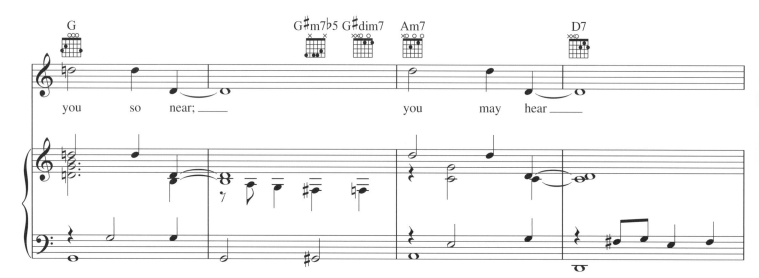

you so near; ___ you may hear ___

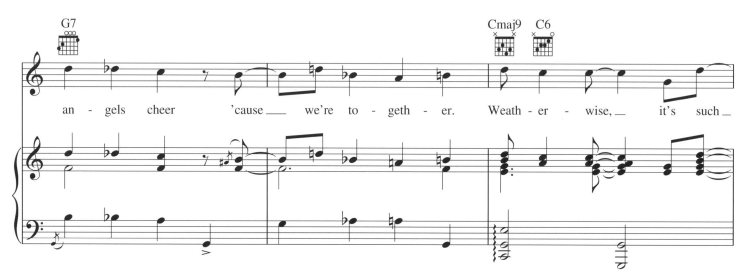

an - gels cheer 'cause ___ we're to - geth - er. Weath - er - wise, __ it's such __

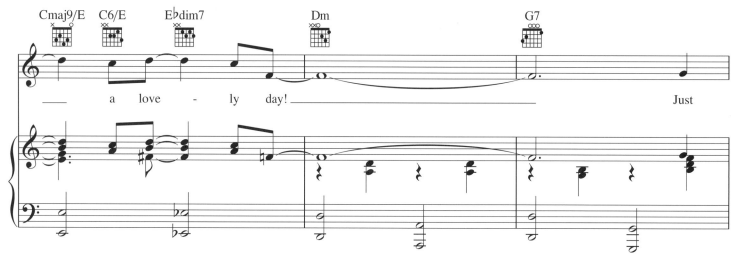

___ a love - ly day! _____ Just

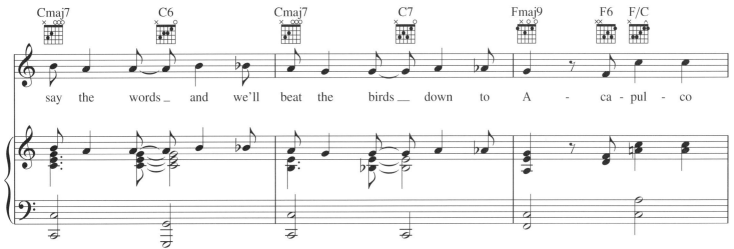

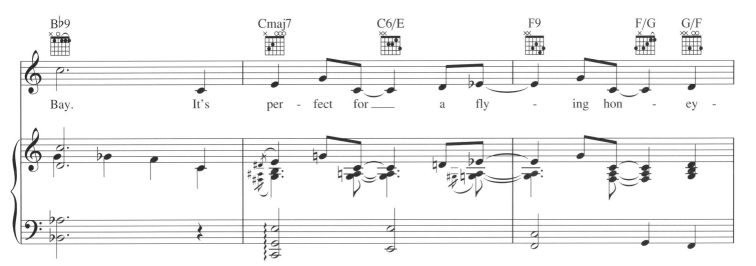

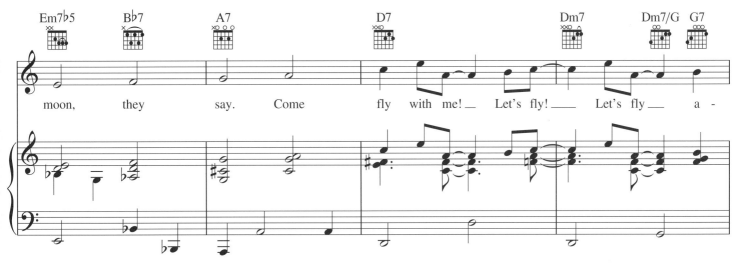

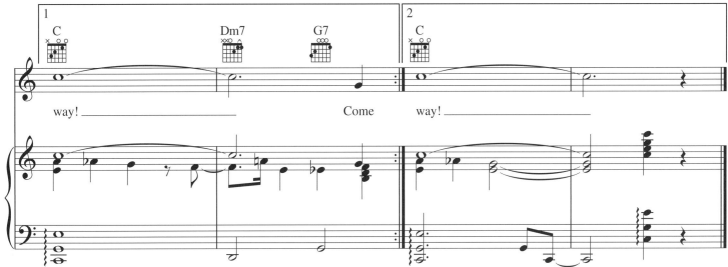

COPACABANA
(At the Copa)

Music by BARRY MANILOW
Lyric by BRUCE SUSSMAN and JACK FELDMAN

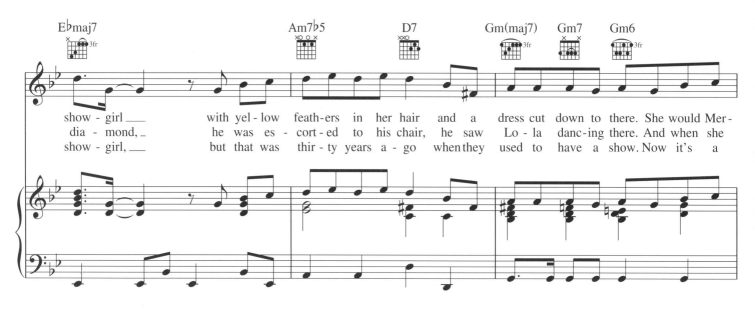

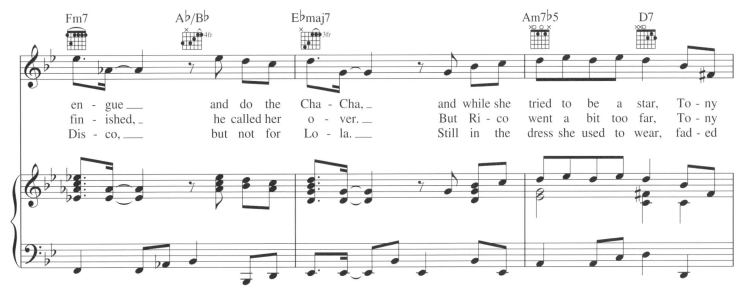

en - gue ___ and do the Cha - Cha, ___ and while she tried to be a star, To - ny
fin - ished, ___ he called her o - ver. ___ But Ri - co went a bit too far, To - ny
Dis - co, ___ but not for Lo - la. ___ Still in the dress she used to wear, fad - ed

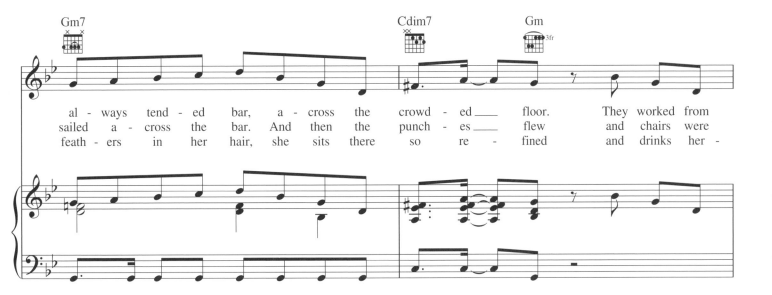

al - ways tend - ed bar, a - cross the crowd - ed ___ floor. They worked from
sailed a - cross the bar. And then the punch - es ___ flew and chairs were
feath - ers in her hair, she sits there so re - fined and drinks her -

eight to ___ four. They were young and they had each oth - er, who could
smashed in ___ two. There was blood and a sin - gle gun - shot, but just
self half ___ blind. She lost her youth and she lost her To - ny, now she's

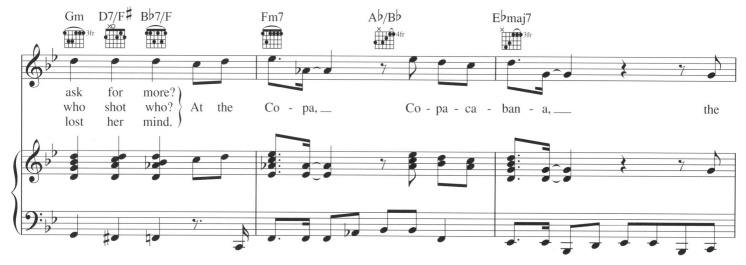

ask for more?
who shot who? } At the Co-pa, __ Co-pa-ca-ban-a, __ the
lost her mind.

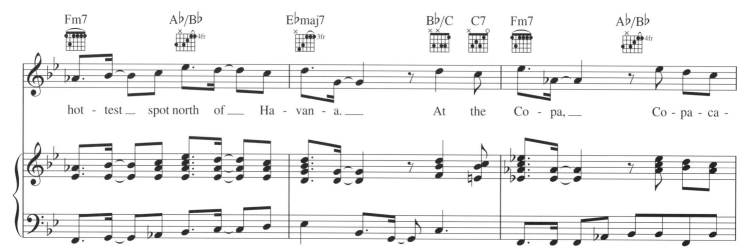

hot-test __ spot north of __ Ha-van-a. __ At the Co-pa, __ Co-pa-ca-

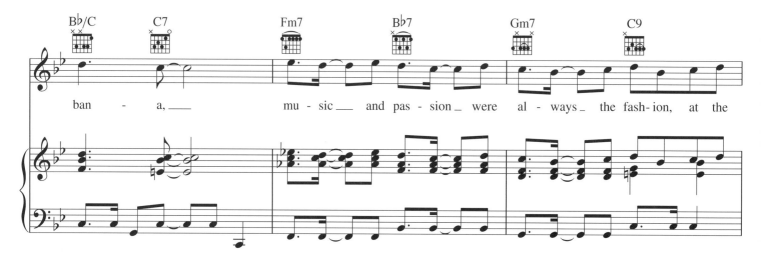

ban - a, __ mu-sic __ and pas-sion __ were al-ways __ the fash-ion, at the

To Coda

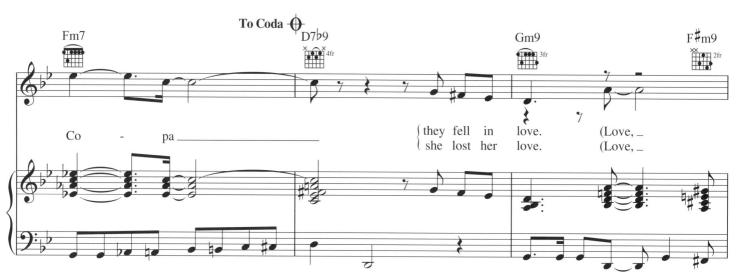

Co - pa _____

they fell in love. (Love, __
she lost her love. (Love, __

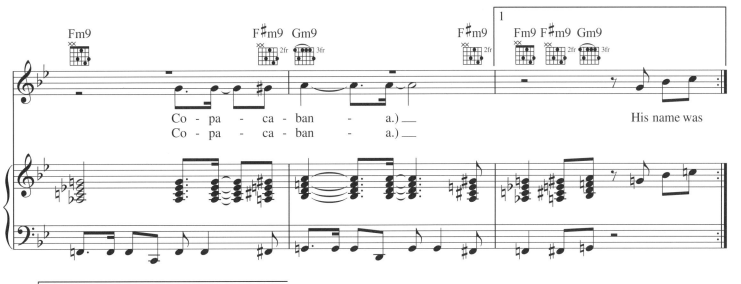

His name was

Co - pa, _____ Co - pa - ca -

poco a poco cresc.

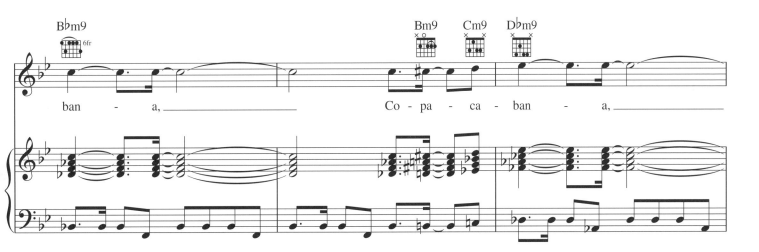

ban - a, _____ Co - pa - ca - ban - a, _____

ah, _____

Instrumental solo ad lib.

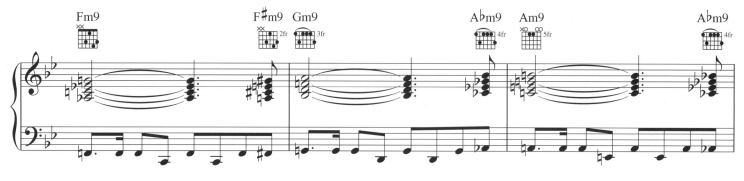

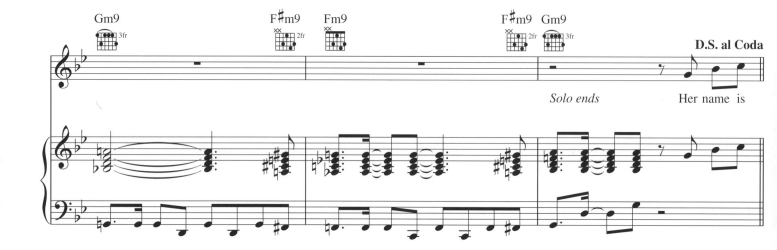

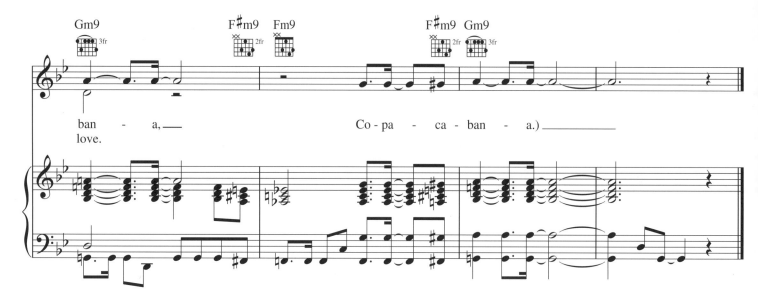

DEFYING GRAVITY
from the Broadway Musical WICKED

Music and Lyrics by
STEPHEN SCHWARTZ

Freely, with quiet intensity

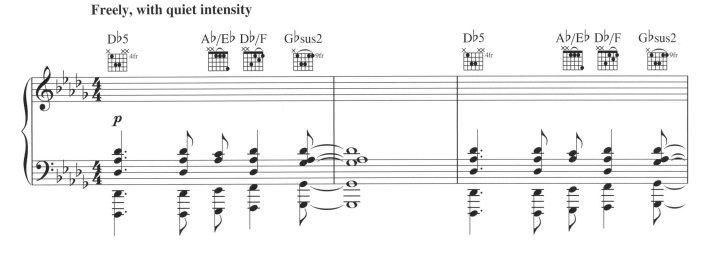

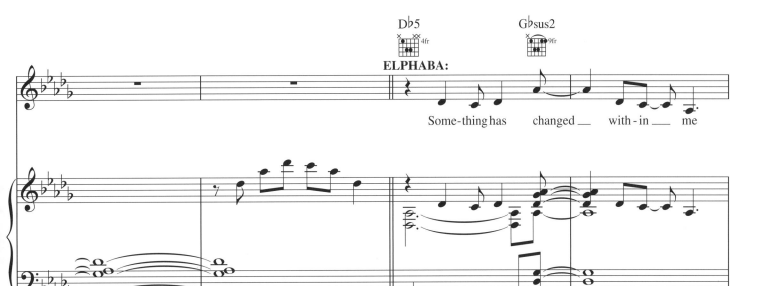

ELPHABA:

Some-thing has changed __ with-in __ me

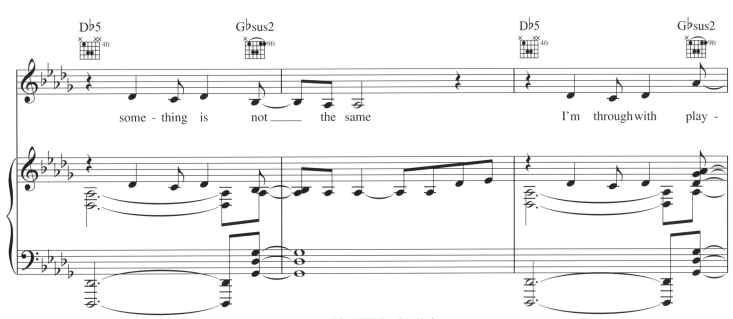

some - thing is not ___ the same   I'm through with play -

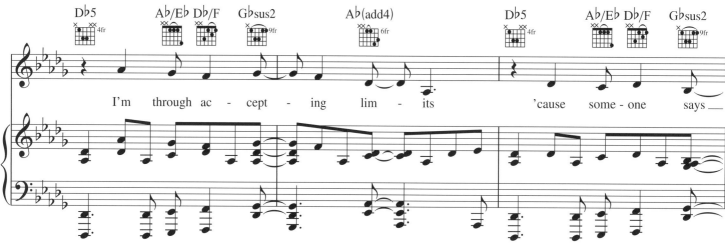

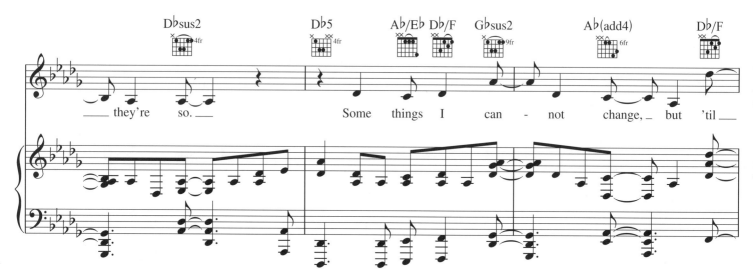

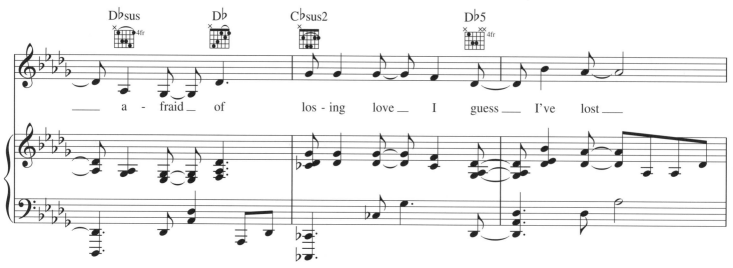

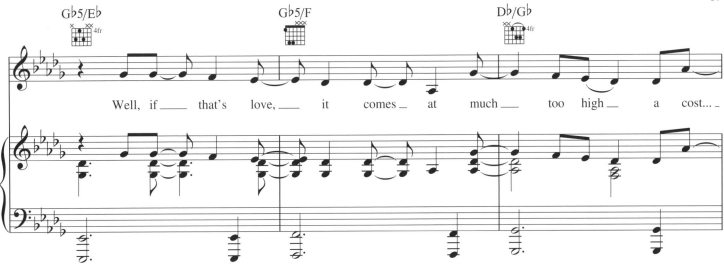

Well, if ___ that's love, ___ it comes ___ at much ___ too high ___ a cost... ___

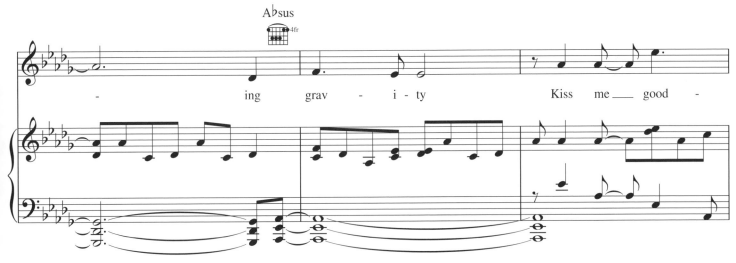

___ I'd soon - er buy de - fy -

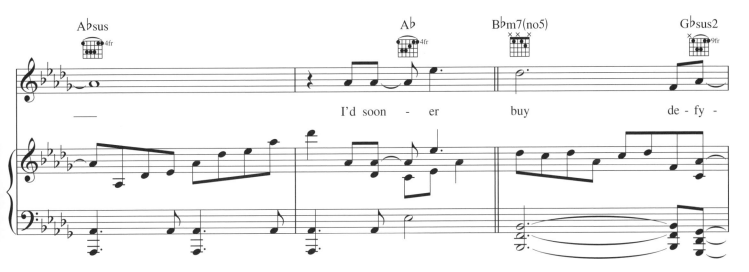

- ing grav - i - ty Kiss me ___ good -

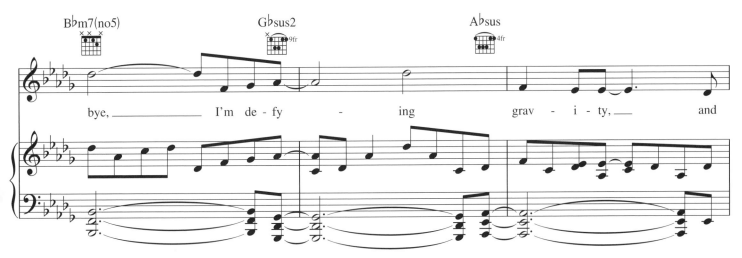

bye, ___ I'm de - fy - ing grav - i - ty, ___ and

Moderato, dreamily

you can't pull __ me down. ____

Un - lim - it - ed... ____ My fu - ture is

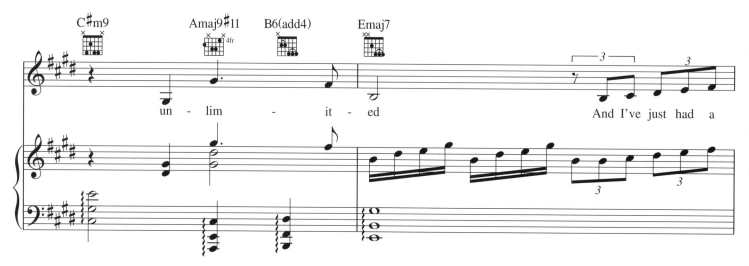

un - lim - it - ed And I've just had a

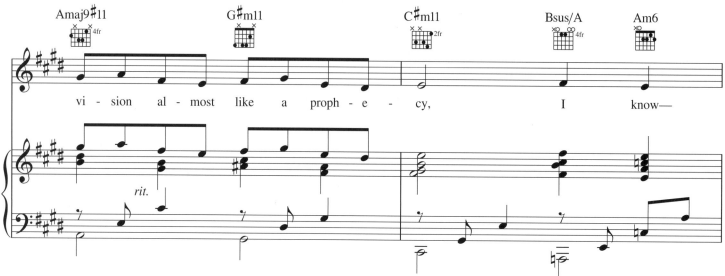

vi - sion al - most like a proph - e - cy, I know—

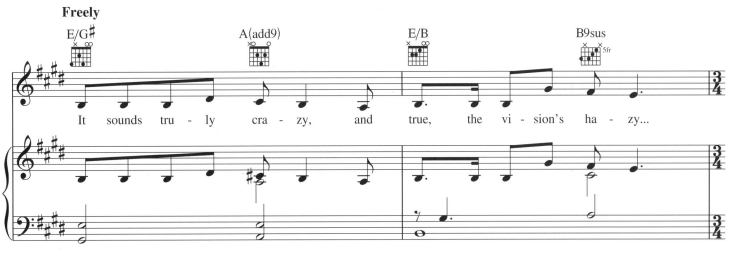

Freely

It sounds tru-ly cra-zy, and true, the vi-sion's ha-zy...

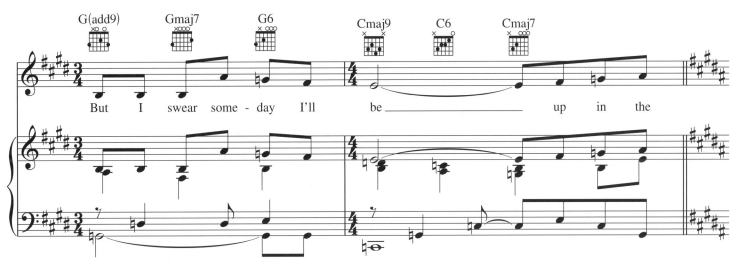

But I swear some-day I'll be _____ up in the

Allegro; as before

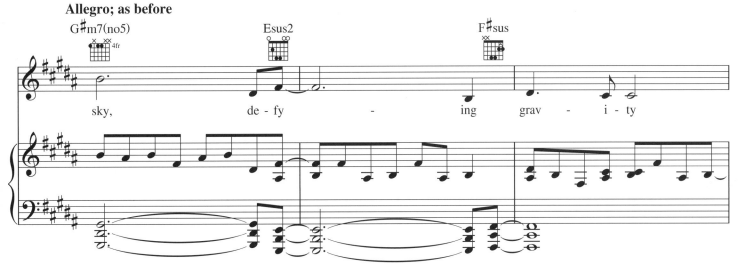

sky, de-fy - ing grav - i-ty

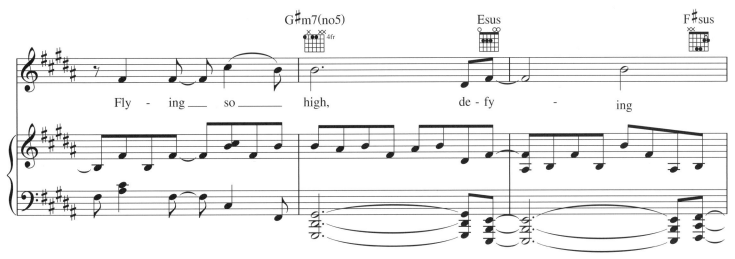

Fly - ing ___ so ___ high, de-fy - ing

grav - i - ty, ___ They'll nev - er pull ___ me down... ___

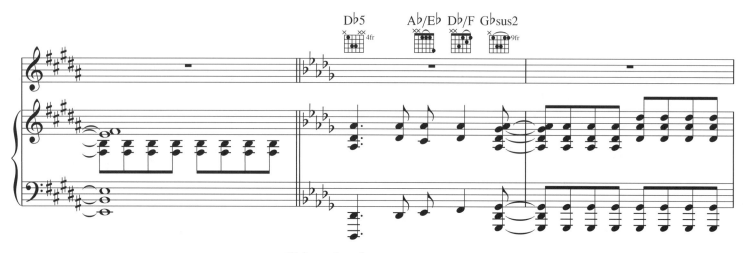

Triumphantly

So if ___ you care ___ to find ___ me,

look ___ to the west - ern sky ___ As some - one told ___

all of Oz, no Wiz-ard that there is or was is ev-er gon-na

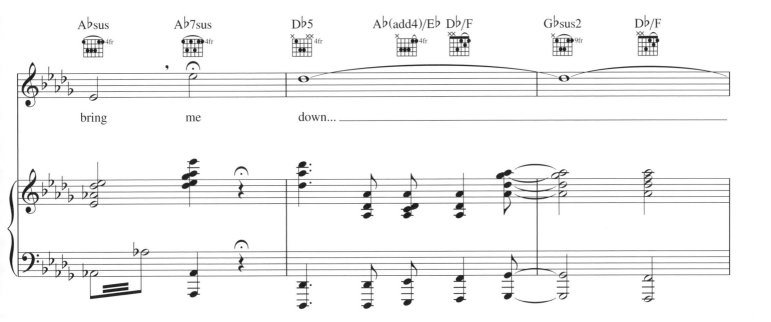

bring me down... _____

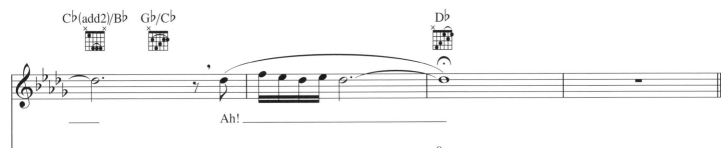

____ Ah! _____

DON'T GO BREAKING MY HEART

Words and Music by CARTE BLANCHE
and ANN ORSON

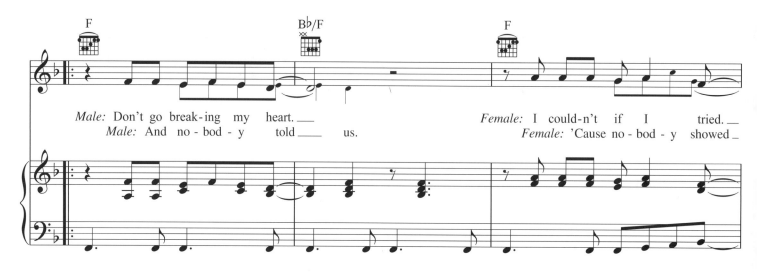

Male: Don't go break-ing my heart. ___
Male: And no-bod-y told ___ us.

Female: I could-n't if I tried. ___
Female: 'Cause no-bod-y showed _

___ us.

Male: Oh, hon-ey, if I ___ get rest-less,
Male: And now ___ it's up ___ to us, ___ babe.

Both: Ooh, hoo, ___ no-bod-y knows ___ it,

Male: but when I was down ___ Female: I was your clown. ___

Both: Ooh, hoo, ___ no-bod-y knows ___ it, (no-bod-y know-

- ows it,) but, right from the start ___ I gave you my heart. ___

Male: Female:

D.S. al Coda

CODA

Both: Don't go break-ing my, don't go break-ing my, don't go break-ing my heart.

Female: I won't go break-ing your heart. don't go break-ing my heart.

EVERY BREATH YOU TAKE

Music and Lyrics by
STING

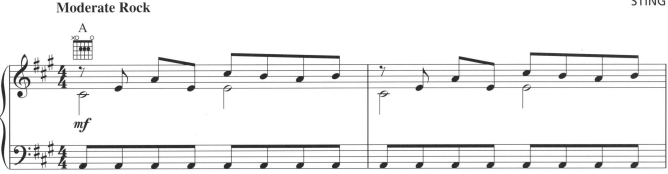

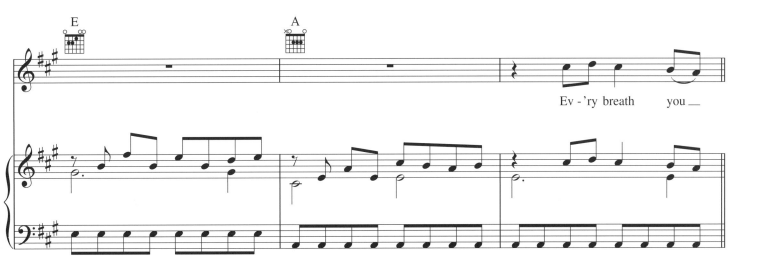

Ev-'ry breath   you __

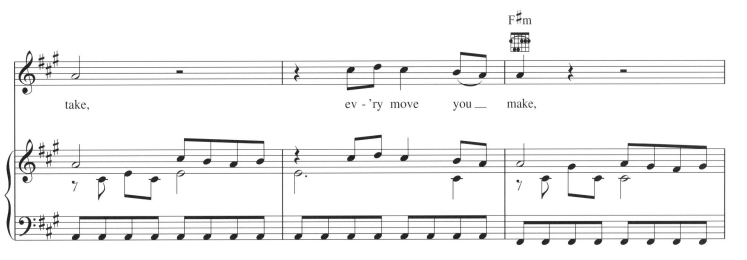

take,   ev-'ry move you __ make,

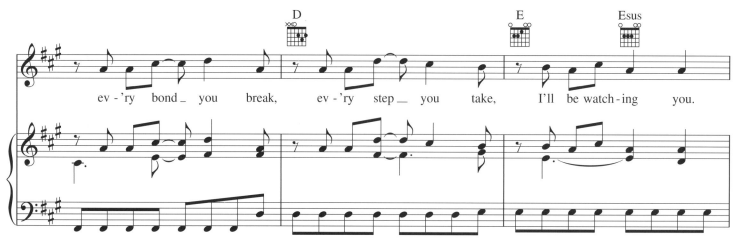

ev-'ry bond _ you break, ev-'ry step _ you take, I'll be watch-ing you.

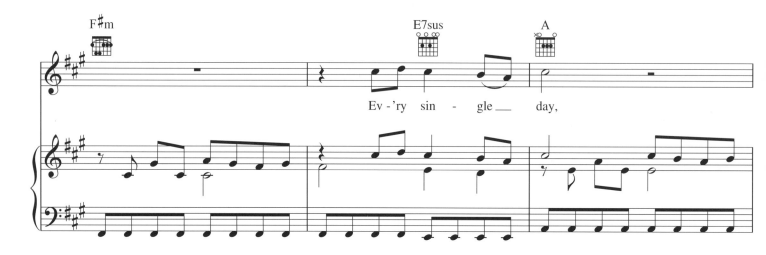

Ev-'ry sin-gle _ day,

ev-'ry word you _ say, ev-'ry game _ you play,

ev-'ry night _ you stay, I'll be watch-ing you.

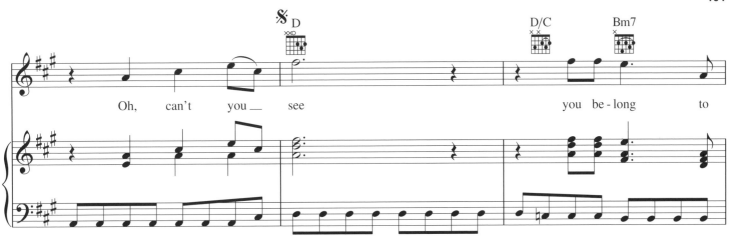

Oh, can't you — see you be-long to

me? How my poor heart _____ aches —

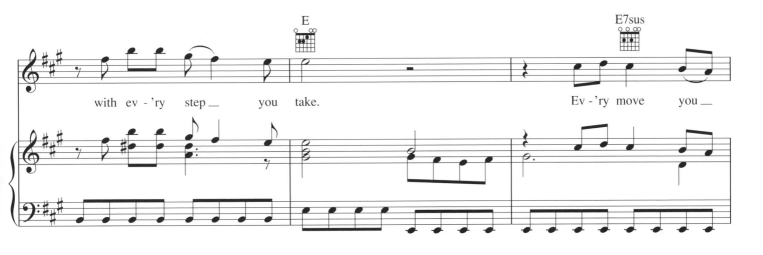

with ev-'ry step — you take. Ev-'ry move you —

make, ev-'ry vow you — break,

ev-'ry smile _ you fake, ev-'ry claim _ you stake, I'll be watch-ing you.

Since you've gone, _ I been lost _

_ with - out _____ a trace, I dream at night I can on - ly see _ your face.

I look a - round, but it's you I can't _ re - place. I feel so cold and I

long for your _ em - brace. I keep cry - ing, ba - by, ba - by, please. _

Oh, can't you ___

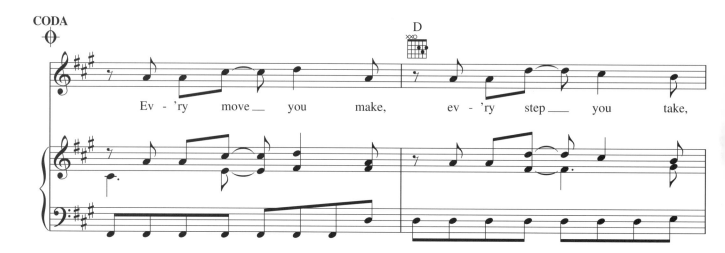

Ev - 'ry move ___ you make, ev - 'ry step ___ you take,

I'll be watch - ing you.

I'll be watch - ing

you.(Ev-'ry breath __ you take, ev-'ry move __ you make, ev-'ry bond __ you break,
you.(Ev-'ry move __ you make, ev-'ry vow __ you break, ev-'ry smile __ you fake,

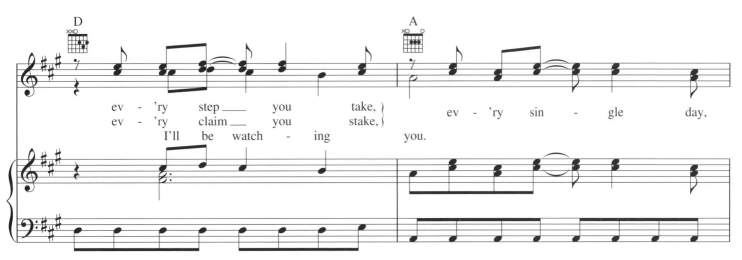

ev-'ry step __ you take,)
ev-'ry claim __ you stake,)
I'll be watch-ing you.
ev-'ry sin-gle day,

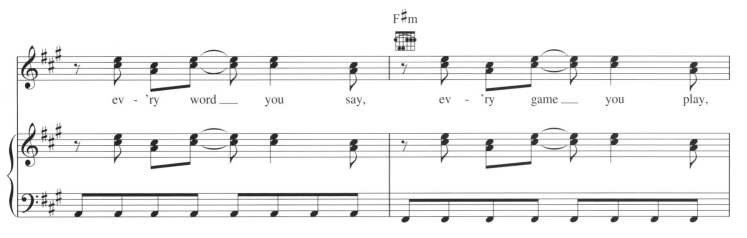

ev-'ry word __ you say, ev-'ry game __ you play,

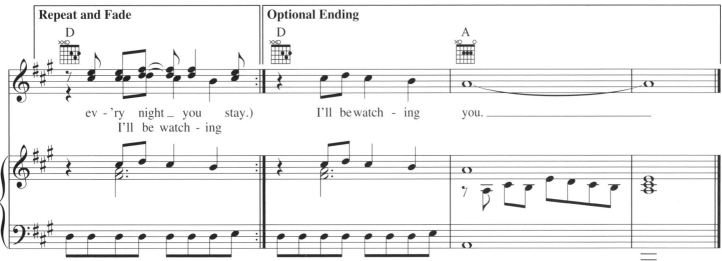

Repeat and Fade

ev-'ry night __ you stay.)
I'll be watch-ing

Optional Ending

I'll be watch-ing you. _____

DON'T STOP BELIEVIN'

Words and Music by STEVE PERRY,
NEAL SCHON and JONATHAN CAIN

Moderately fast

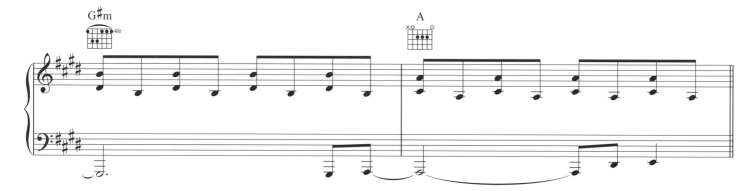

Just a small-town girl, ____
Just a cit-y boy, ____

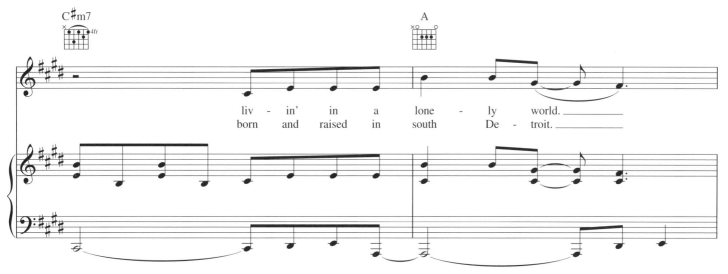

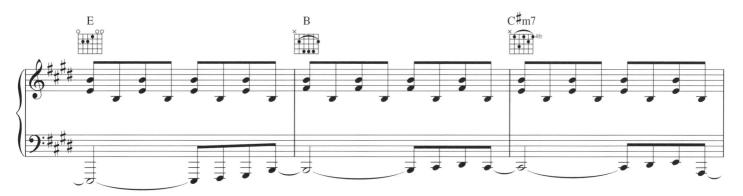

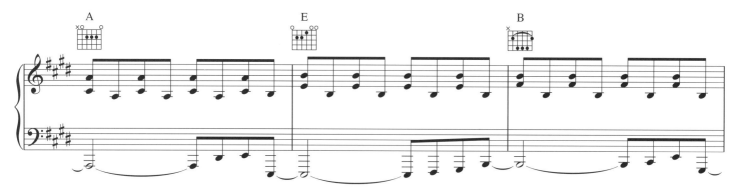

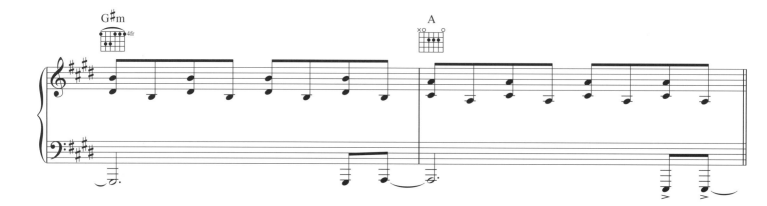

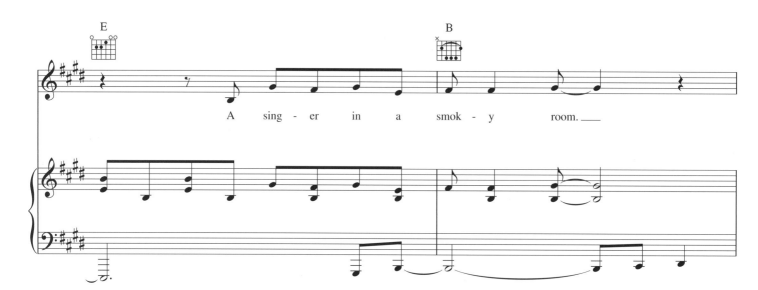

share the night. It goes on and on ___ and on ___ and on. ___

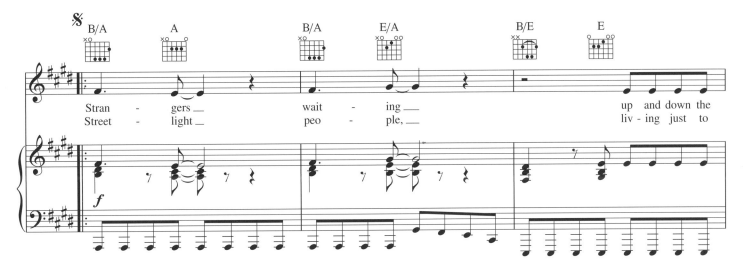

Stran - gers ___ wait - ing ___ up and down the
Street - light ___ peo - ple, ___ liv - ing just to

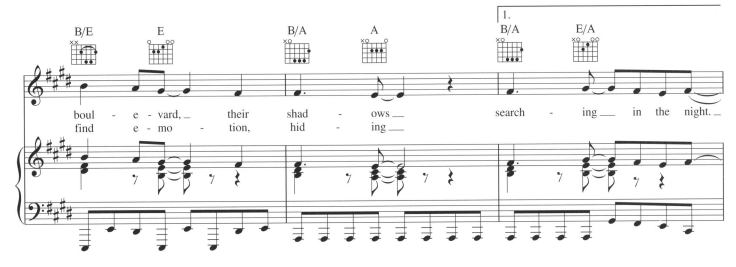

boul - e - vard, ___ their shad - ows ___ search - ing ___ in the night. ___
find e - mo - tion, hid - ing ___

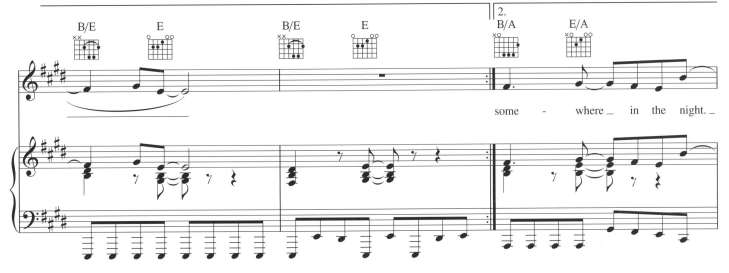

some - where ___ in the night. ___

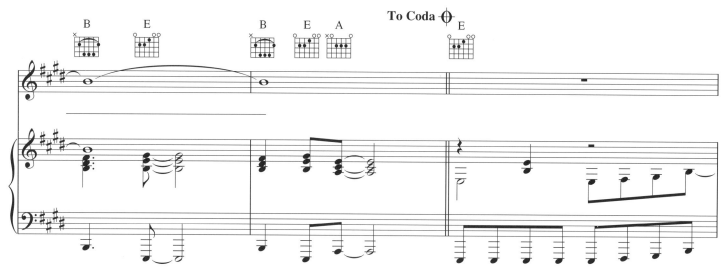

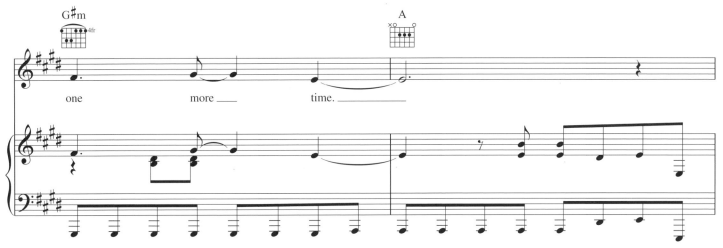

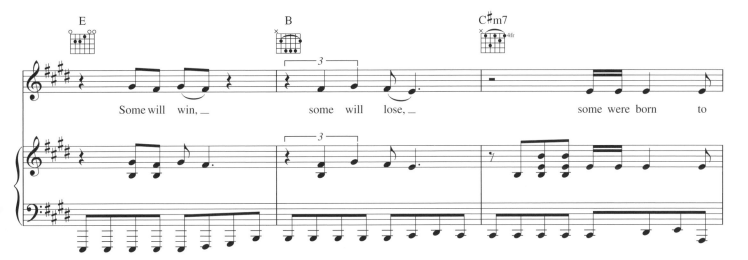

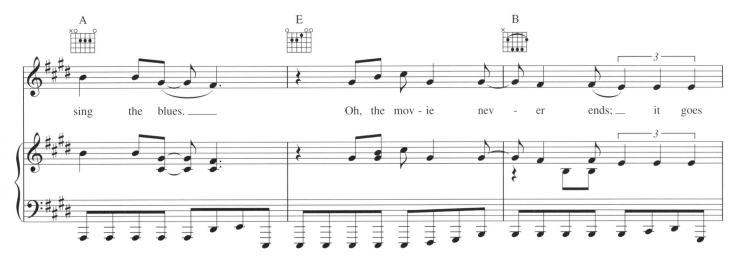

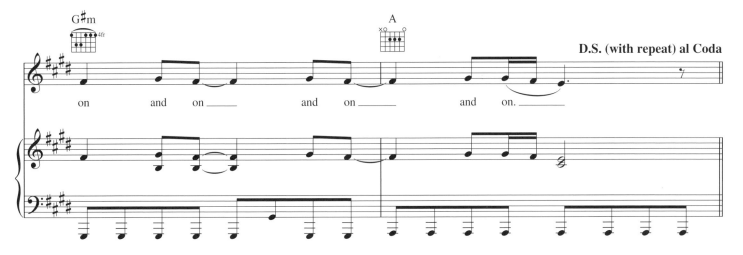

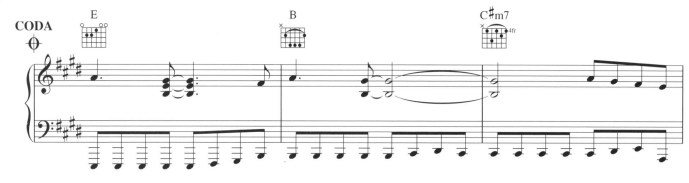

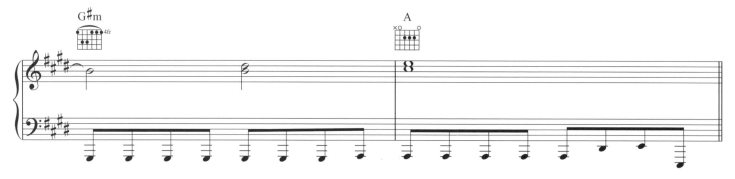

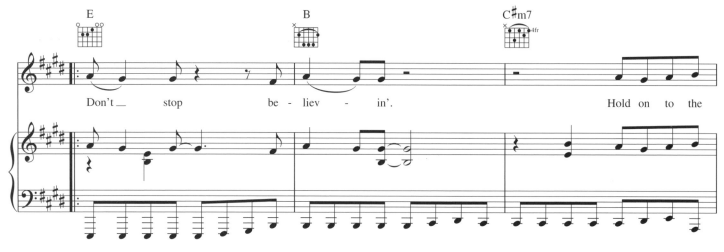

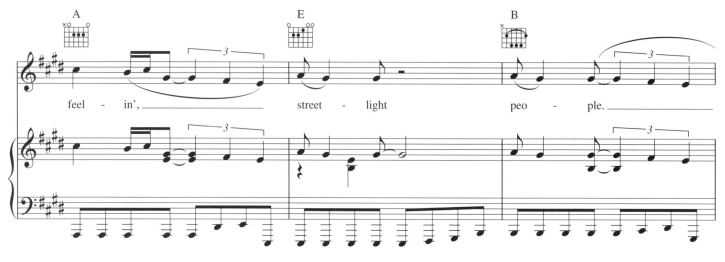

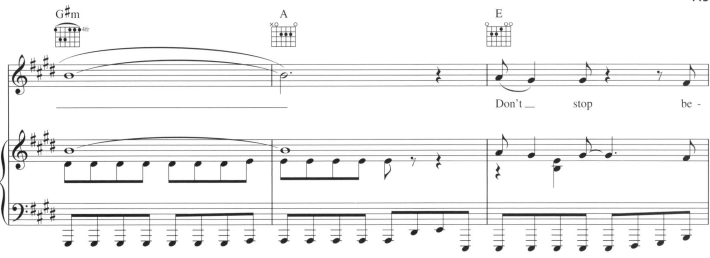

Don't stop be -

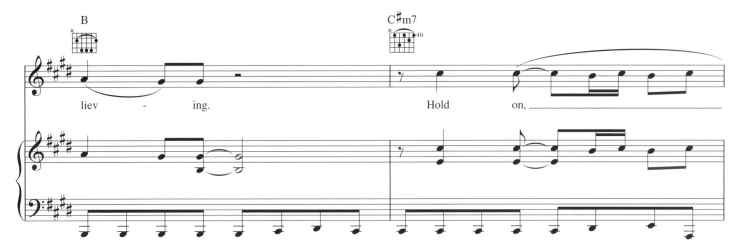

liev - ing. Hold on,

street - light

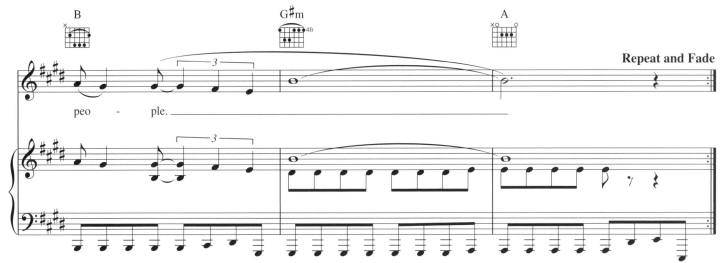

peo - ple.

Repeat and Fade

FEVER

Words and Music by JOHN DAVENPORT
and EDDIE COOLEY

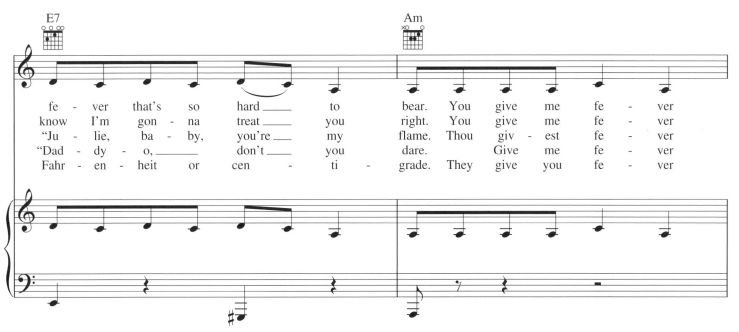

E7   Am

fe - ver	that's	so	hard ____	to	bear. You	give	me	fe - ver
know	I'm	gon - na	treat ____	you	right. You	give	me	fe - ver
"Ju -	lie,	ba - by,	you're ____	my	flame. Thou	giv - est	fe - ver
"Dad - dy -	o, ____	don't ____	you	dare.	Give	me	fe - ver
Fahr - en - heit	or	cen - ti -	grade.	They	give	you	fe - ver

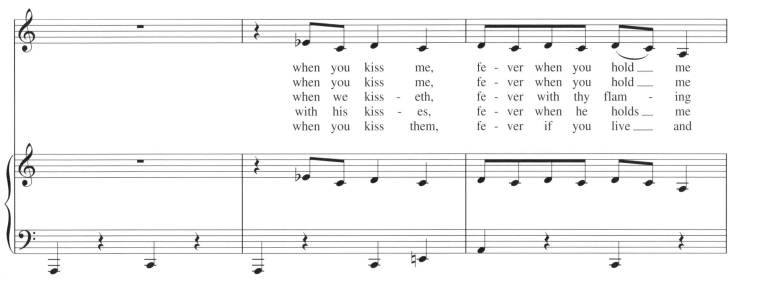

when	you	kiss	me,	fe - ver	when	you	hold ____	me
when	you	kiss	me,	fe - ver	when	you	hold ____	me
when	we	kiss - eth,	fe - ver	with	thy	flam - ing
with	his	kiss - es,	fe - ver	when	he	holds ____	me
when	you	kiss	them,	fe - ver	if	you	live ____	and

tight,	fe - ver	in the	morn - ing,
tight,	fe - ver	in the	morn - ing,
youth.	Fe - ver,	I'm a - fire. ____
tight.	Fe - ver,	I'm his	mis - sus.	Oh,
learn.	Fe - ver	till you	siz - zle,

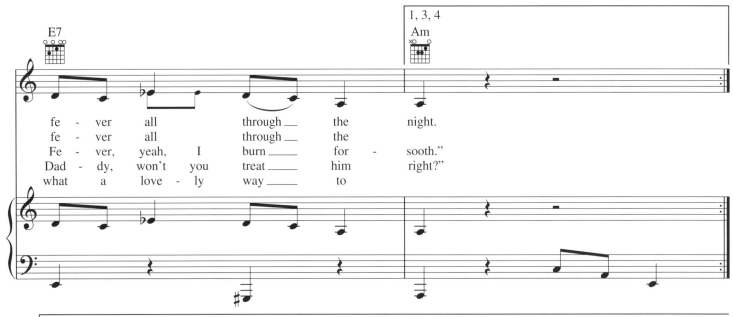

fe - ver all through __ the night.
fe - ver all through __ the
Fe - ver, yeah, I burn _____ for - sooth."
Dad - dy, won't you treat _____ him right?"
what a love - ly way _____ to

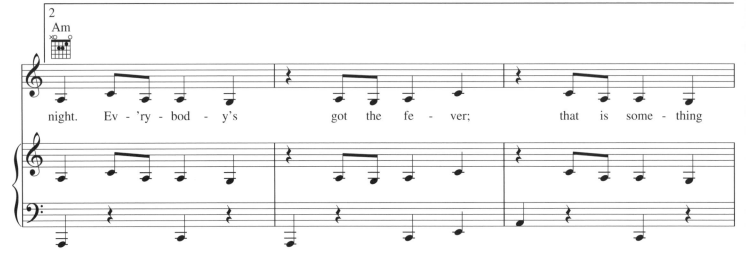

night. Ev - 'ry - bod - y's got the fe - ver; that is some - thing

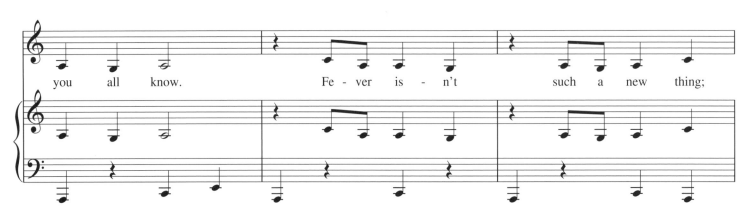

you all know. Fe - ver is - n't such a new thing;

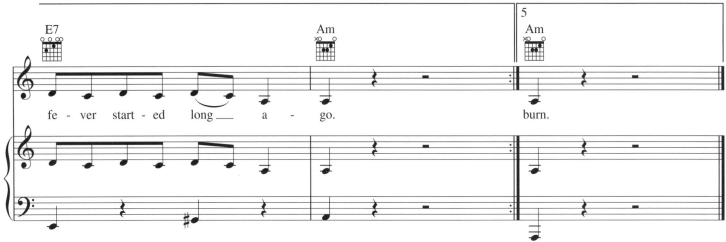

fe - ver start - ed long __ a - go. burn.

HIT ME WITH YOUR BEST SHOT

Words and Music by
EDDIE SCHWARTZ

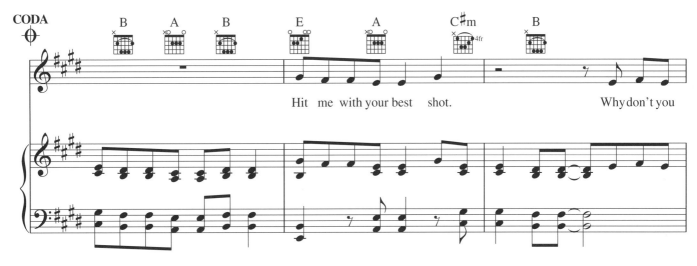

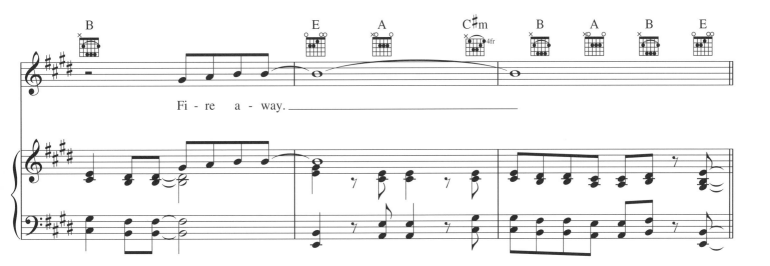

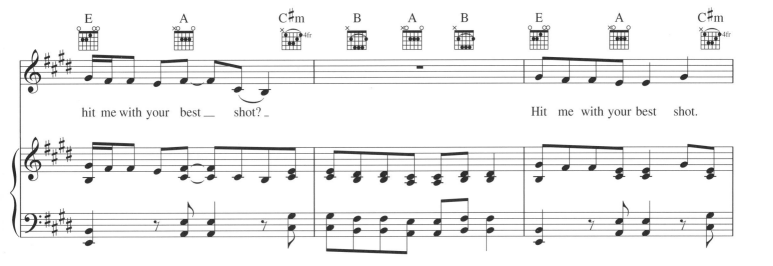

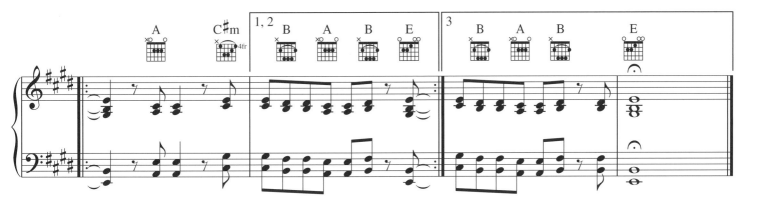

GLORY OF LOVE
Theme from KARATE KID PART II

Words and Music by DAVID FOSTER,
PETER CETERA and DIANE NINI

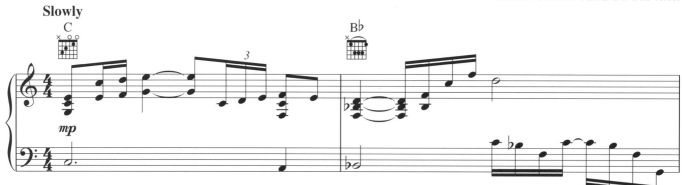

To- night_ it's ver- y clear, as we're both stand- ing here, _

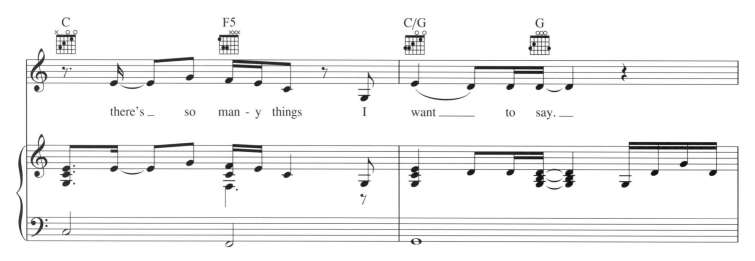

there's _ so man- y things I want _____ to say. ___

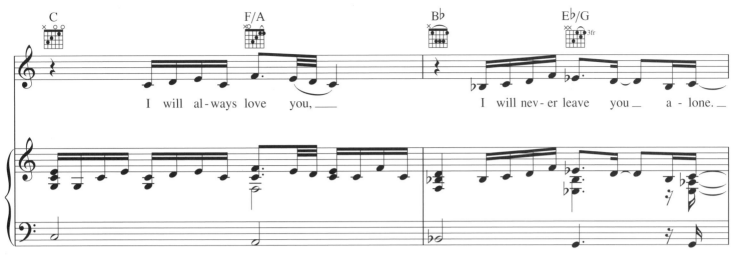

I will al-ways love you, ____ I will nev-er leave you ____ a - lone. ____

Some-times I just for - get, say things I might re - gret, ____
You keep me stand-ing tall, you help me through it all, ____

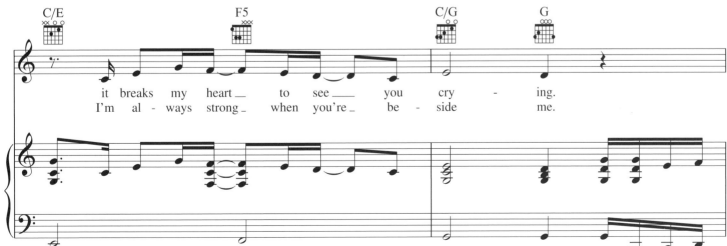

it breaks my heart ____ to see ____ you cry - ing.
I'm al - ways strong ____ when you're ____ be - side me.

I am the man who will fight for your hon - or, I'll be the he - ro that you're dream-ing of.

We're gon-na live for-ev - er, know-ing to-geth - er that we did it all for the glo - ry of love.

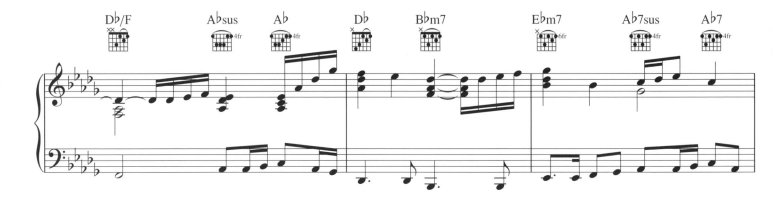

GOODBYE YELLOW BRICK ROAD

Words and Music by ELTON JOHN
and BERNIE TAUPIN

When are you gon-na come down? When are you going to land?
What do you think you'll do then? I bet that'll shoot down your plane.

I should have stayed on the farm. I should have
It -'ll take you a cou-ple of vod-ka and ton-ics to

lis-tened to my old man. You know you can't hold me for-ev-
set you on your feet a-gain. May-be you'll get a re-place-

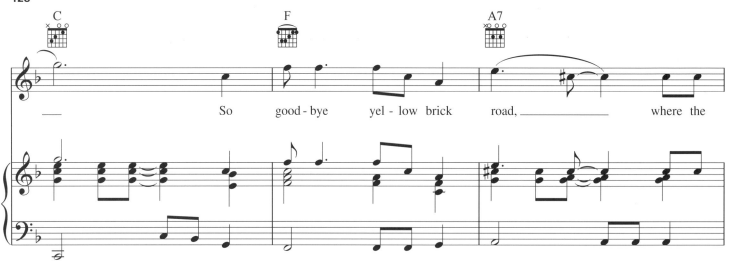

So good-bye yel-low brick road, _____ where the

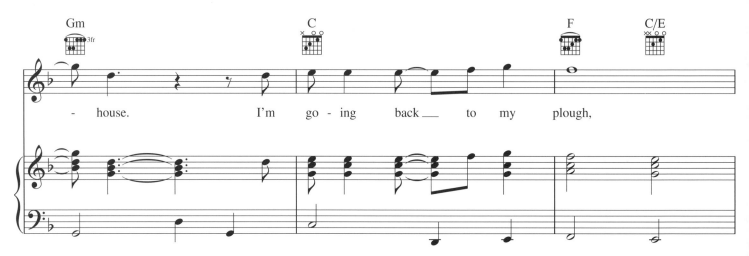

dogs of so-ci-e-ty howl. ___ You can't plant me in your pent-

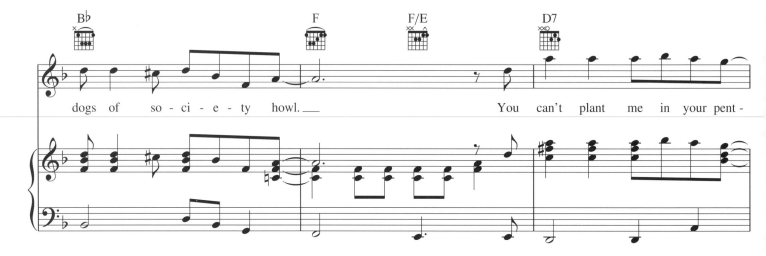

- house. I'm go-ing back ___ to my plough,

back to the howl-ing old owl ___ in the woods, _ hunt-ing the horn-y-backed

HALLELUJAH

Words and Music by
LEONARD COHEN

Moderately slow, in 2

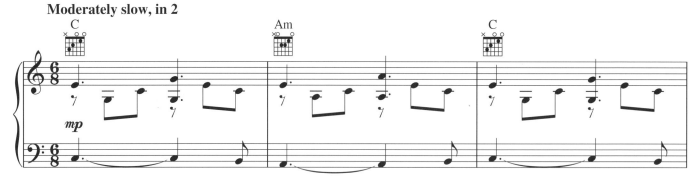

1. I've heard there was a se-cret chord ___ that
2. faith was strong but you need-ed proof. ___ You
3. be I have been here be-fore. ___ I
4.,5. *(See additional lyrics)*

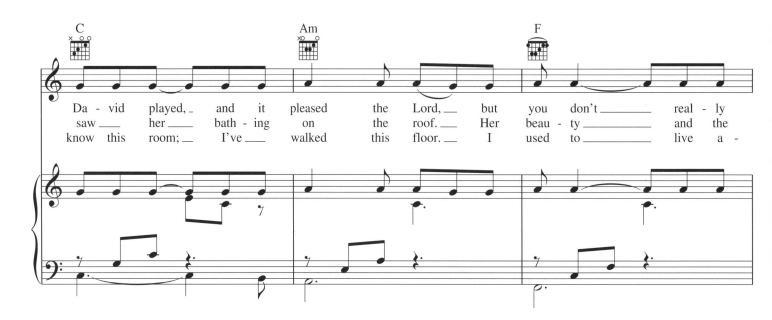

Da-vid played, ___ and it pleased the Lord, ___ but you don't ___ real-ly
saw ___ her ___ bath-ing on the roof. ___ Her beau-ty ___ and the
know this room; ___ I've walked this floor. ___ I used to ___ live a-

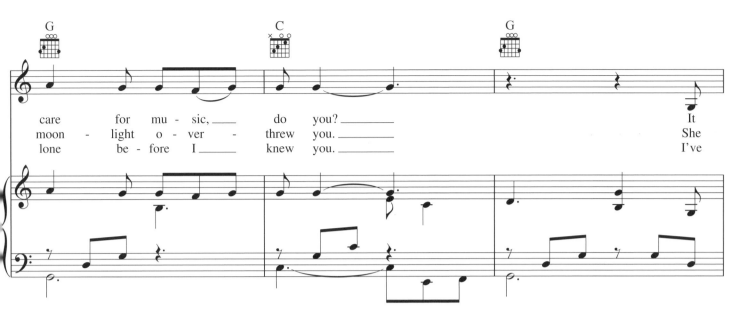

care for mu - sic, ____ do you? ____ It
moon - light o - ver - threw you. ____ She
lone be - fore I ____ knew you. ____ I've

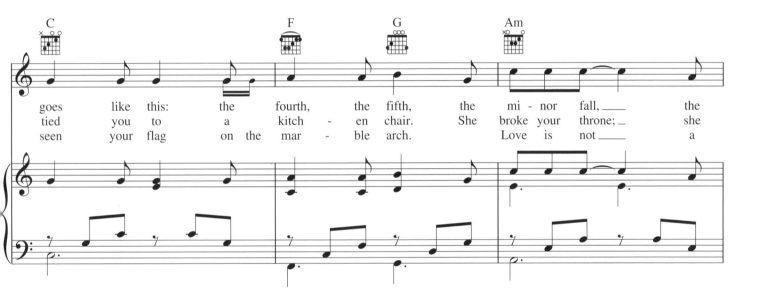

goes like this: the fourth, the fifth, the mi - nor fall, ____ the
tied you to a kitch - en chair. She broke your throne; ____ she
seen your flag on the mar - ble arch. Love is not ____ a

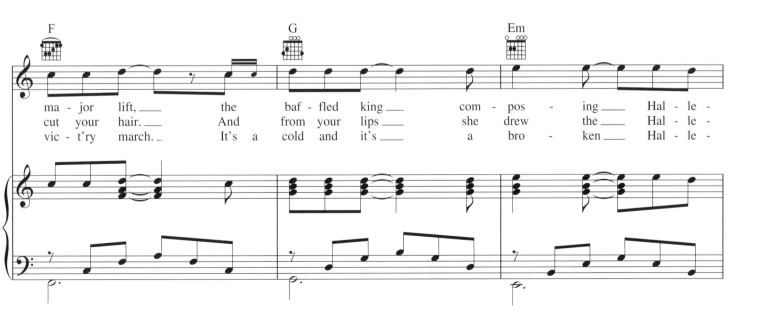

ma - jor lift, ____ the baf - fled king ____ com - pos - ing ____ Hal - le -
cut your hair. ____ And from your lips ____ she drew the ____ Hal - le -
vic - t'ry march. _ It's a cold and it's ____ a bro - ken ____ Hal - le -

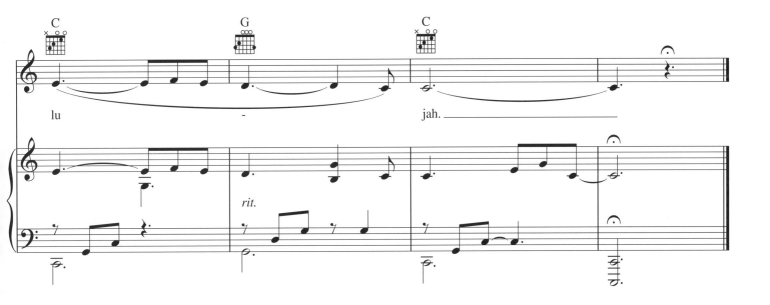

Additional Lyrics

4. There was a time you let me know
   What's real and going on below.
   But now you never show it to me, do you?
   And remember when I moved in you.
   The holy dark was movin', too,
   And every breath we drew was Hallelujah.
   Chorus

5. Maybe there's a God above,
   And all I ever learned from love
   Was how to shoot at someone who outdrew you.
   And it's not a cry you can hear at night.
   It's not somebody who's seen the light.
   It's a cold and it's a broken Hallelujah.
   Chorus

HEY JUDE

Words and Music by JOHN LENNON
and PAUL McCARTNEY

Hey Jude,_____ don't make it bad; take a
don't make it bad; take a

sad song_____ and make it bet - ter._____ Re-
sad song_____ and make it bet - ter._____ Re-

mem - ber to let her in - to your heart; then you can start____
mem - ber to let her un - der your skin, then you be - gin____

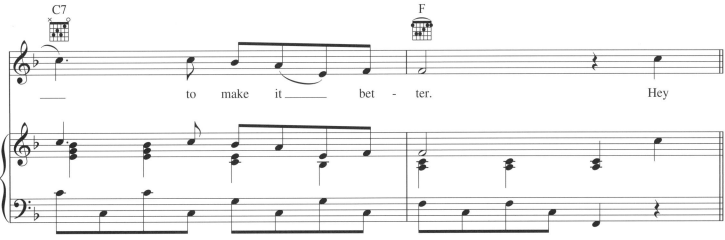

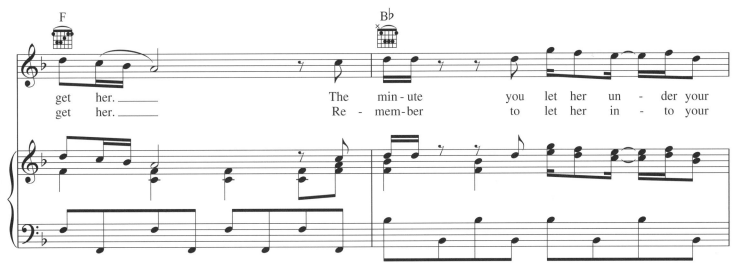

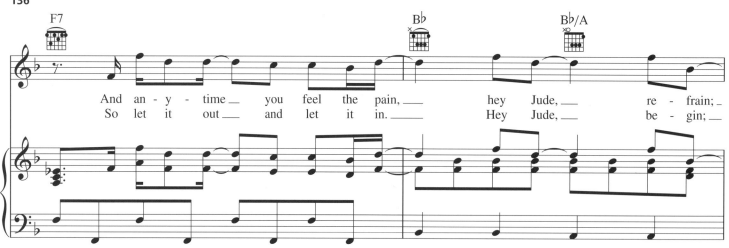

And an - y - time ___ you feel the pain, ___ hey Jude, ___ re - frain;
So let it out ___ and let it in. ___ Hey Jude, ___ be - gin;

___ don't car - ry the world ___ up - on ___ your shoul - ders. _
___ you're wait - ing for some - one to ___ per - form ___ with. _

For well you know ___ that it's a fool ___ who plays ___ it cool ___
And don't you know ___ that it's just you? ___ Hey Jude, ___ you'll do. ___

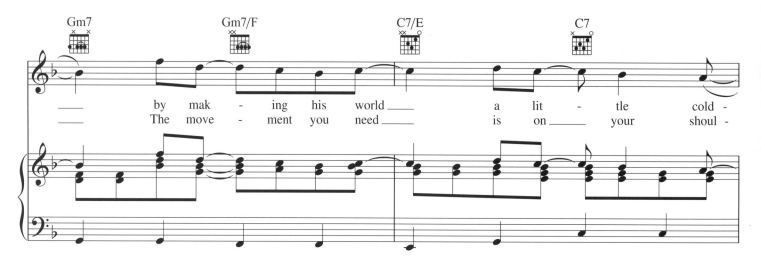

___ by mak - ing his world ___ a lit - tle cold -
___ The move - ment you need ___ is on ___ your shoul -

HEY, SOUL SISTER

Words and Music by PAT MONAHAN,
ESPEN LIND and AMUND BJORKLAND

Moderately

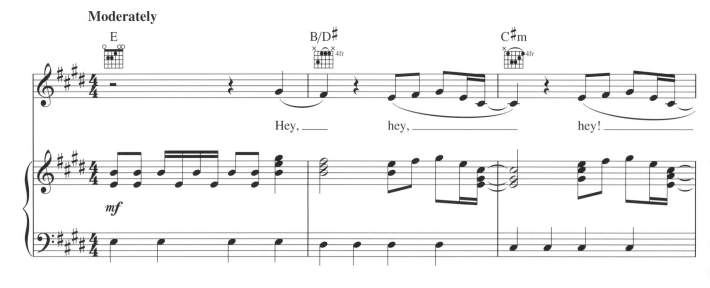

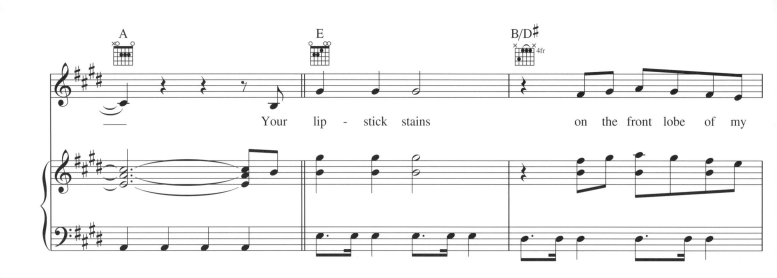

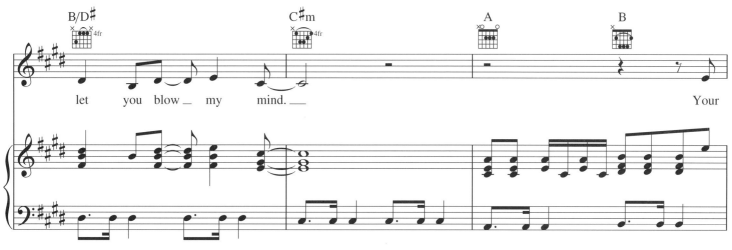

let you blow __ my mind. __   Your

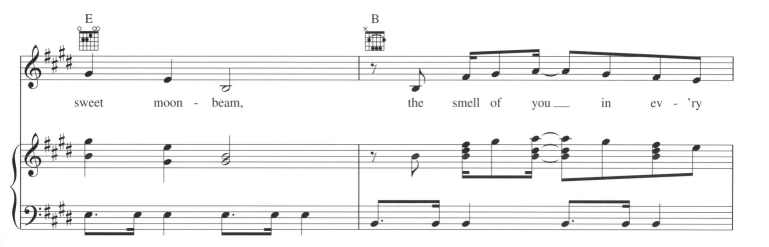

sweet moon - beam,   the smell of you __ in ev - 'ry

sin - gle dream I __ dream, __   I knew when we col - lid -

- ed you're the one __ I have de - cid - ed who's one of my __ kind. __

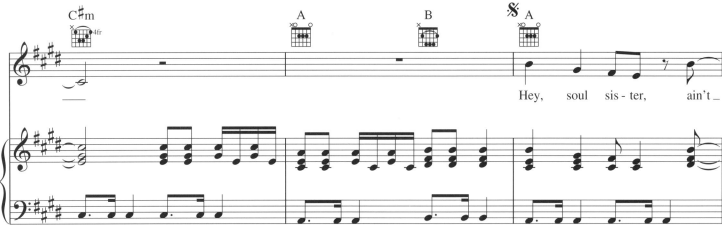

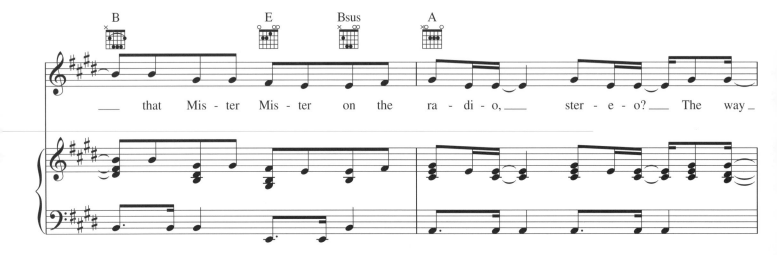

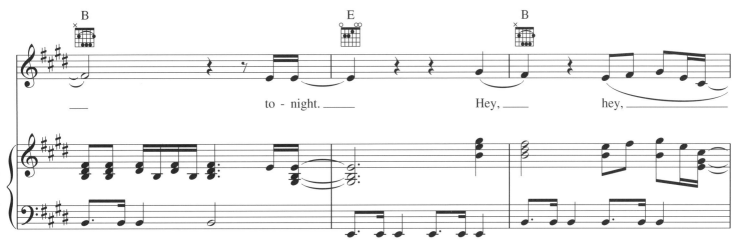

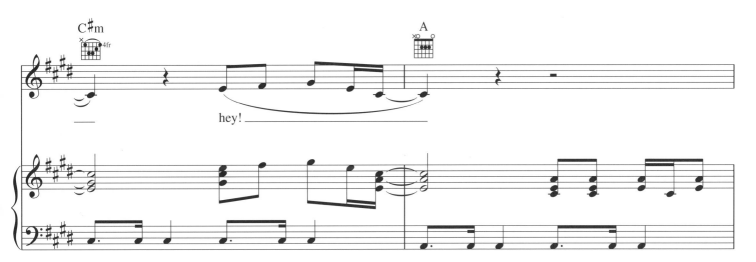

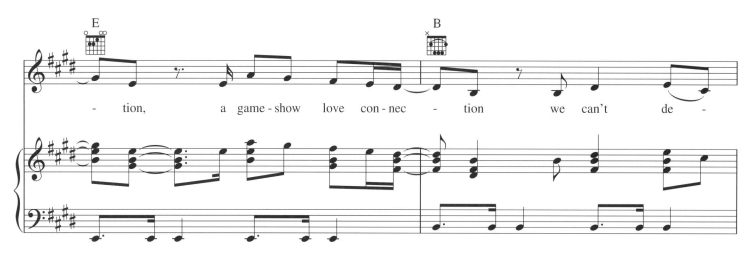

-tion, a game-show love con-nec - tion we can't de -

ny. I, I, _____ I, _____ I'm so ob-sessed.

My heart is bound to beat right out my un-trimmed __ chest.

__ I be-lieve __ in you. __ Like a vir - gin, you're Ma-don-

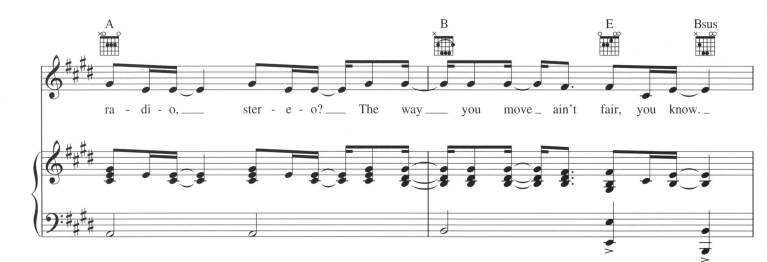

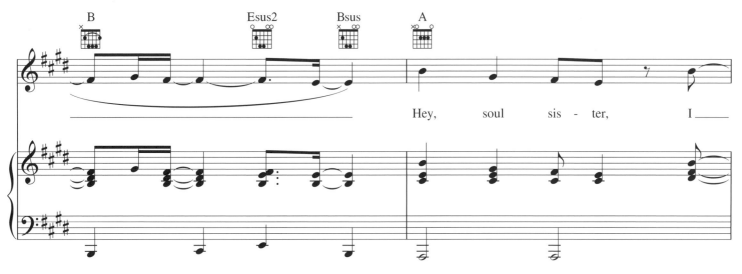

I LOVE ROCK 'N ROLL

Words and Music by ALAN MERRILL
and JAKE HOOKER

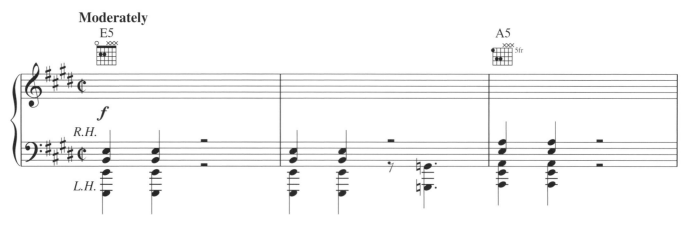

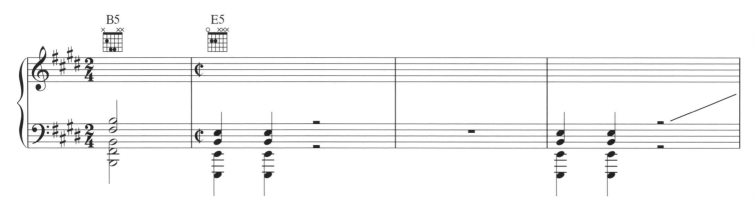

I saw him danc-ing there ___ by the rec-ord ma-
smiled, so I got up ___ and asked ___ for his

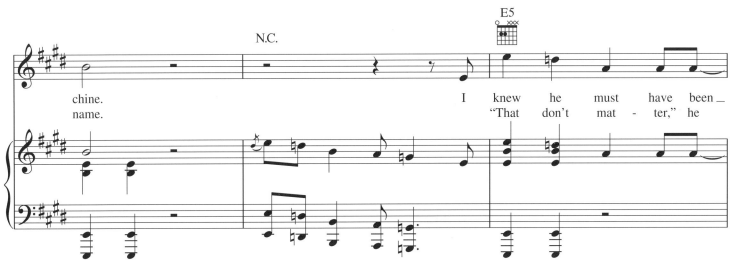

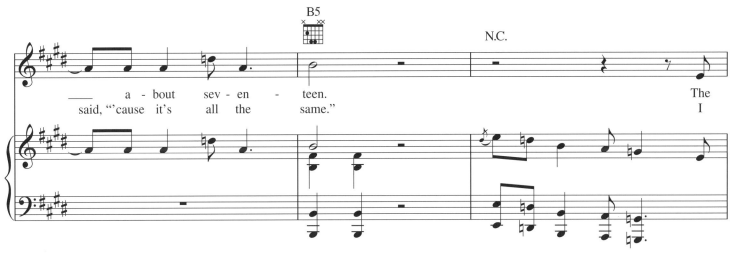

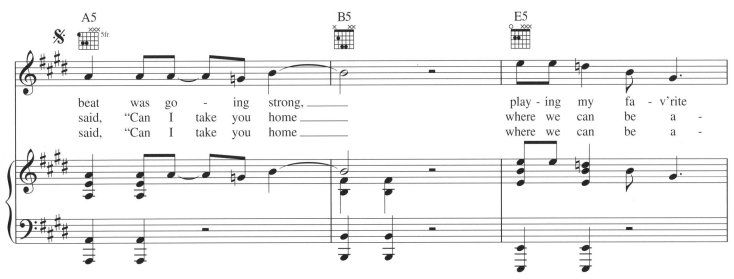

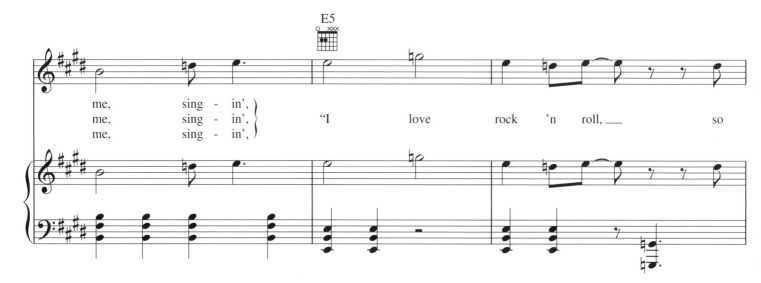

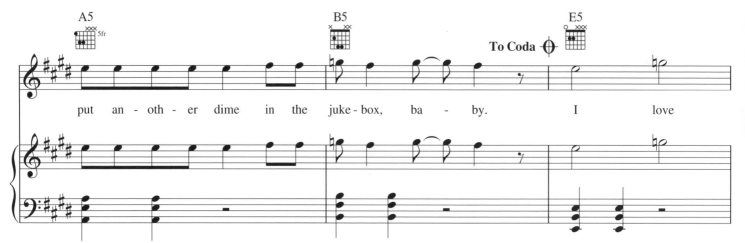

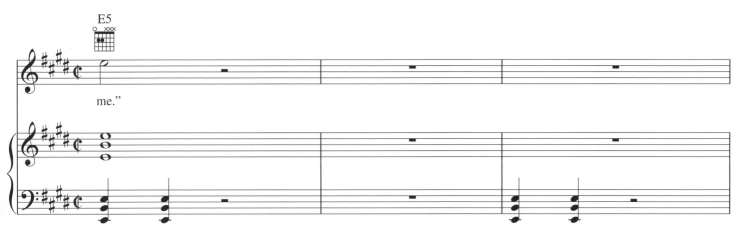

me."

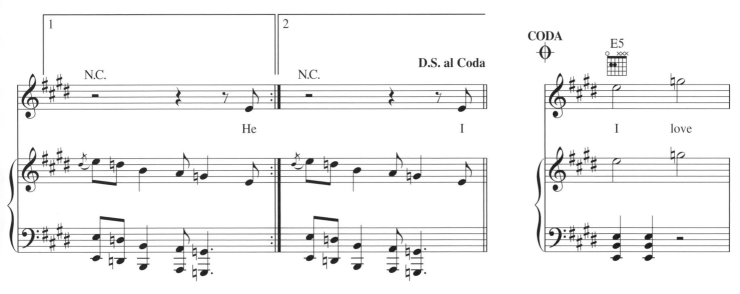

D.S. al Coda

CODA

He

I

I love

rock 'n roll, ___ so come and take your time and dance with me."

I WILL ALWAYS LOVE YOU

Words and Music by
DOLLY PARTON

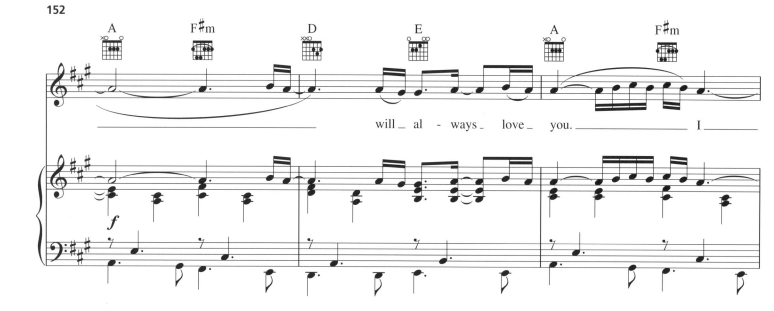

will al - ways love you. I

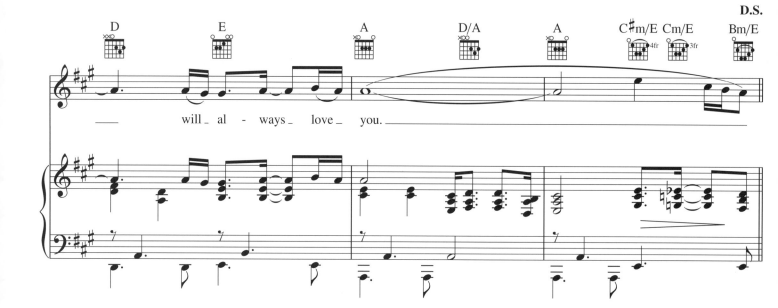

will al - ways love you.

D.S.

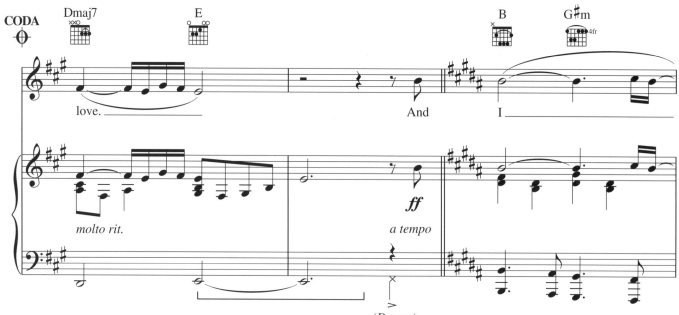

CODA

love. And I

molto rit.

a tempo

(Drums)

will _ al - ways _ love _ you. _____ I will al - ways _____ love _

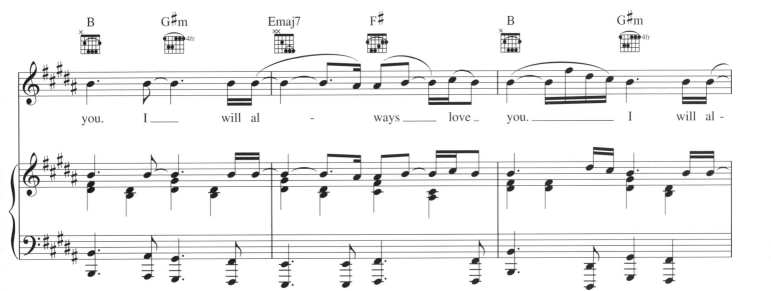

you. I ____ will al - ways _____ love _ you. _____ I will al -

- ways _ love you. _____ I will _ al - ways love

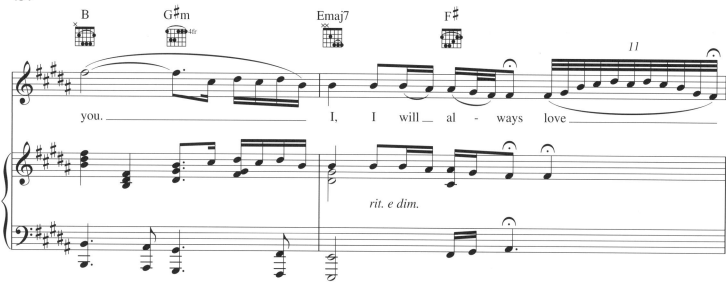

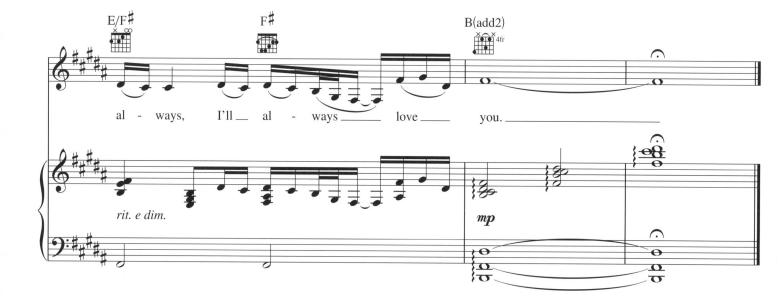

Additional Lyrics

3. I hope life treats you kind.
   And I hope you have all you've dreamed of.
   And I wish to you, joy and happiness.
   But above all this, I wish you love.

I WILL SURVIVE

Words and Music by DINO FEKARIS
and FREDERICK J. PERREN

Fmaj7   Bm7♭5   E7sus

Weren't you the one who tried to hurt me with good-bye? Did you think I'd crum-ble, did you think I'd

E7   Am   Dm

lay down — and die? Oh no, not I, I will sur-vive. — Oh, — as

G   Cmaj7   Fmaj7

long as I know how to love, I know I'll stay a-live. I've got all my life to live, I've got

Bm7♭5   E7sus   **1** E7   **2** E7   **D.S. and Fade**

all my love to give and I'll sur-vive, I will sur-vive! It took vive! Now

I'M A BELIEVER

featured in the DreamWorks Motion Picture SHREK

Words and Music by
NEIL DIAMOND

I thought love was on - ly true in
I thought love was more or less a

fair - y tales,   meant for some - one else but not for
giv - in' thing;   seems the more I gave the less I

me.
got.   (2., D.S.) What's the use in try - in'?   Love   was   out   to   get   me.

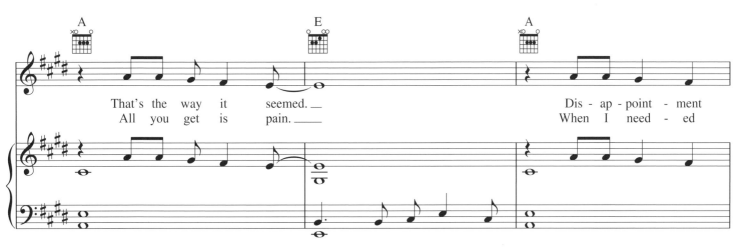

That's the way it seemed. ___
All you get is pain. ___
Dis - ap - point - ment
When I need - ed

haunt - ed all my dreams.
sun - shine I got rain.
Then I saw her face; ___

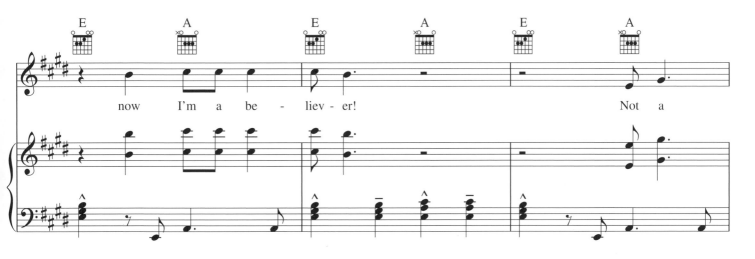

now I'm a be - liev - er! Not a

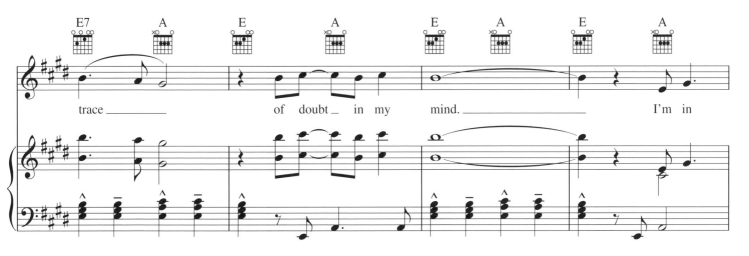

trace ___ of doubt _ in my mind. ___ I'm in

love, and I'm a be - liev - er! I could - n't

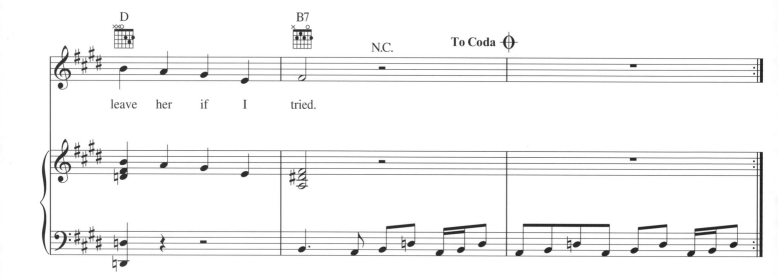

leave her if I tried.

D.S. al Coda

CODA

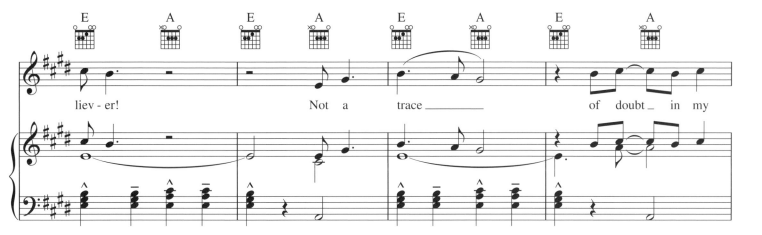

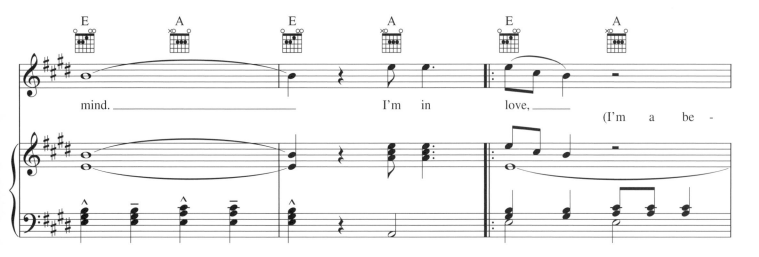

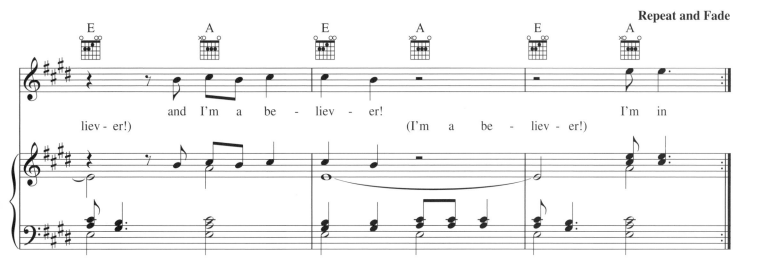

I'M YOURS

Words and Music by
JASON MRAZ

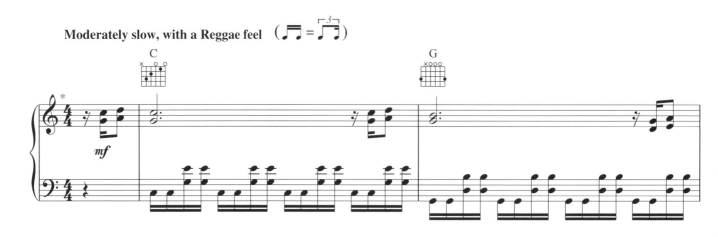

Well,

you done done _ me in; you bet I felt _ it. I tried to be chill, _ but you're so hot that I melt - ed. I

*Recorded a half step lower.

fell right through the cracks. _____ Now I'm try-ing to get _ back. _____ Be-fore the

cool done run out, I'll be giv-ing it my best - est, and noth-ing's gon-na stop me but di-vine in - ter - ven - tion. I

reck - on it's a - gain my turn _ to win some _ or learn _ some. But

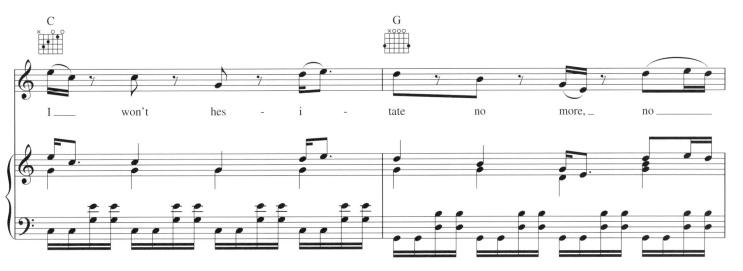

I _ won't hes - i - tate no more, _ no _____

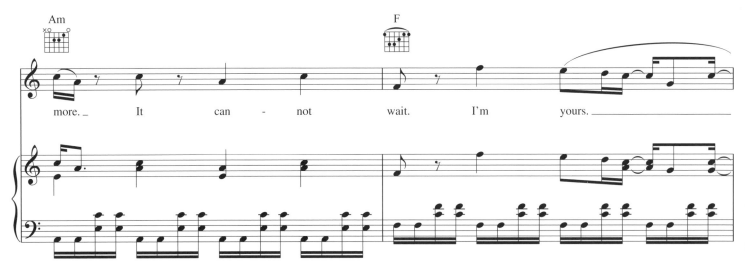

Am   F

more._ It can- not wait. I'm yours._

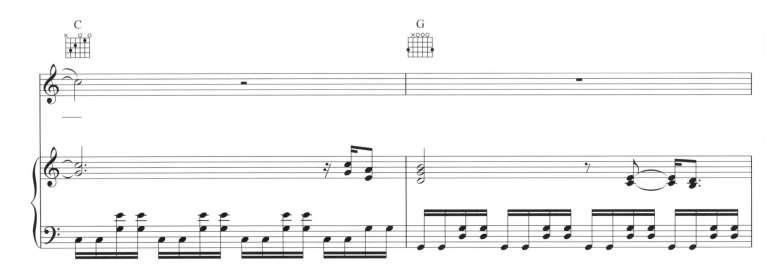

C   G

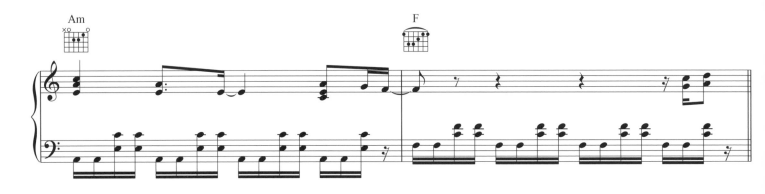

Am   F

C   G

Well, o- pen up your mind and see_ like me._ O- pen up your plans and, damn,_ you're free.

more. ___ It can - not wait. I'm sure. _____ There's no

need ___ to com - pli - cate. Our ___ time ___ is _____

short. ___ This is our fate. I'm yours. _____ *Scat sing...*

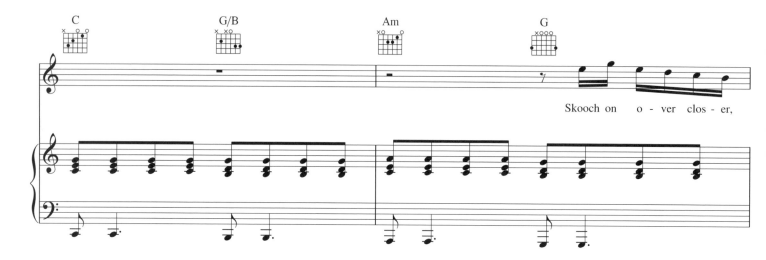

Skooch on o - ver clos - er,

dear,   and I will nib - ble your ear. _____   *Scat sing...*

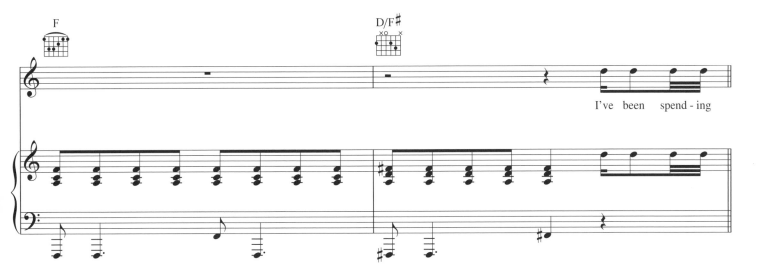

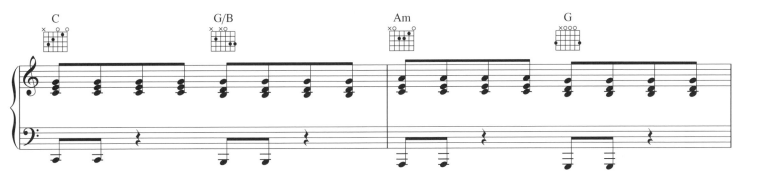

I've been spend - ing

way too long _ check-ing my tongue in the mir - ror   and bend-ing o - ver back-wards just to try to see it clear - er.   But

my breath fogged _ up the glass, _ and so I drew a new face _ and I laughed. _____ I

guess what I'll be say-ing is there ain't no bet-ter rea-son to rid your-self of van-i-ties and just go with the sea-sons. It's

what we aim to do. Our ____ name is ____ our vir - tue. But

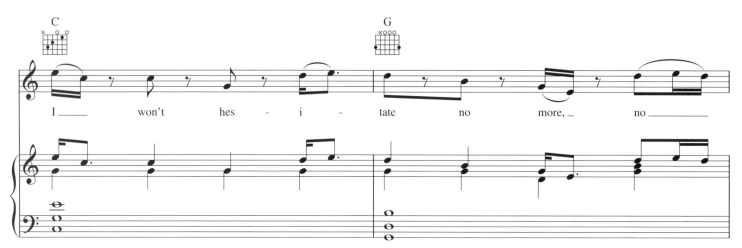

I ____ won't hes - i - tate no more, _ no _____

more. __ It can - not wait. I'm yours. _____

O - pen up your mind ___ and see like me. ___ O - pen up your plans ___ and, damn, __ you're __ free. __
(I won't hes - i - tate no more, no

____ Look in - to your heart __ and you'll __ find __ that the sky __ is yours. _____ So
more. It can - not wait. I'm sure. _____ No

please don't, please don't, please don't... There's no need _ to com - pli - cate 'cause our time _
need to com - pli - cate. Our time is

_ is short. _ This is, this is, this is our fate. I'm yours. _____ *Scat sing...*
short. This is our fate. I'm yours.) _____

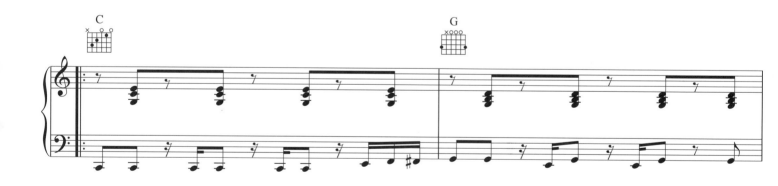

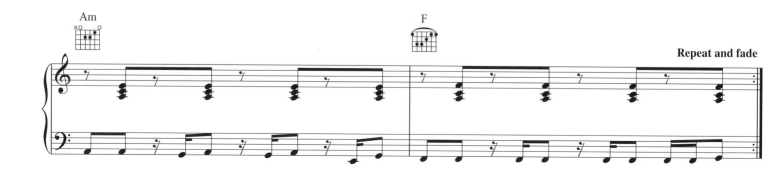

Repeat and fade

THE JOKER

Words and Music by STEVE MILLER,
EDDIE CURTIS and AHMET ERTEGUN

speak of the pom-pa-tus of love. _____

Peo - ple talk __ a - bout _____ me, ba - by, _____

say I'm do - ing you wrong, __ do - ing you wrong. _____

Well, don't you wor - ry, ba - by, don't wor - ry 'cause I'm

right here, right here, right here, right here at home. __ 'Cause I'm a

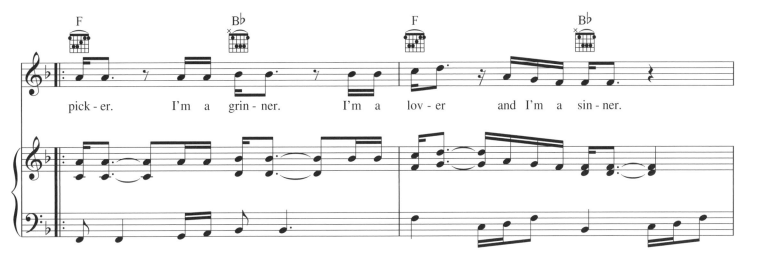

pick-er. I'm a grin-ner. I'm a lov-er and I'm a sin-ner.

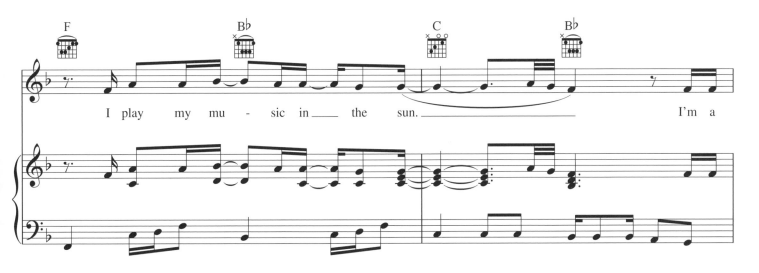

I play my mu-sic in __ the sun. __ I'm a

jok-er. I'm a smok-er. I'm a mid-night __ tok-er.

I sure don't want to hurt no one. I'm a

I get my lov-ing on the run. Oo, hoo.

Oo, hoo.

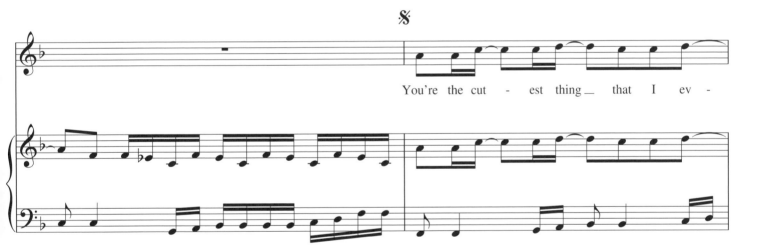

You're the cut - est thing __ that I ev -

- er did see. _____ I real - ly love __ your peach - es, wan - na

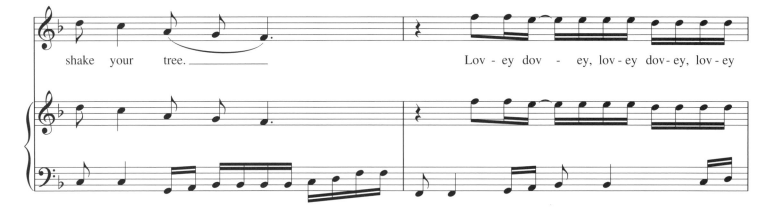

shake your tree. _____ Lov-ey dov - ey, lov-ey dov-ey, lov-ey

To Coda ⊕

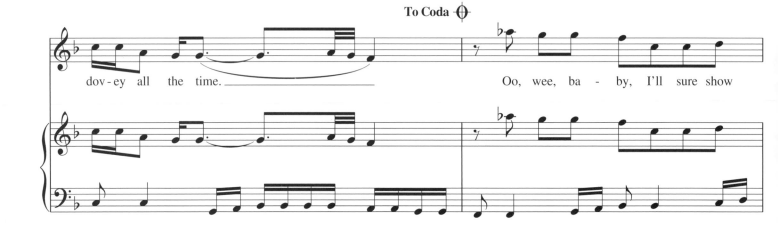

dov-ey all the time. _____ Oo, wee, ba - by, I'll sure show

you a good time. _____ 'Cause I'm a pick-er. I'm a grin-ner. I'm a

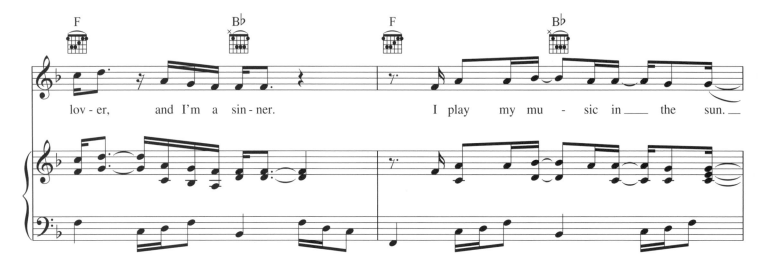

lov-er, and I'm a sin-ner. I play my mu - sic in___ the sun.___

I'm a jok - er. I'm a smok - er. I'm a

mid - night __ tok - er. I get my lov - ing on __ the run. __

I'm a   I sure don't want __ to hurt __ no one. __

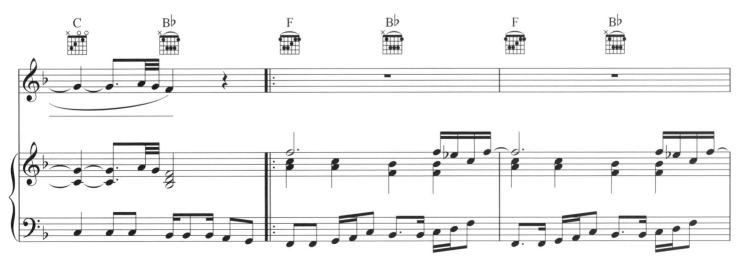

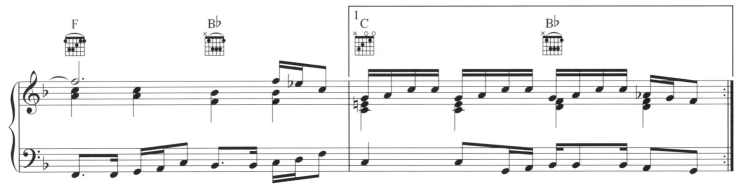

Oo, hoo. _____ Oo, hoo. _____

Peo - ple keep talk - in' a - bout _____ me, ba - by.

They say I'm do - ing you wrong. _____

Well, don't you wor-ry. Don't wor - ry. No, don't wor - ry, ma - ma,

D.S. al Coda

'cause I'm right here at home.

CODA

Come on, babe, __ and I'll show you a good time.

Repeat and Fade **Optional Ending**

IMAGINE

Words and Music by
JOHN LENNON

Slowly

I-mag-ine there's no heav-en.

It's eas-y if you try. No hell be-low us,

a-bove us on-ly sky.

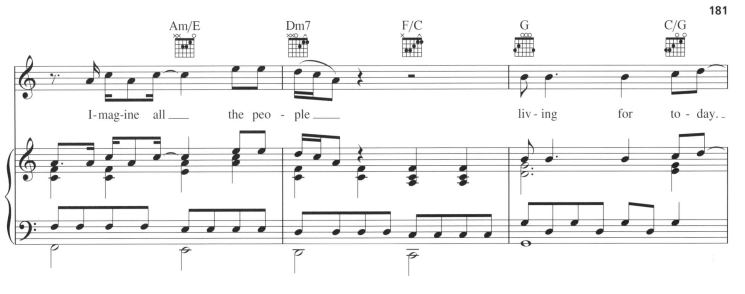

I-mag-ine all ___ the peo - ple ___ liv - ing for to - day. __

__ Ah. _____ I - mag-ine there's no coun - tries.
sions.

It is - n't hard _____ to do. _____
I won - der if you ___ can. ____

Noth-ing to kill ___ or die _____ for,
No need for greed _ or hun - ger,

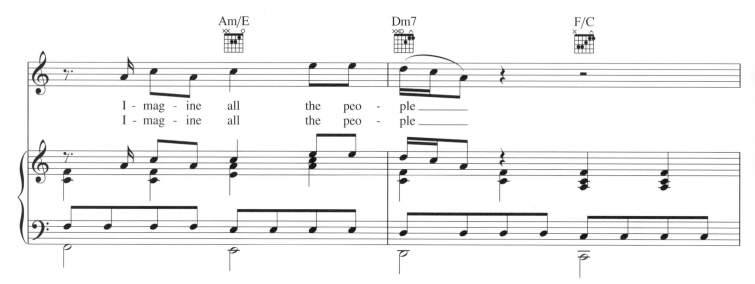

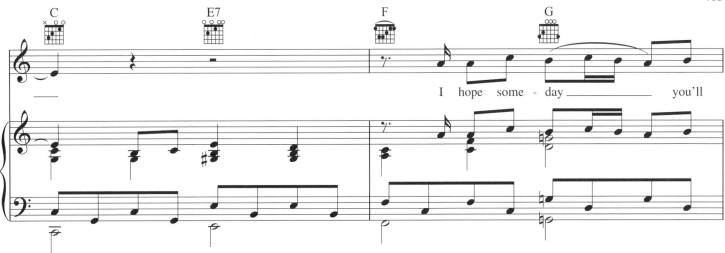

I hope some-day _____ you'll

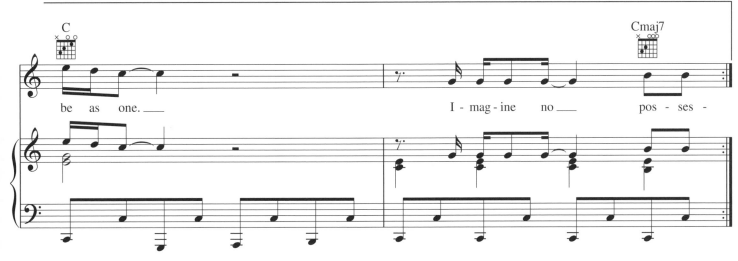

join us _____ and the world _____ will

be as one. ____ I - mag - ine no ____ pos - ses -

and the world _____ will live as one. ____

IT'S TOO LATE

Words and Music by CAROLE KING
and TONI STERN

Stayed in bed all morn-in' just to pass the time. ___
used to be so eas-y, liv-in' here with you. ___

There's some-thin' wrong here, there can be no de-ny-in'. One of us ___ is chang-in', or
You were light and breez-y, an' I knew ___ just what to do. Now you look so un-hap-py, and I ___

may-be we've just ___ stopped try-in'. ___
___ feel ___ like a fool. ___

And it's too ___

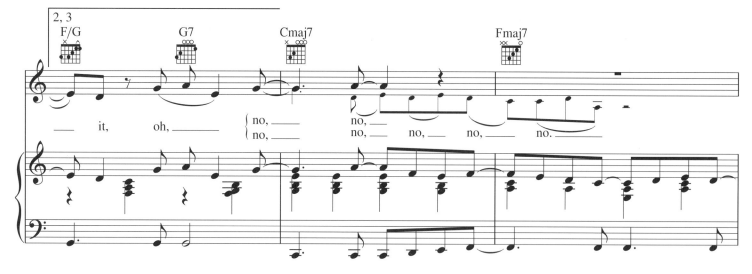

it, oh, _____ { no, _____ no, _____ no, _____ no, _____ no.
no, _____

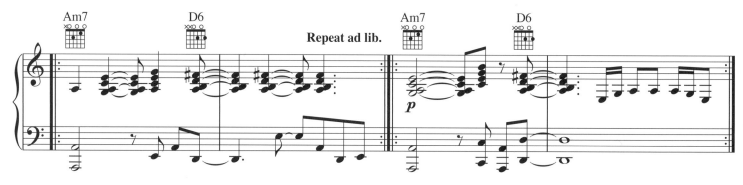

To Coda ⊕

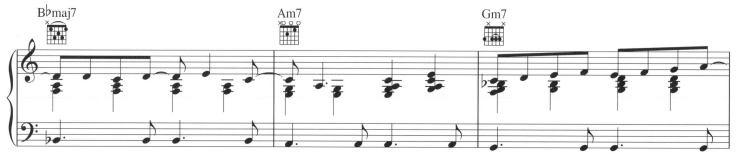

Repeat ad lib.

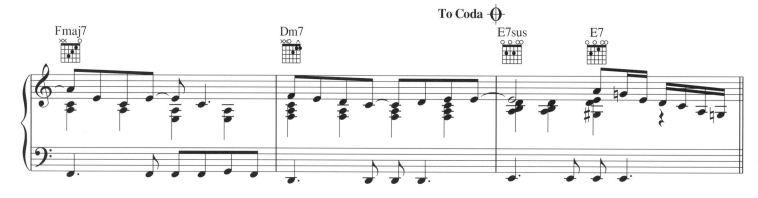

There'll be good times _ a - gain for me and _ you, _____ but we just can't stay to-geth - er; don't you

feel it too? __ Still I'm glad for what we __ had __ and how I ___ once __ loved __

D.S. al Coda
(take 2nd ending)

CODA

___ you. __ But it's too ___ It's too late, __

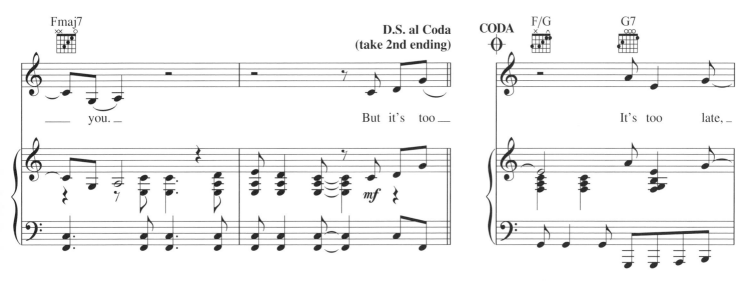

ba - by, it's too ___ late ___ now, __ dar -

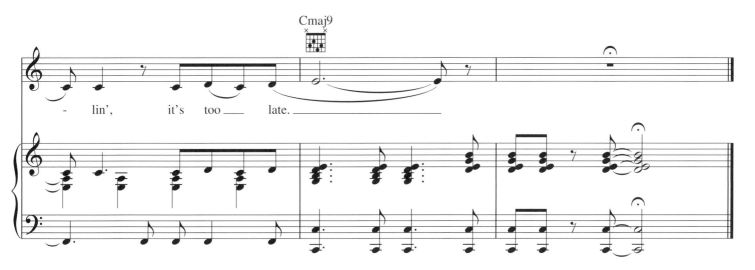

- lin', it's too ___ late. _____

JESSIE'S GIRL

Words and Music by
RICK SPRINGFIELD

KANSAS CITY

Words and Music by JERRY LEIBER
and MIKE STOLLER

Medium Blues

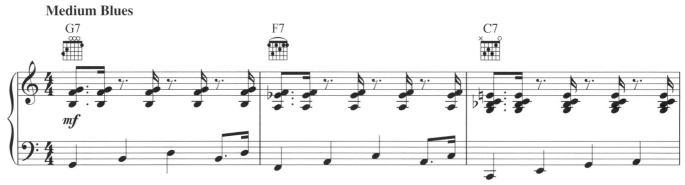

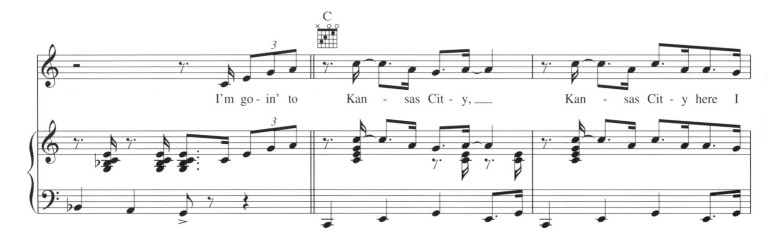

I'm go-in' to Kan-sas Cit-y,___ Kan-sas Cit-y here I

come.___ I'm go-in' to Kan-sas Cit-y,___

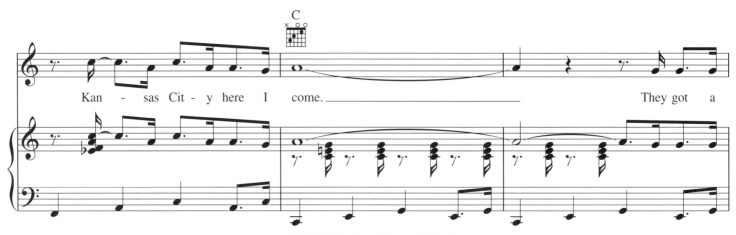

Kan-sas Cit-y here I come.___ They got a

cra - zy way of lov - in' there and I'm gon - na get me some. _

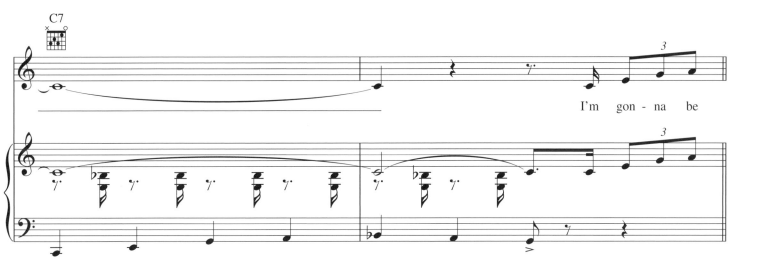

I'm gon - na be

stand - in' on the cor - ner _ Twelfth Street and Vine. _
pack _ my clothes, _ leave at the _ crack of dawn. _

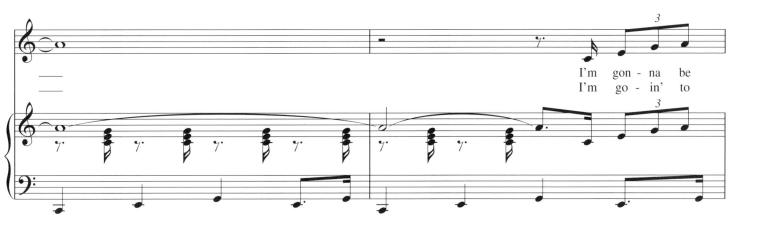

I'm gon - na be
I'm go - in' to

standin' on the cor - ner ___ Twelfth Street and Vine, ___
pack ___ my clothes, _____ leave at the ___ crack of dawn. ___

___ with my
My old

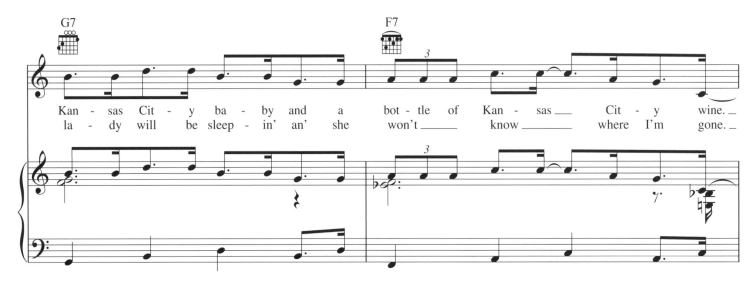

Kan - sas Cit - y ba - by and a bot - tle of Kan - sas ___ Cit - y wine. ___
la - dy will be sleep - in' an' she won't ___ know ___ where I'm gone. ___

Well, ___ I
'Cause if I

might take a train, _____ I might take a plane, _____ but
stay with that wom - an I know I'm gon - na die, _____ got - ta

if I have to walk _____ I'm goin' just the same. _ I'm go - in' to
find a brand - new ba - by and that's the rea - son why I'm go - in' to

Kan - sas Cit - y, _____ Kan - sas Cit - y here I

come. _____ They got a

cra - zy way of lov - in' there and I'm gon - na get me some.

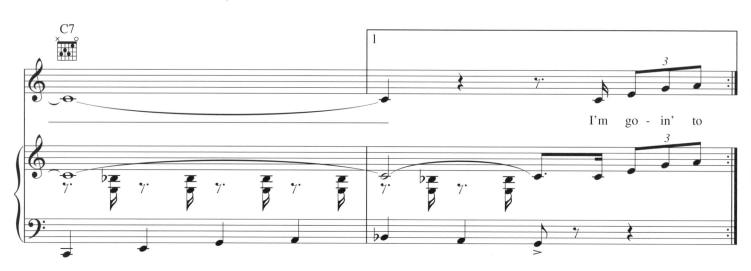

I'm go - in' to

They got a cra - zy way of lov - in' there and

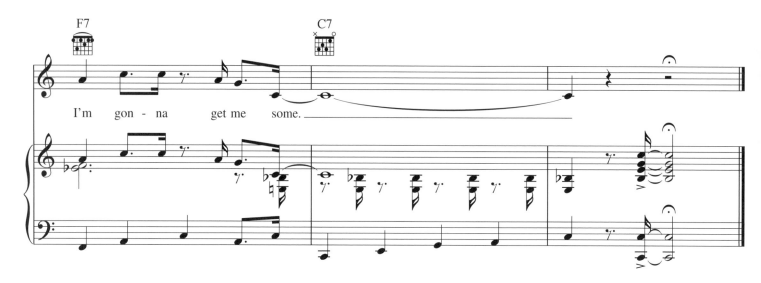

I'm gon - na get me some.

KEEP HOLDING ON

from the Twentieth Century Fox Motion Picture ERAGON

Words and Music by AVRIL LAVIGNE
and LUKASZ GOTTWALD

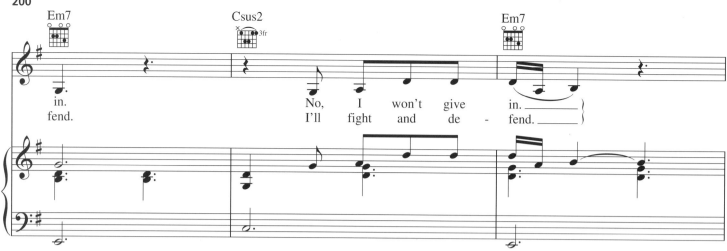

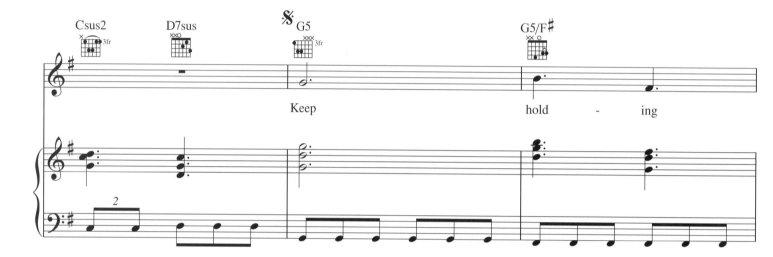

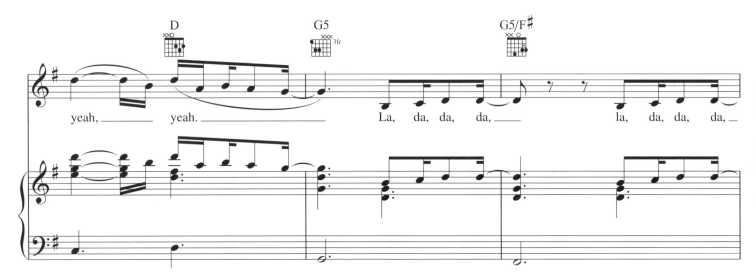

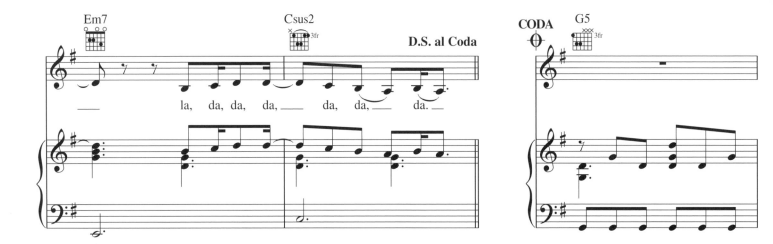

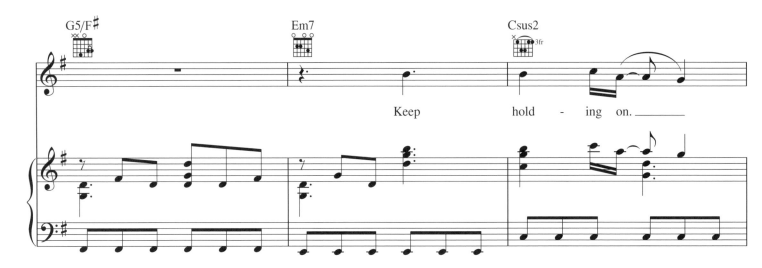

LADY IN RED

Words and Music by
CHRIS DeBURGH

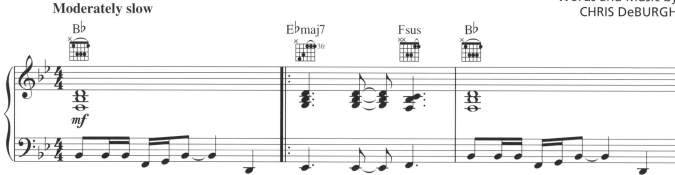

Moderately slow

I've nev-er seen you look-ing so love-ly as you did __ to-night;
I've nev-er seen you look-ing so gor-geous as you did __ to-night;

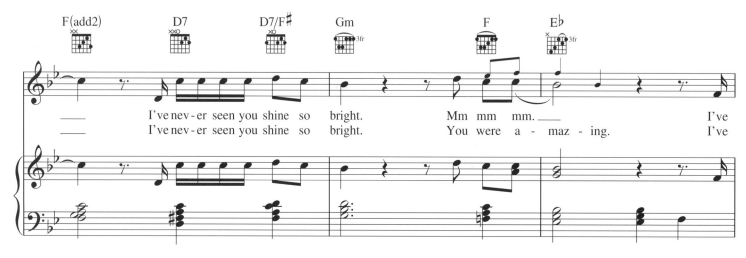

__ I've nev-er seen you shine so bright.   Mm mm mm. __   I've
__ I've nev-er seen you shine so bright.   You were a-maz-ing.   I've

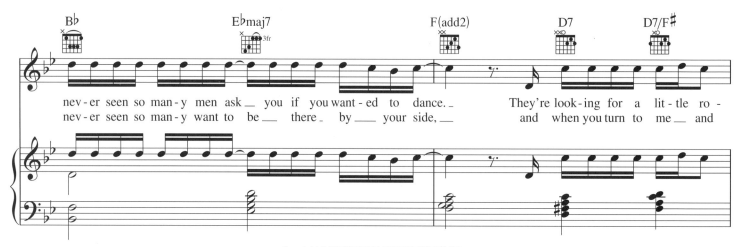

nev-er seen so man-y men ask __ you if you want-ed to dance. __   They're look-ing for a lit-tle ro-
nev-er seen so man-y want to be __ there __ by __ your side,   and when you turn to me __ and

mance, given half _____ a chance. I have
smiled, it took my breath _____ a - way. I have

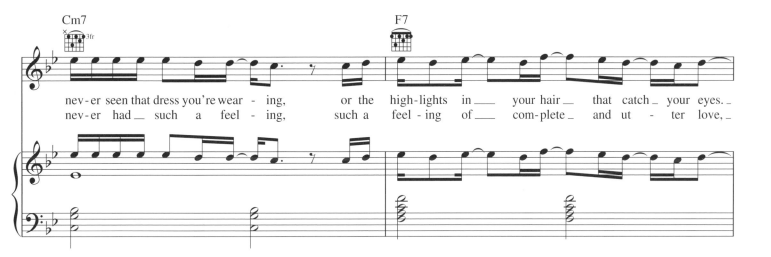

nev-er seen that dress you're wear - ing, or the high-lights in ___ your hair ___ that catch ___ your eyes. ___
nev-er had ___ such a feel - ing, such a feel - ing of ___ com-plete ___ and ut - ter love, ___

I have ___ been blind. ___
as I ___ do to - night.

The la - dy in red. _____

is danc - ing ___ with me, cheek ___ to cheek. ___

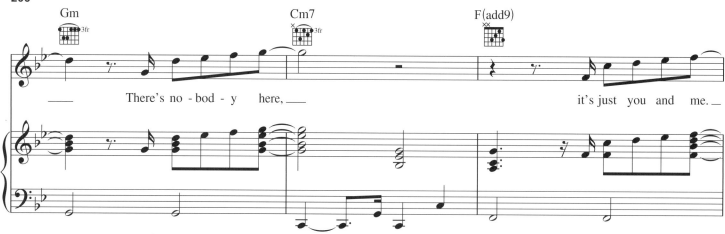

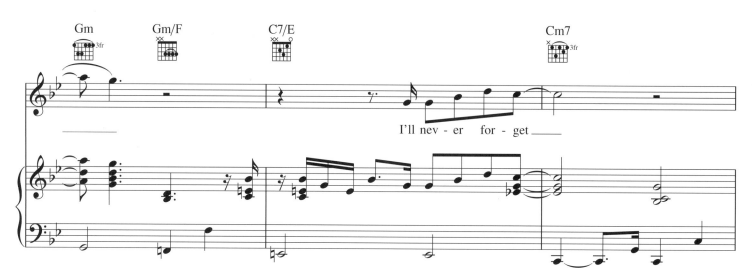

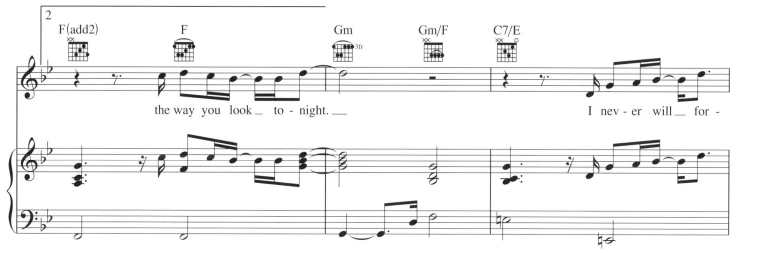

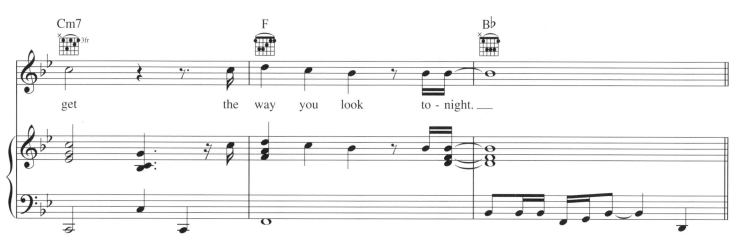

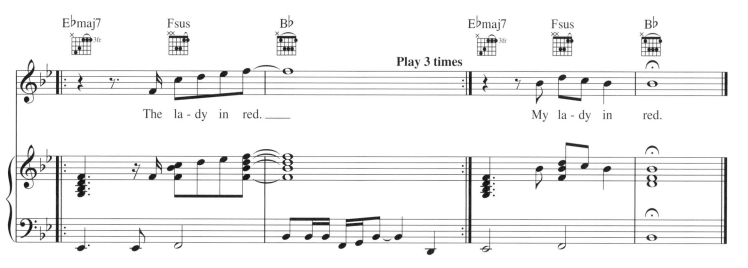

LEAN ON ME

Words and Music by
BILL WITHERS

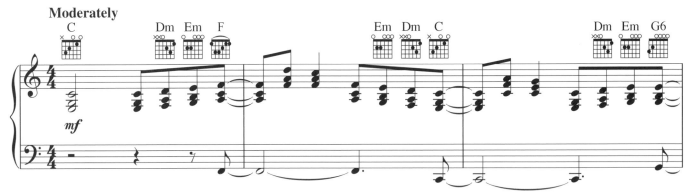

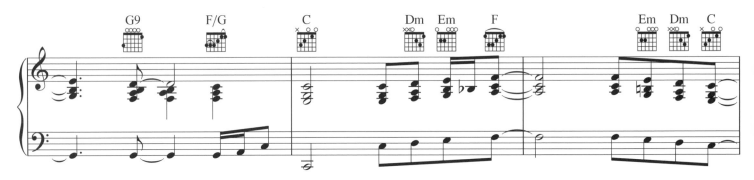

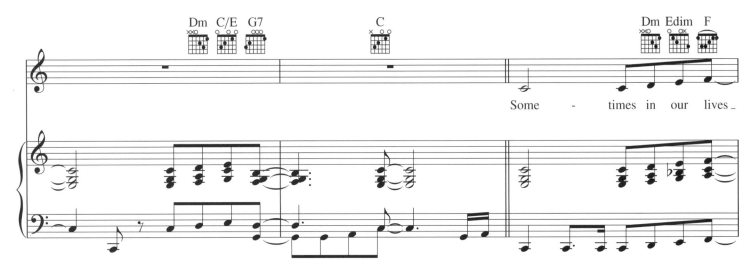

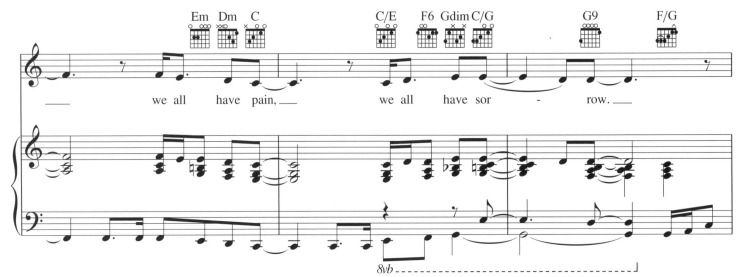

Some - times in our lives _ we all have pain, ___ we all have sor - row. ___

But if we are wise, _____ we know that there's _____

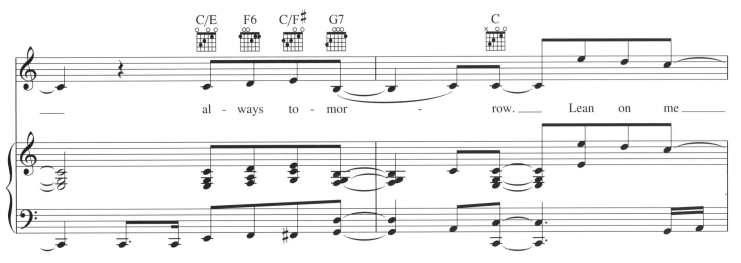

_____ al - ways to - mor - row. _____ Lean on me _____

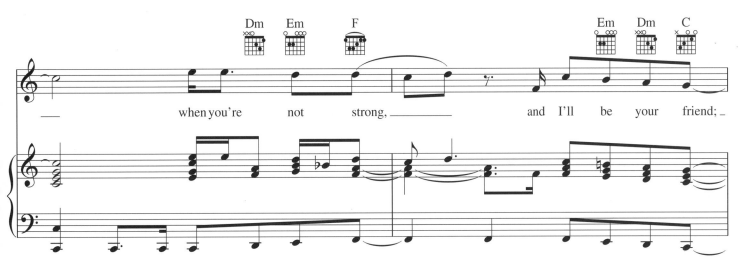

_____ when you're not strong, _____ and I'll be your friend; _

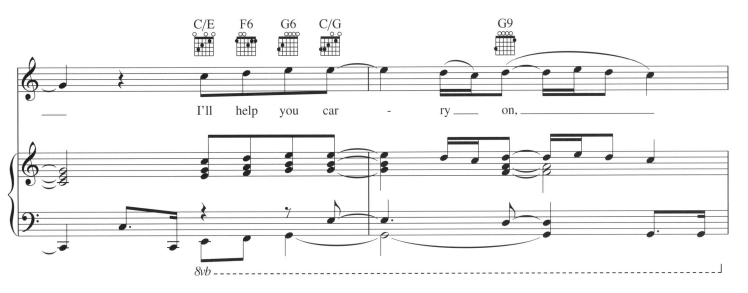

_____ I'll help you car - ry _____ on, _____

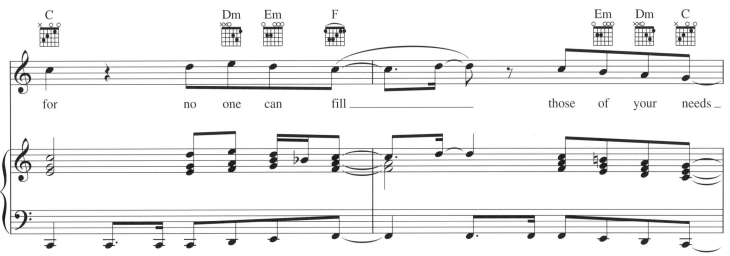

for no one can fill _____ those of your needs ___

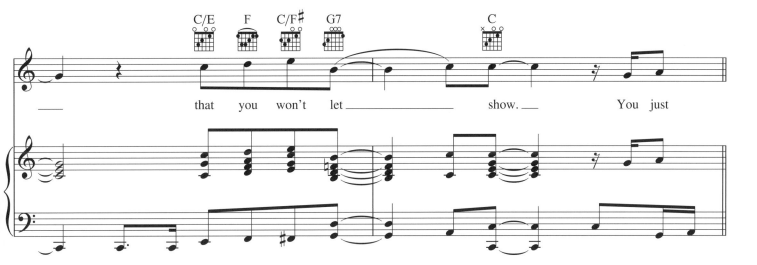

___ that you won't let _____ show. ___ You just

call on me, broth - er, when you need a ___ hand. ___ We all ___

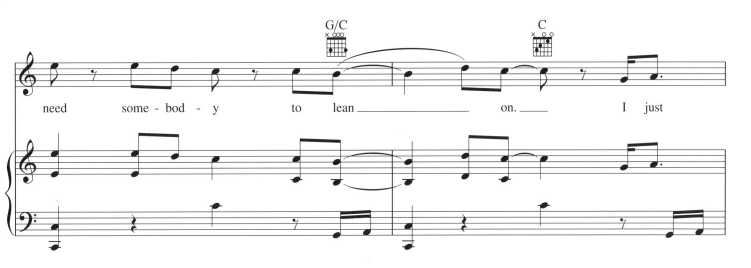

need some - bod - y to lean _____ on. ___ I just

might have a prob-lem that you'll un-der-stand. ___ We all ___

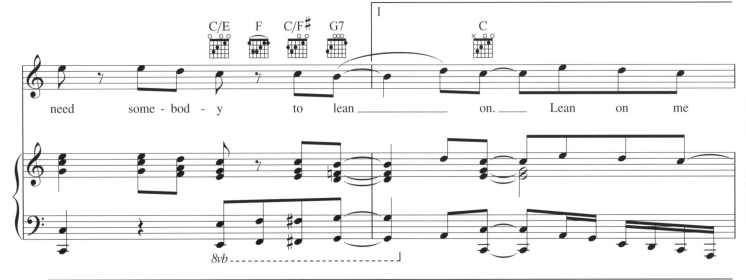

need some-bod-y to lean ___ on. ___ Lean on me

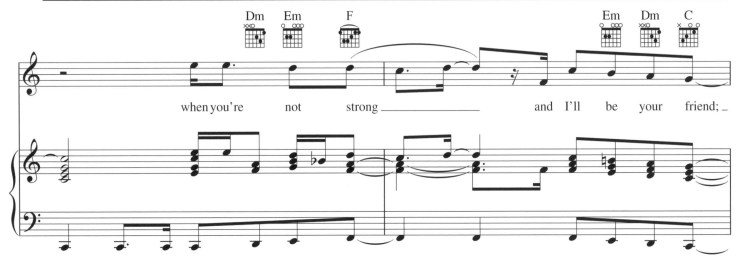

when you're not strong ___ and I'll be your friend; ___

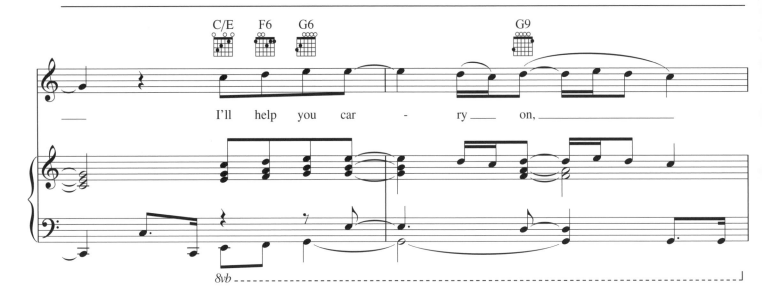

___ I'll help you car - ry ___ on, ___

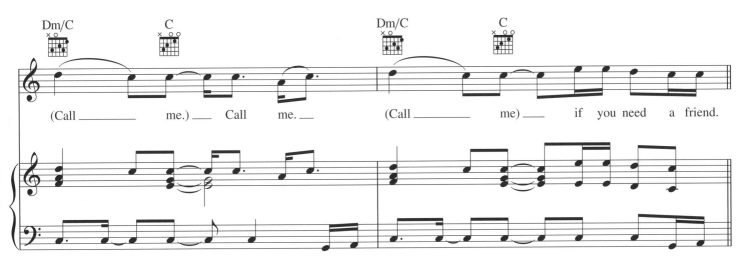

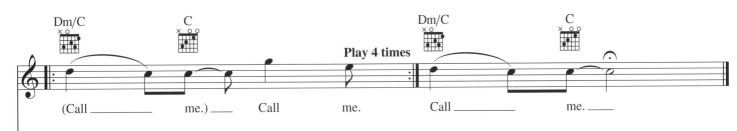

LIKE A VIRGIN

Words and Music by BILLY STEINBERG
and TOM KELLY

ver - y first time.   Like a vir - gin, ___

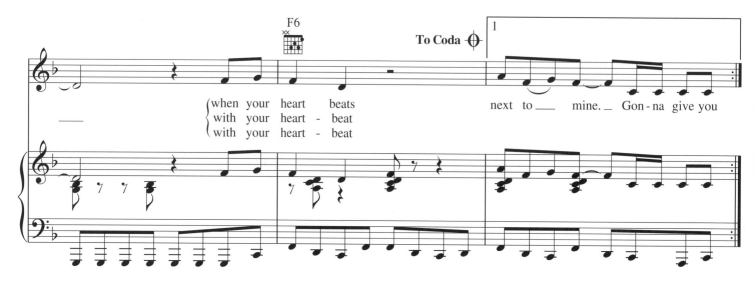

when your heart   beats
with your heart - beat   next to ___ mine. ___ Gon - na give you
with your heart - beat

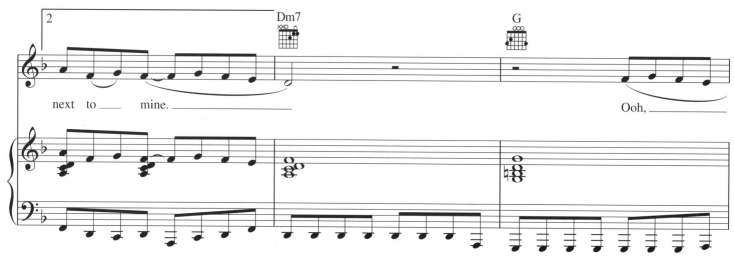

next to ___ mine. ___   Ooh, ___

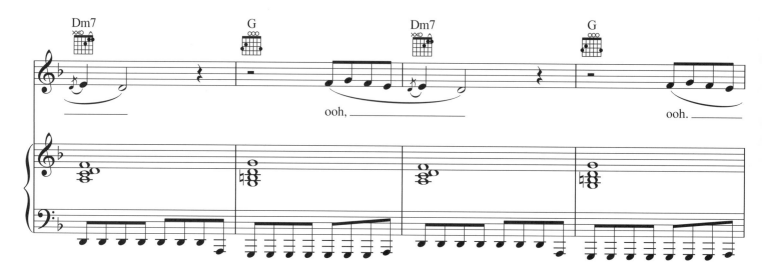

___   ooh, ___   ooh. ___

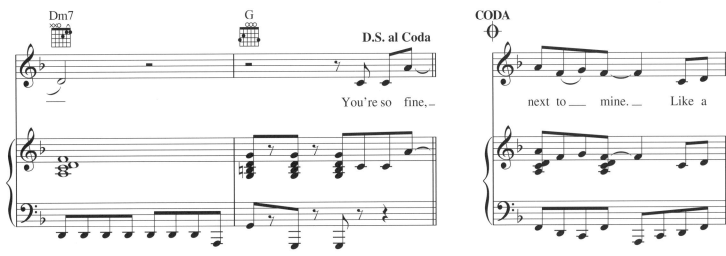

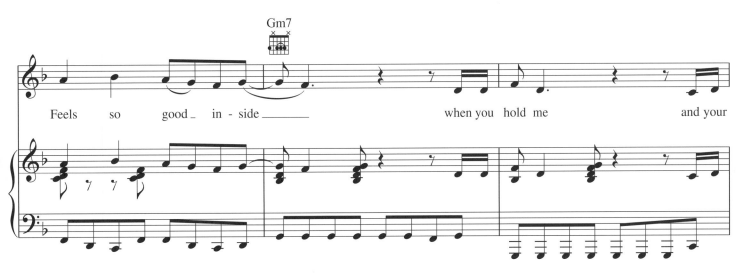

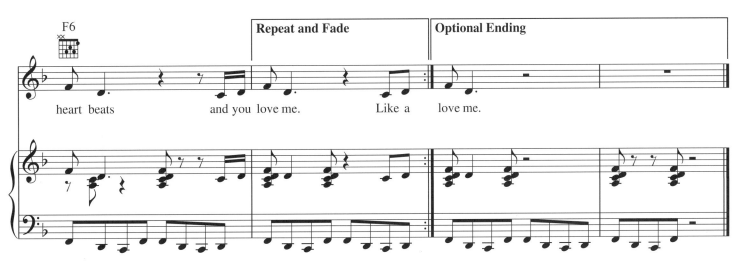

LOVE SHACK

Words and Music by CATHERINE E. PIERSON,
FREDERICK W. SCHNEIDER, KEITH J. STRICKLAND
and CYNTHIA L. WILSON

Moderate Rock

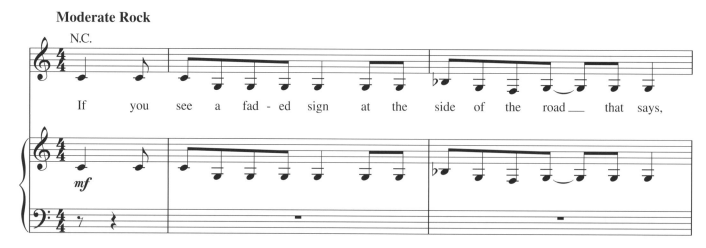

If you see a fad-ed sign at the side of the road __ that says,

"Fif - teen miles to the Love _____ Shack." __

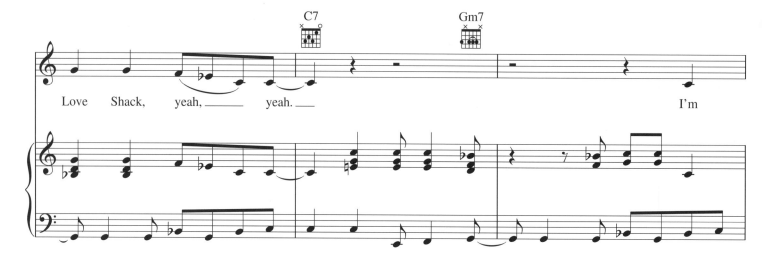

Love Shack, yeah, _____ yeah. __   I'm

head - ed down the At - lan - ta____ high - way,

look - in' for the love get - a - way,

head - in'____ for the love____ get - a - way. I got me a car.____ It's as
Hop in my Chry - sler, it's as

big as a whale,____ and we're head - in' on down to the Love Shack. I
big as a whale,____ and it's a - bout to set sail. I

got me a Chrys - ler, it seats a - bout twen - ty. So, hur - ry up and bring your
got me a car, _____ it seats a - bout twen - ty. So, come on and bring your

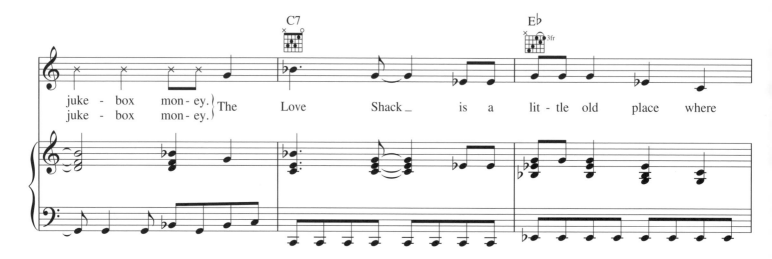

juke - box mon - ey.} The Love Shack _ is a lit - tle old place where
juke - box mon - ey.

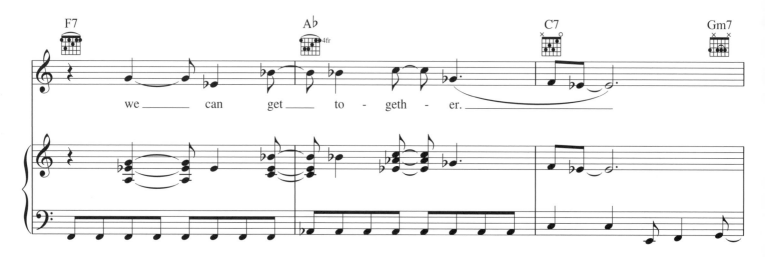

we _____ can get _____ to - geth - er. _____

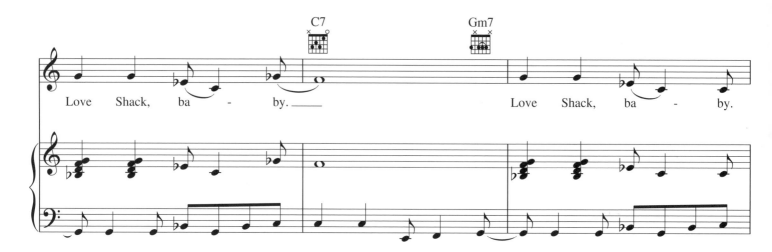

Love Shack, ba - by. _____ Love Shack, ba - by.

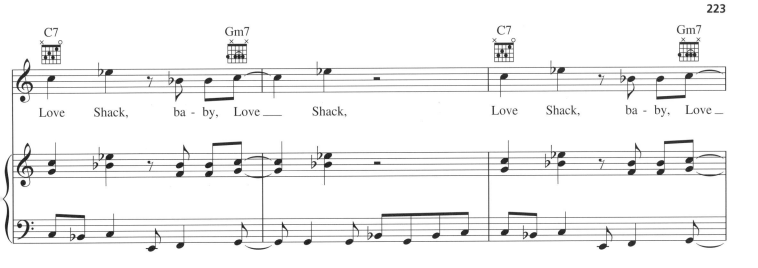

Love Shack, ba - by, Love ___ Shack, Love Shack, ba - by, Love ___

___ Shack, Love Shack, ba - by, Love ___ Shack,

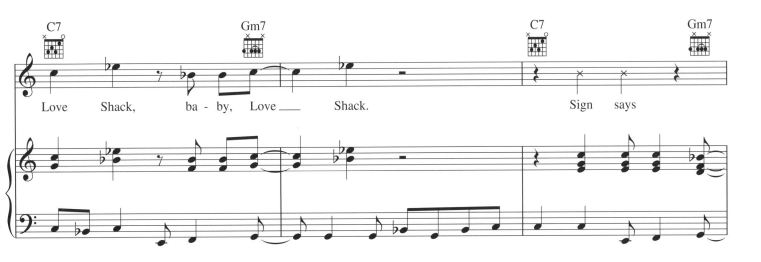

Love Shack, ba - by, Love ___ Shack. Sign says

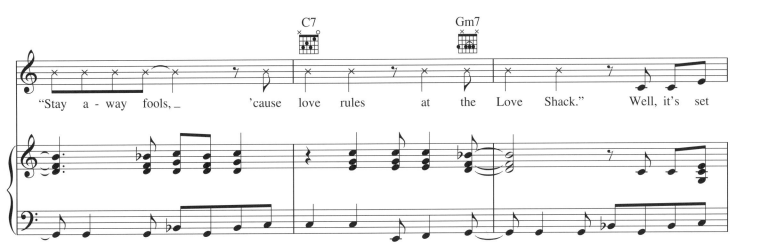

"Stay a - way fools, ___ 'cause love rules at the Love Shack." Well, it's set

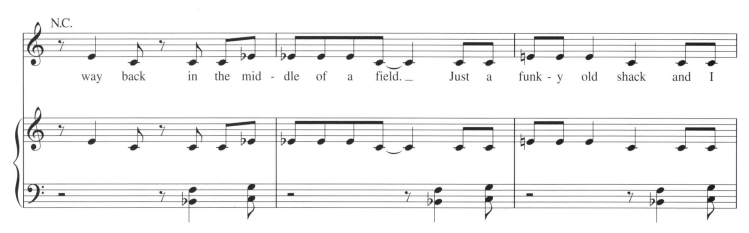

way back in the mid-dle of a field. __ Just a funk-y old shack and I

got-ta get back. __ Glit-ter on the mat-tress, __

glit-ter on the high-way, __ glit-ter on the front porch, __

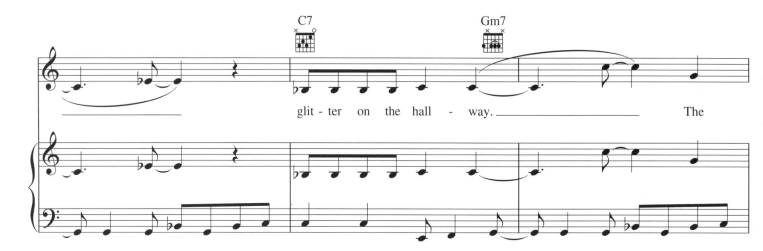

__ glit-ter on the hall-way. __ The

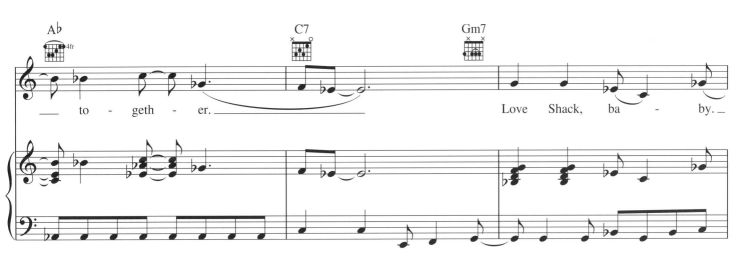

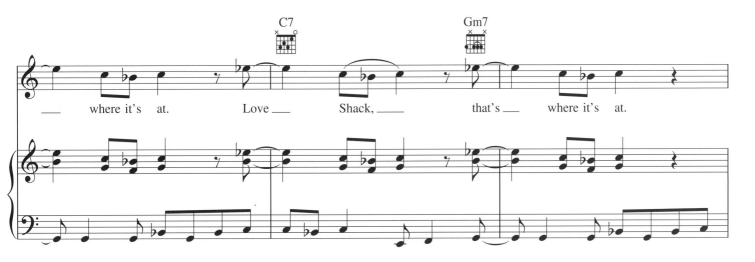

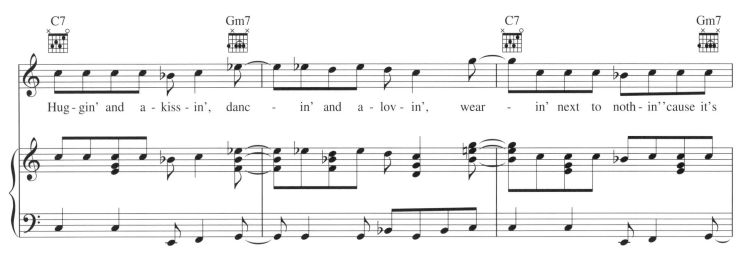

Hug - gin' and a - kiss - in', danc - in' and a - lov - in', wear - in' next to noth - in' 'cause it's

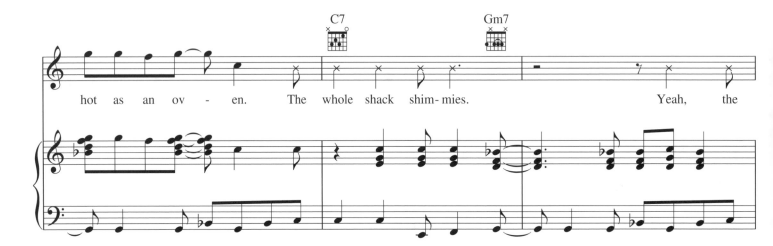

hot as an ov - en. The whole shack shim - mies. Yeah, the

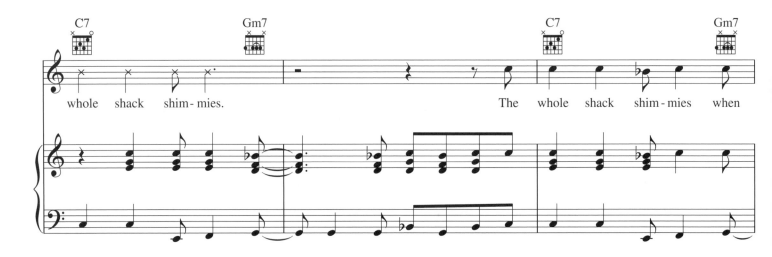

whole shack shim - mies. The whole shack shim - mies when

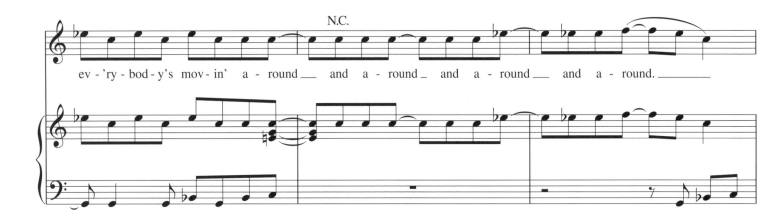

ev - 'ry - bod - y's mov - in' a - round___ and a - round___ and a - round___ and a - round.___

Ev-'ry-bod-y's mov-in', ev - 'ry-bod-y's groov-in', ba - by. Folks lin-in' up out-side

just to get down. Ev-'ry-bod-y's mov-in', ev - 'ry-bod-y's groov-in', ba - by.

Funk-y lit-tle shack, funk - y lit-tle shack.

D.S. al Coda

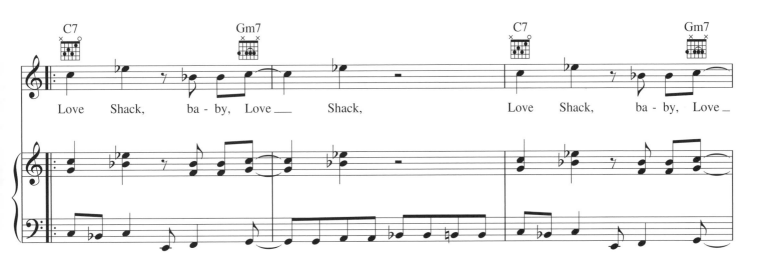

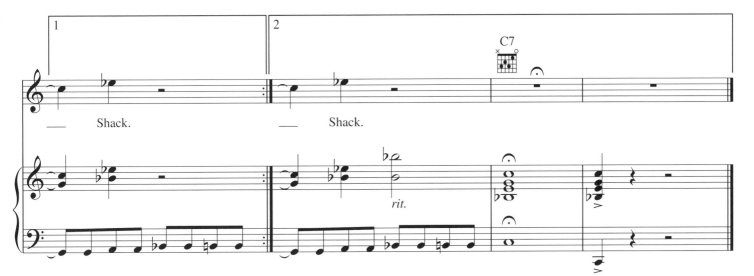

LOVE STORY

Words and Music by
TAYLOR SWIFT

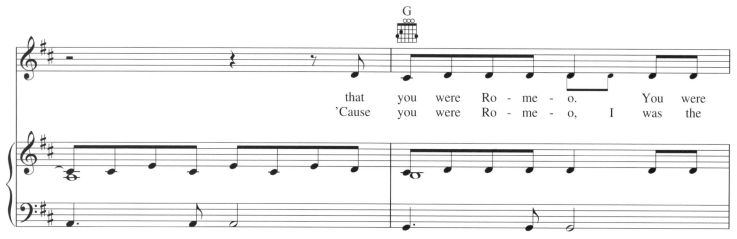

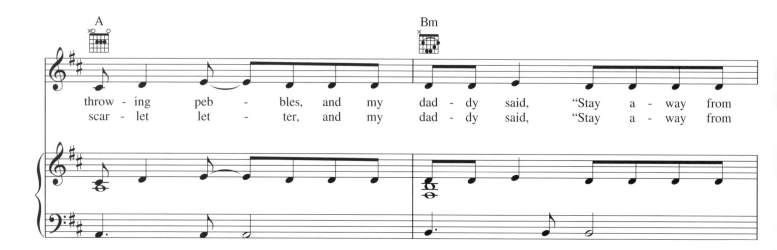

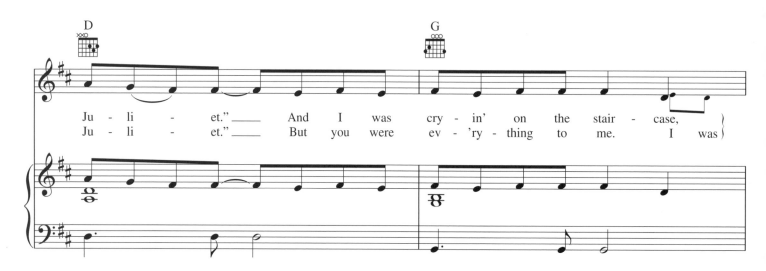

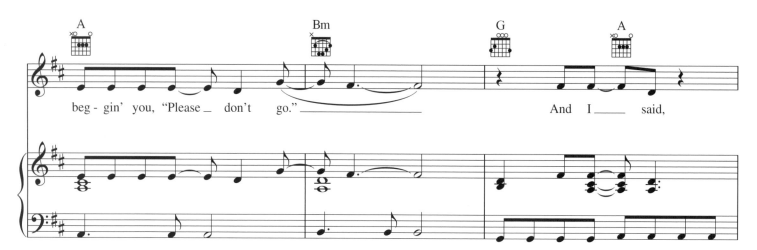

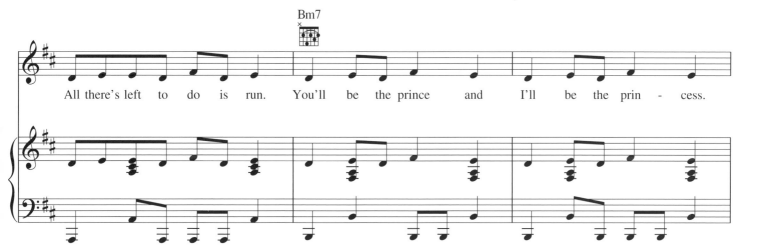

This love is dif - fi - cult, but it's __ real. ____ Don't be a - fraid. We'll

make it out of this mess. It's a love sto - ry. __ Ba - by, just say __ yes."

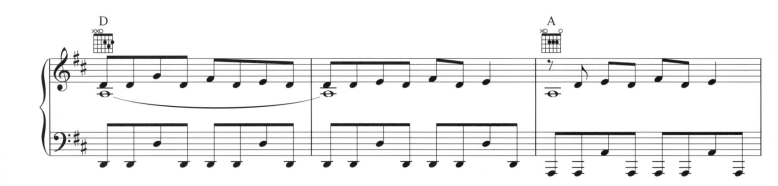

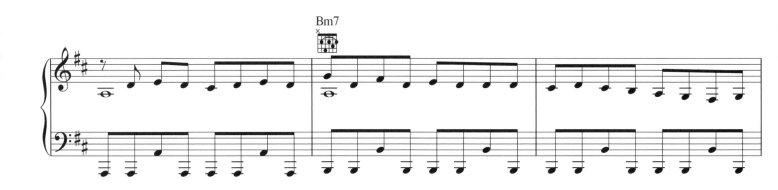

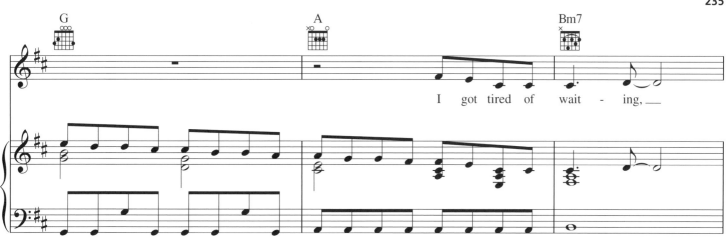

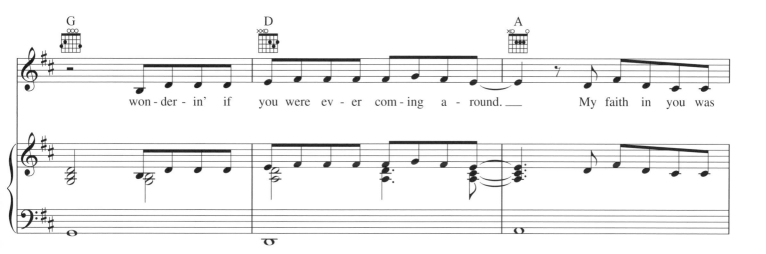

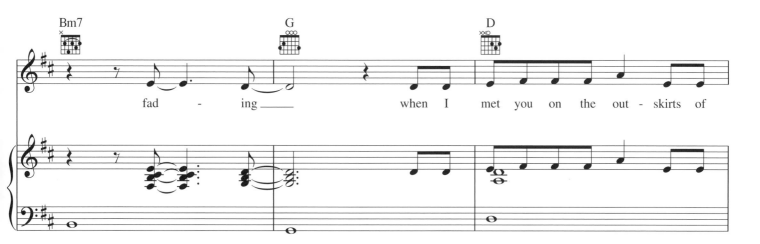

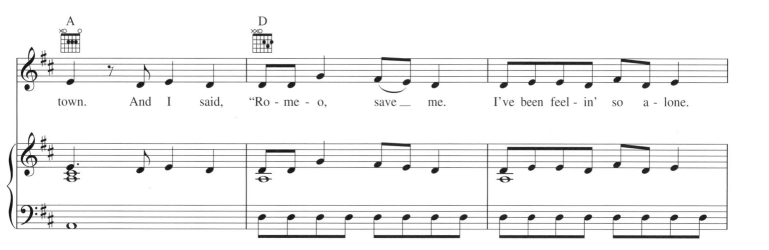

I keep wait - ing for you, but you nev - er come. Is this in my head? I don't

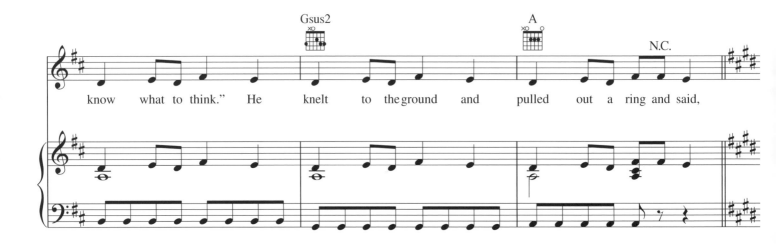

know what to think." He knelt to the ground and pulled out a ring and said,

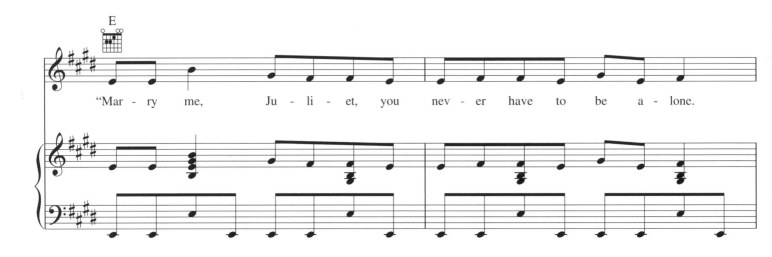

"Mar - ry me, Ju - li - et, you nev - er have to be a - lone.

I love you __ and that's all I real - ly know. I talked to your dad. Go

pick out a white dress. It's a love sto - ry. ___ Ba - by, just say ___

yes." ___ Oh, oh, oh, ___

C#m7

oh, oh, oh, ___ oh. 'Cause

we were both young when I first saw ___ you. ___

MAMMA MIA

Words and Music by BENNY ANDERSSON,
BJÖRN ULVAEUS and STIG ANDERSON

DONNA:

I was cheat-ed by you ___ and I think you know when. ___
I was an-gry and sad ___ when I knew we were through. ___

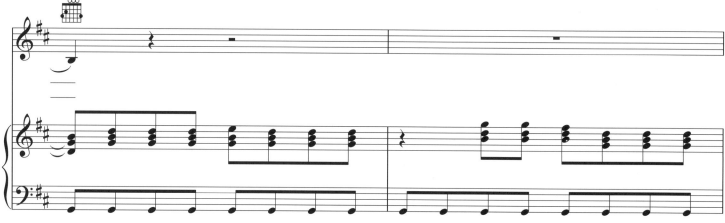

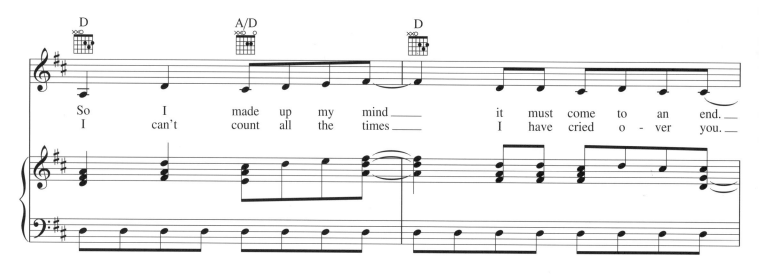

So I made up my mind ___ it must come to an end.
I can't count all the times ___ I have cried o-ver you.

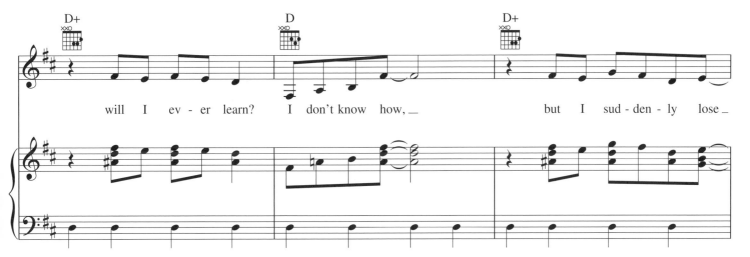

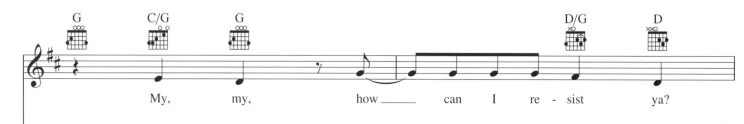

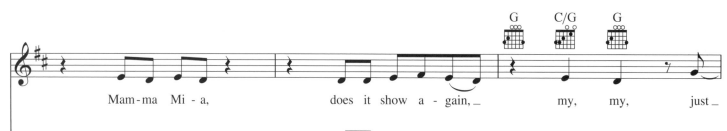

how much I've missed ya? Yes, ___ I've been bro - ken - heart - ed,

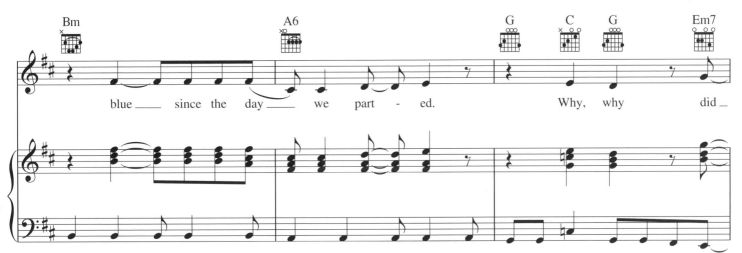

blue ___ since the day ___ we part - ed. Why, why did ___

___ I ev - er let you go? ___ Mam-ma Mi - a, now I real - ly know, ___

To Coda

my, my, I ___ should not have let you go. ___

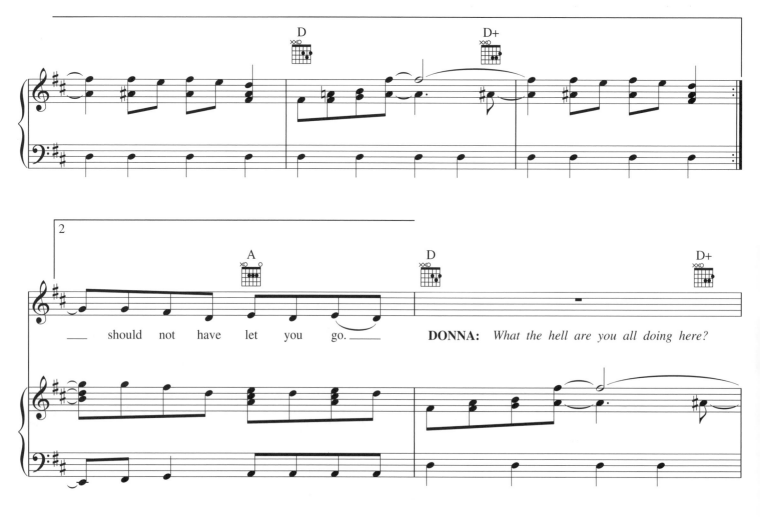

D | D+

D | D+

DONNA: *What the hell are you all doing here?*

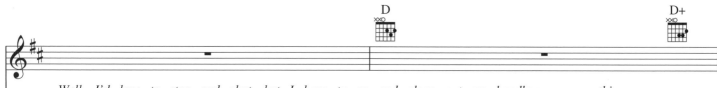

should not have let you go.

D | D+

Well, I'd love to stop and chat, but I have to go and clean out my handbag or something.

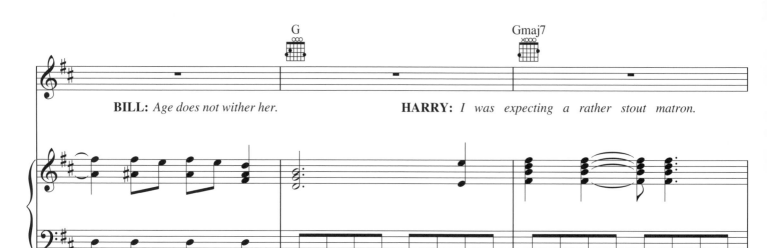

G | Gmaj7

BILL: *Age does not wither her.*   **HARRY:** *I was expecting a rather stout matron.*

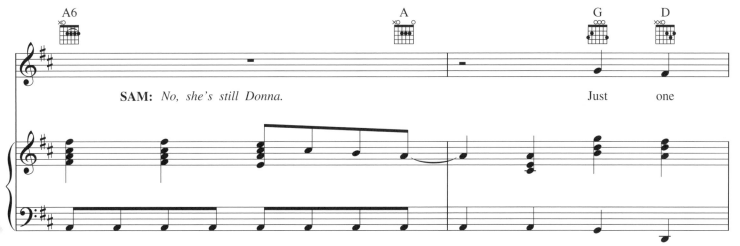

SAM: *No, she's still Donna.*

Just one

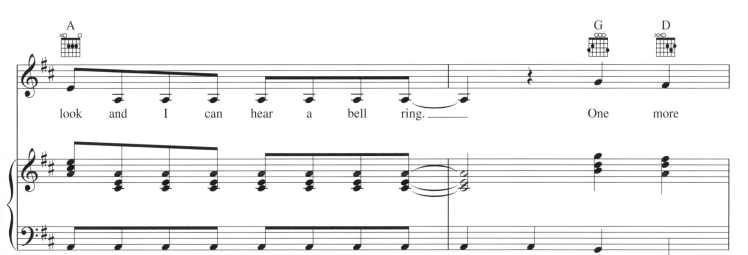

look and I can hear a bell ring. _____ One more

D.S. al Coda

look and I for - get ev - 'ry - thing, _____ oh, _____ oh. _____

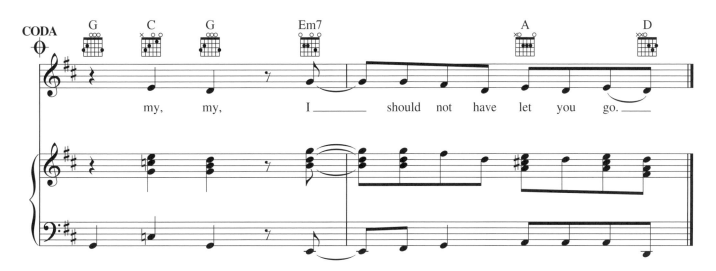

CODA

my, my, I _____ should not have let you go. _____

MISSING YOU

Words and Music by JOHN WAITE,
CHARLES SANFORD and MARK LEONARD

Moderately

miles _ a - way _ and I'm won - d'rin' why _ you left. There's a

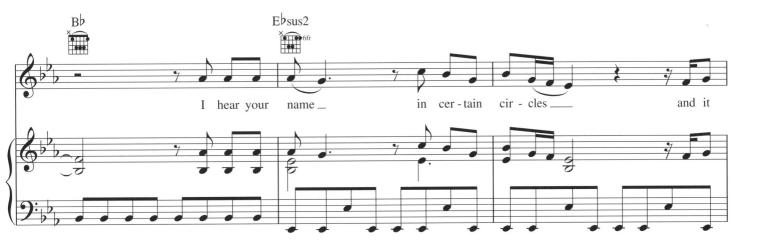

storm that's rag - in' through my fro - zen heart to - night.

I hear your name _ in cer - tain cir - cles _ and it

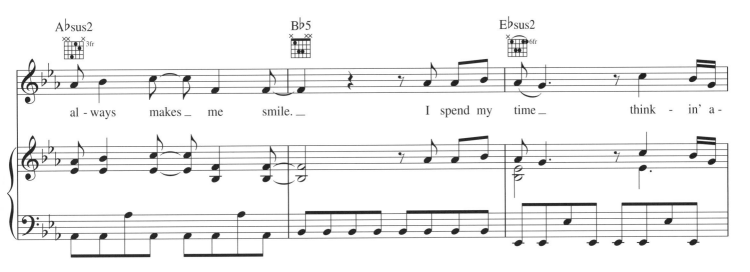

al - ways makes _ me smile. _ I spend my time _ think - in' a -

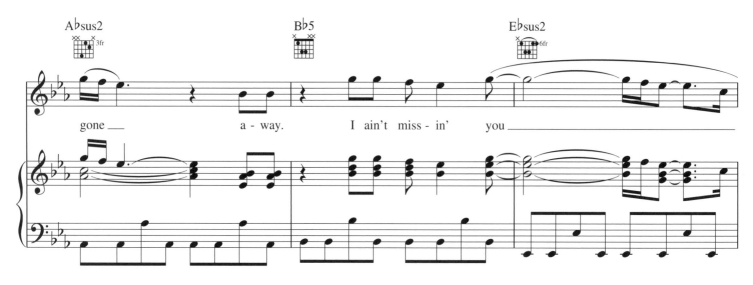

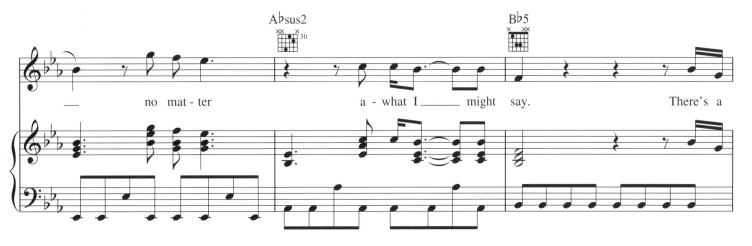

no mat - ter a - what I _____ might say. There's a

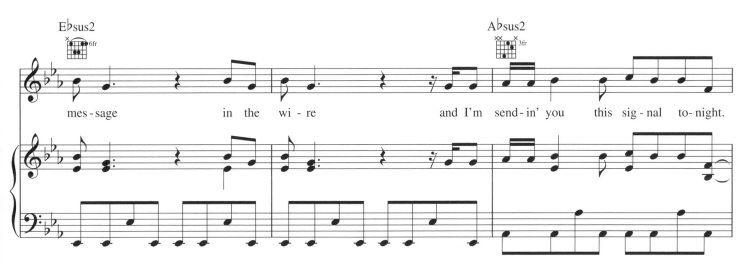

mes - sage in the wi - re and I'm send - in' you this sig - nal to - night.

You don't know ___ how des - p'rate I've be - come ___ and it

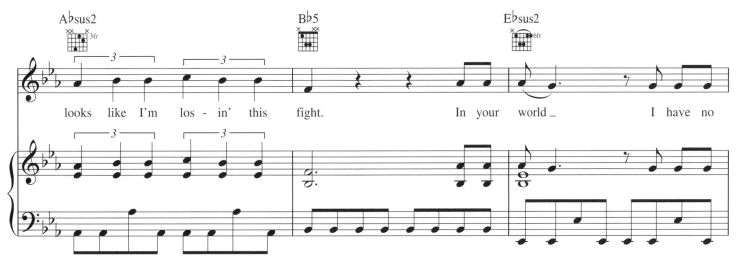

looks like I'm los - in' this fight. In your world ___ I have no

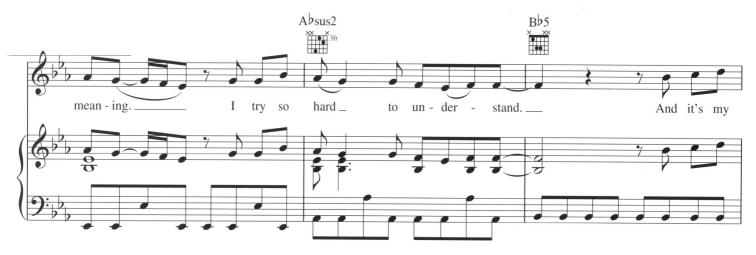

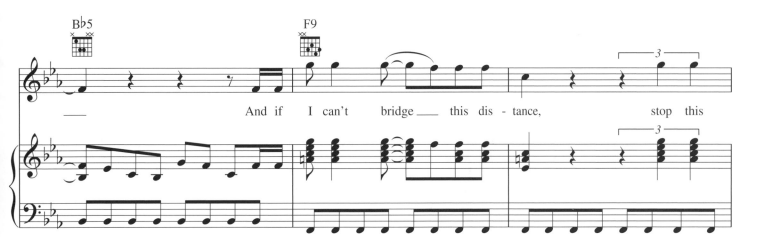

since you've been gone _____ a - way. I ain't miss- in' you _____

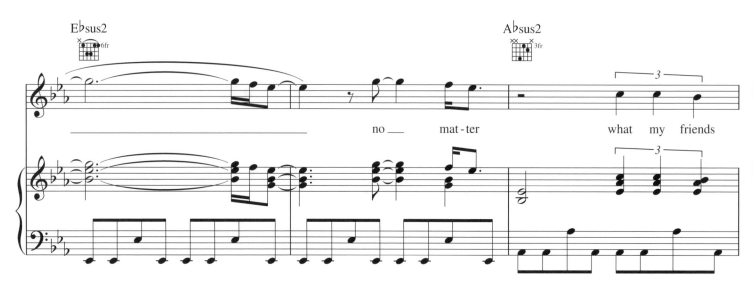

no _____ mat - ter what my friends

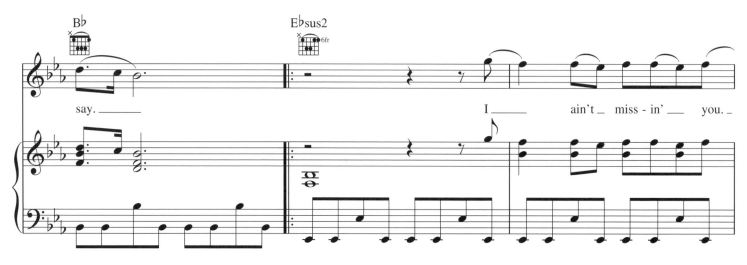

say. _____ I _____ ain't _____ miss - in' _____ you. _____

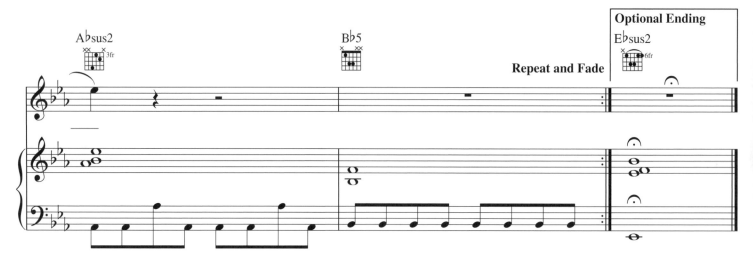

Optional Ending

Repeat and Fade

MRS. ROBINSON

from THE GRADUATE

Words and Music by
PAUL SIMON

Moderately bright

And here's to you, ___ Mis-sus Rob - in - son, ___ Je-sus loves you more ___

___ than you ___ will know. _____ (Wo, wo, wo.) ___

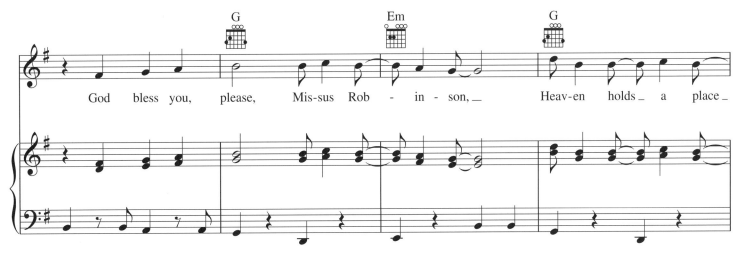

God bless you, please, Mis-sus Rob - in - son, ___ Heav-en holds ___ a place ___

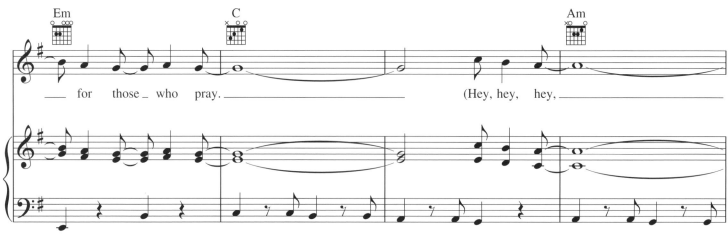

for those _ who pray. _____ (Hey, hey, hey, _____

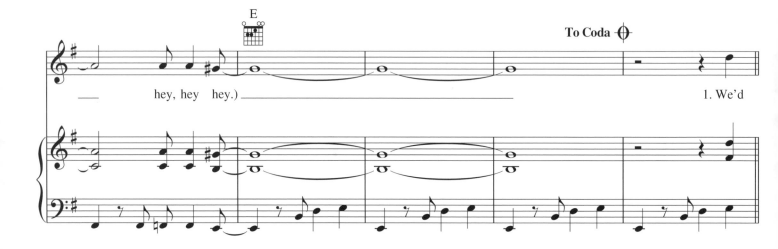

_ hey, hey hey.) _____ **To Coda** ⊕ 1. We'd

like to know a lit - tle bit _ a - bout _ you for our files, _____

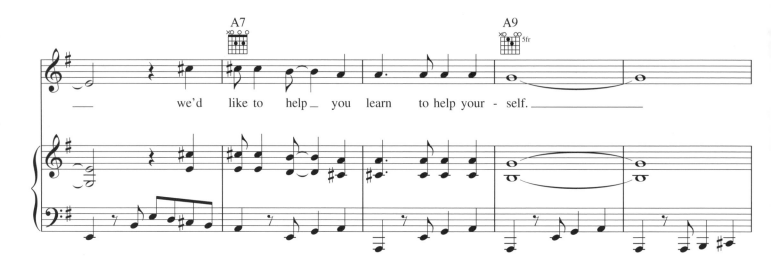

_ we'd like to help _ you learn to help your - self. _____

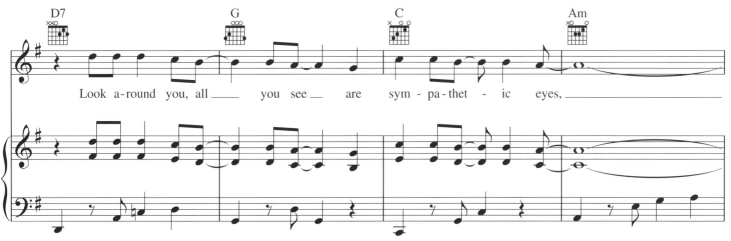

Look a-round you, all _____ you see ___ are sym-pa-thet - ic eyes, _____

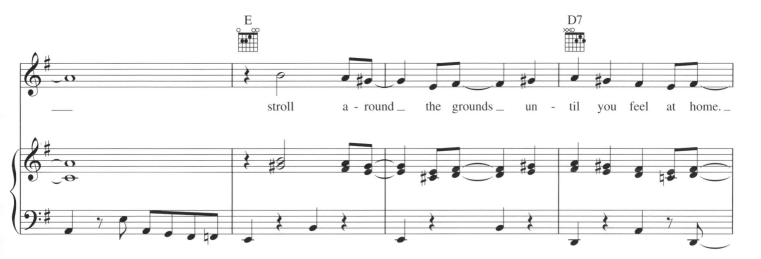

_____ stroll a - round ___ the grounds ___ un - til you feel at home. ___

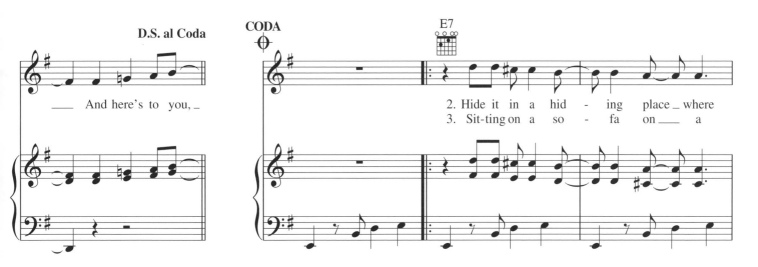

D.S. al Coda

____ And here's to you, _

CODA

2. Hide it in a hid - ing place __ where
3. Sit-ting on a so - fa on ___ a

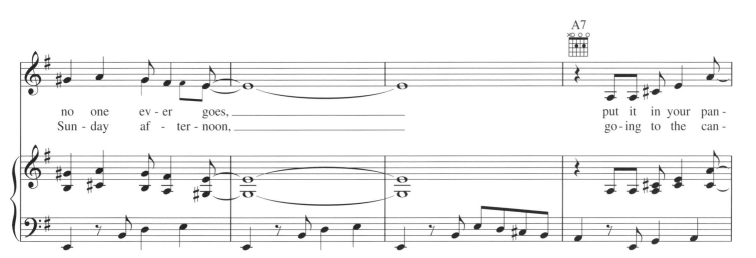

no one ev - er goes, _____ put it in your pan-
Sun - day af - ter-noon, _____ go-ing to the can-

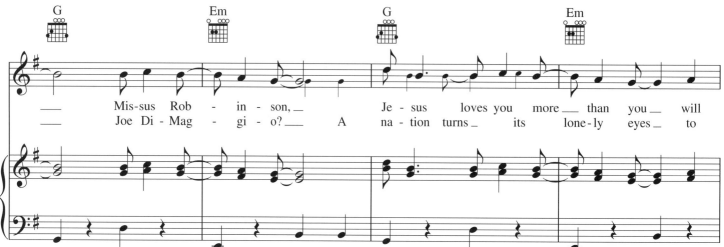

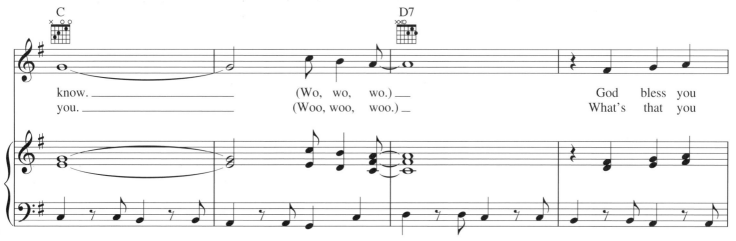

know. _____ (Wo, wo, wo.) __ God bless you
you. _____ (Woo, woo, woo.) __ What's that you

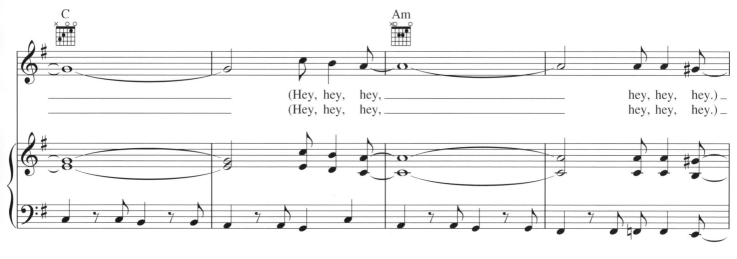

please, Mis-sus Rob - in - son, __ Heav-en holds __ a place __ for those __ who pray. __
say, Mis-sus Rob - in - son, __ "Jolt-in' Joe" __ has left and gone __ a - way. __

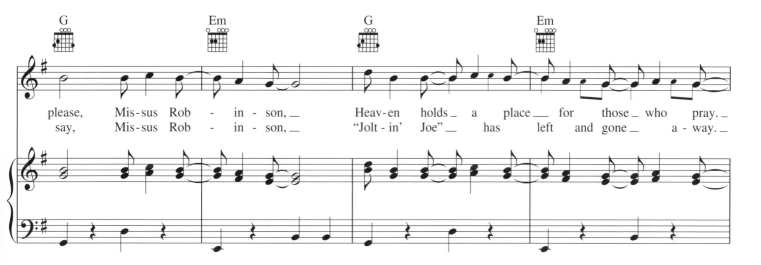

(Hey, hey, hey, _____ hey, hey, hey.) __
(Hey, hey, hey, _____ hey, hey, hey.) __

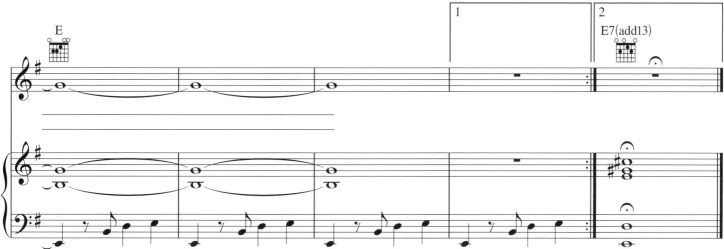

MY HEART WILL GO ON
(Love Theme from 'Titanic')
from the Paramount and Twentieth Century Fox Motion Picture TITANIC

Music by JAMES HORNER
Lyric by WILL JENNINGS

Ev - 'ry night in my dreams I see you, I

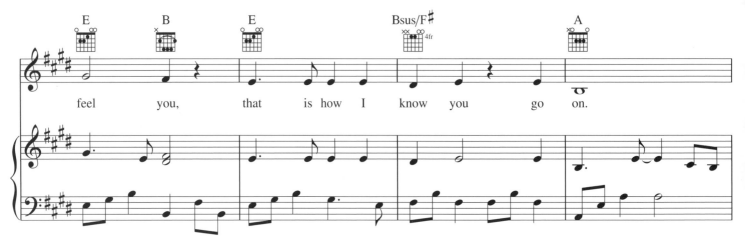

feel you, that is how I know you go on.

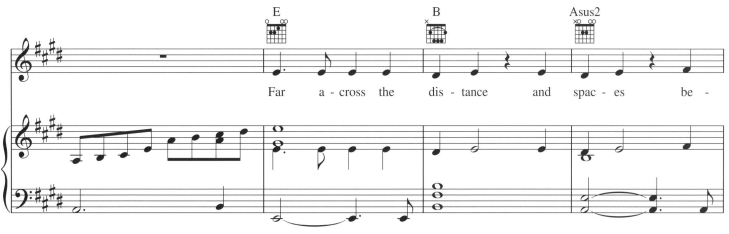

Far a-cross the dis-tance and spac-es be-

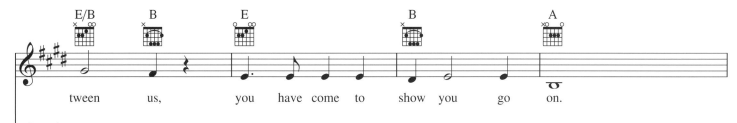

tween us, you have come to show you go on.

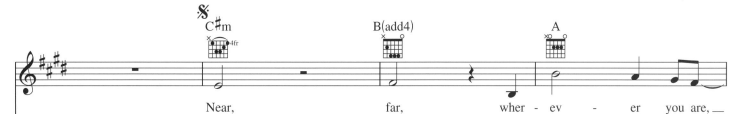

Near, far, wher-ev-er you are,__

__ I be-lieve that the heart does go on. _____

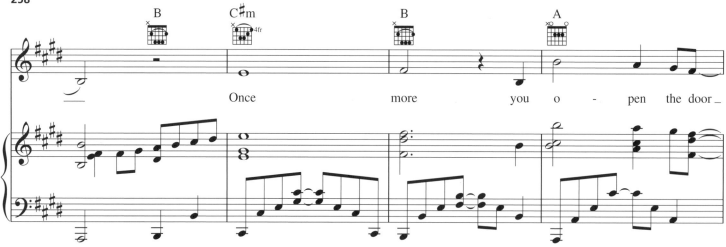

Once more you o - pen the door _

_ and you're here in my heart, and my heart will go

To Coda

on and on.

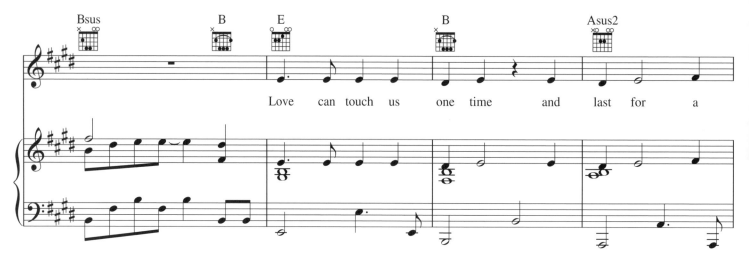

Love can touch us one time and last for a

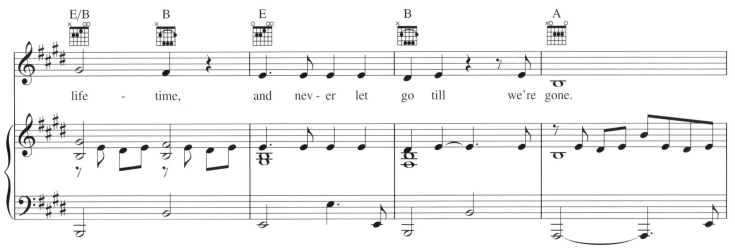

life - time, and nev - er let go till we're gone.

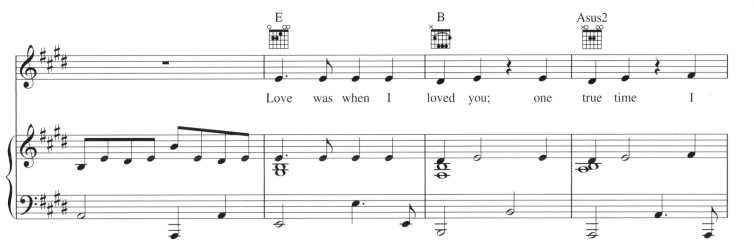

Love was when I loved you; one true time I

hold to. In my life we'll al - ways go on.

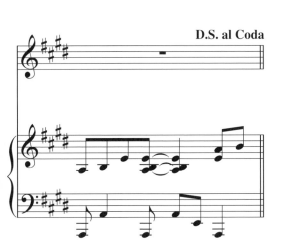

D.S. al Coda

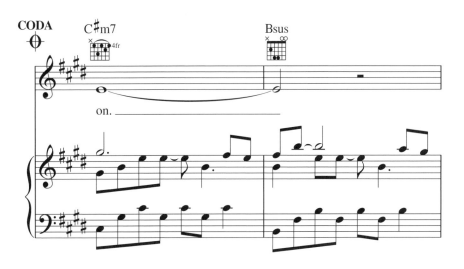

CODA

on. _____

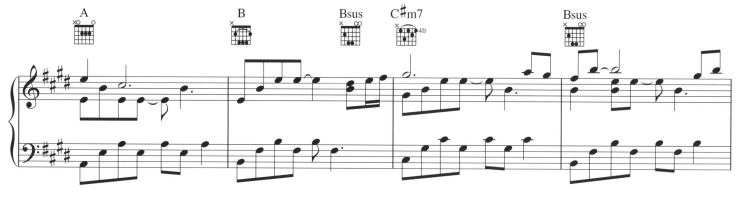

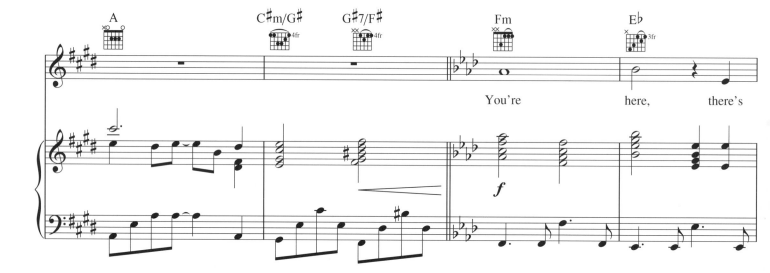

You're here, there's

noth - ing I fear __ and I know __ that my heart will go

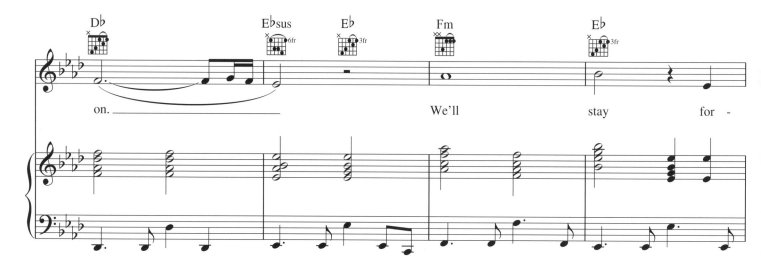

on. _____ We'll stay for -

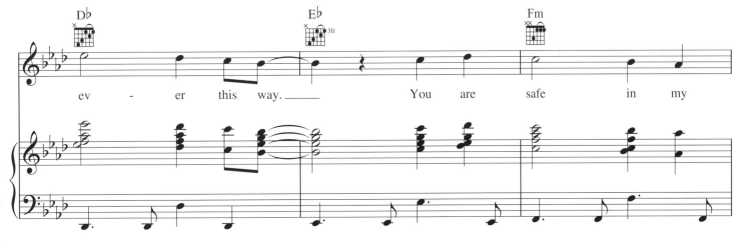

ev - er this way. ____ You are safe in my

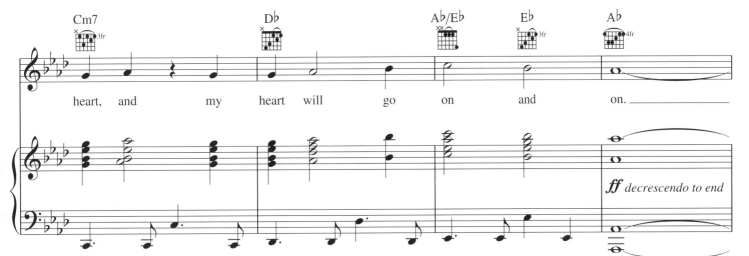

heart, and my heart will go on and on. ____

ff decrescendo to end

Mm. ____

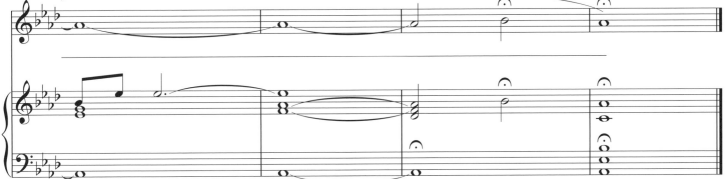

MY WAY

English Words by PAUL ANKA
Original French Words by GILLES THIBAULT
Music by JACQUES REVAUX
and CLAUDE FRANCOIS

off more than I could chew. But through it all, when there was

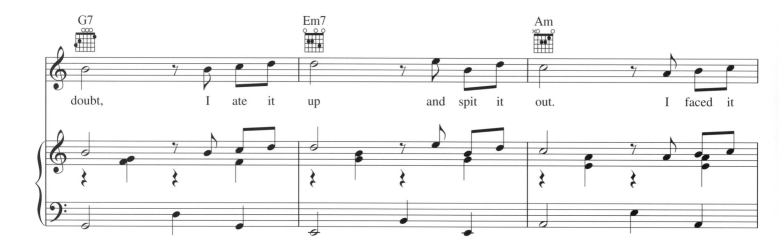

doubt, I ate it up and spit it out. I faced it

all, and I stood tall, and did it my

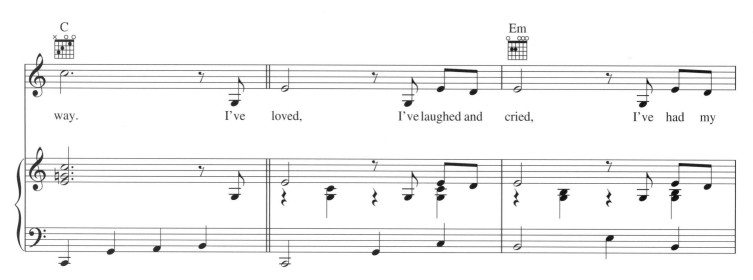

way. I've loved, I've laughed and cried, I've had my

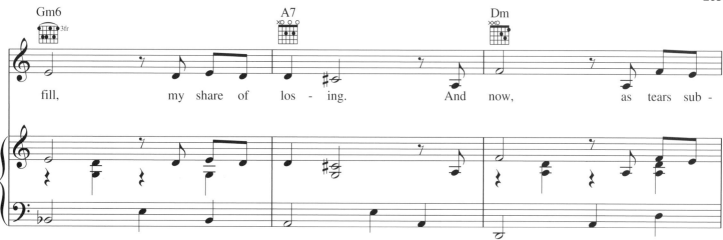

fill,   my share of los - ing.   And now,   as tears sub -

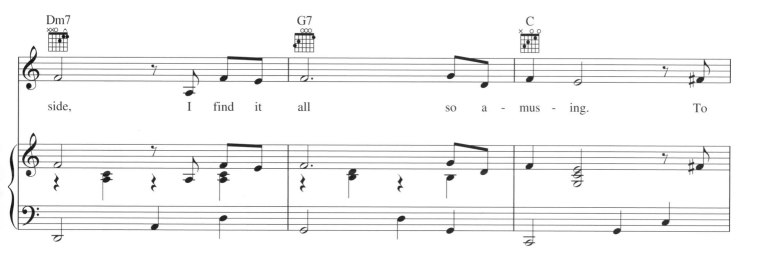

side,   I find it all   so a - mus - ing.   To

think   I did all that,   and may I say,   not in a

shy way,   "Oh no,   oh, no, not me,   I did it my

way." For what is a man, what has he got? If not him-

self, then he has naught. To say the things he tru - ly

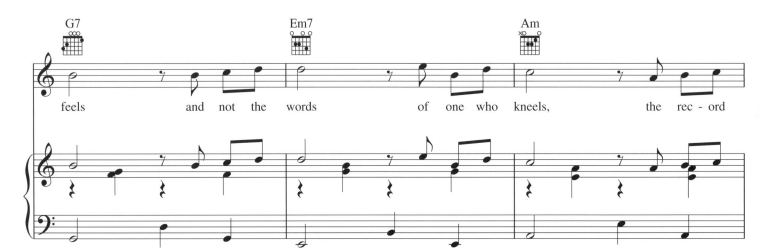

feels and not the words of one who kneels, the rec - ord

shows I took the blows, and did it my way.

NIGHT FEVER

from SATURDAY NIGHT FEVER

Words and Music by BARRY GIBB,
ROBIN GIBB and MAURICE GIBB

Moderate Disco beat

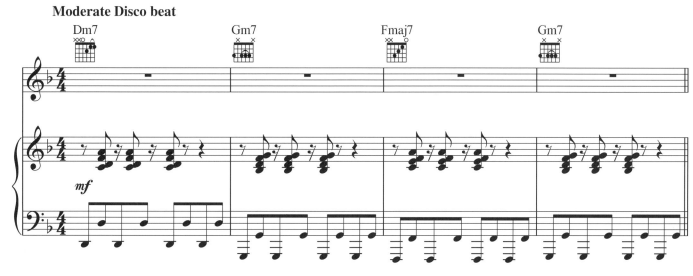

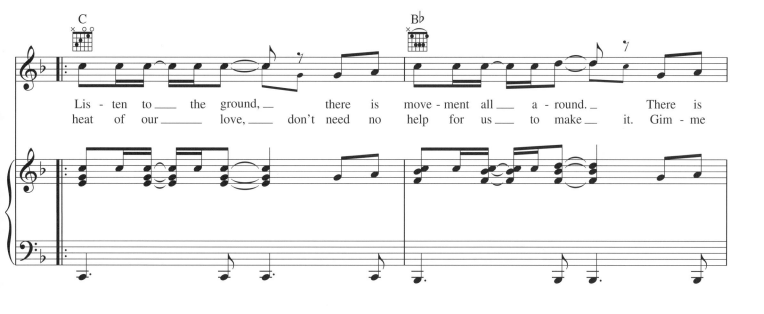

Lis-ten to ___ the ground, ___ there is move-ment all ___ a-round. ___ There is
heat of our ___ love, ___ don't need no help for us ___ to make ___ it. Gim-me

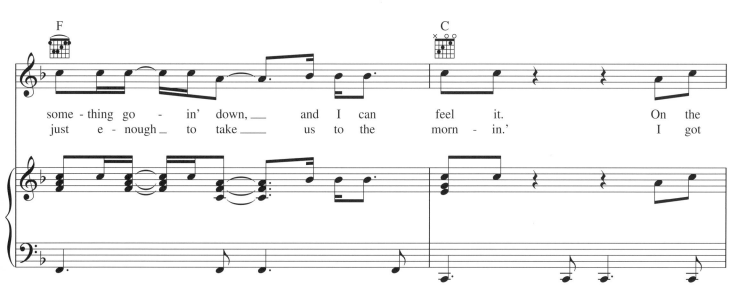

some-thing go-in' down, ___ and I can feel it. On the
just e-nough ___ to take ___ us to the morn-in.' I got

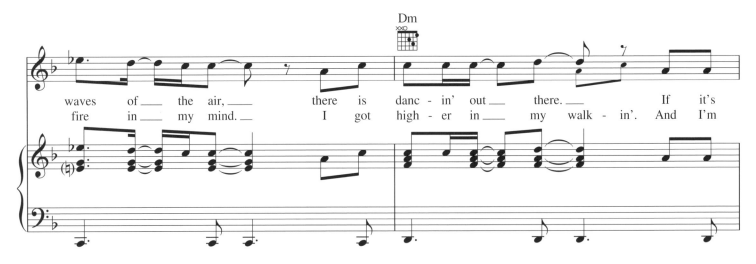

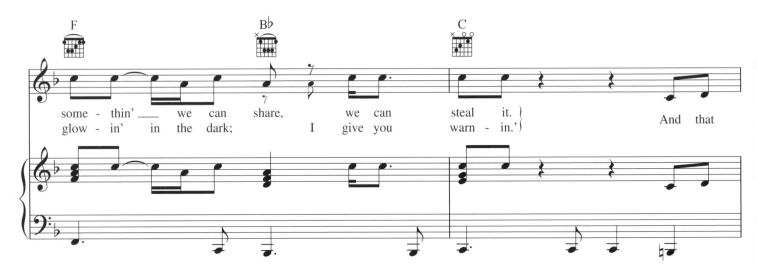

reach out for me, ___ yeah, and the feel - in' is ___ bright, then I get

night fe - ver, night fe - ver. _____ We know how to do ___

___ it. Gim - me that

night fe - ver, night fe - ver. _____ We know how to show ___

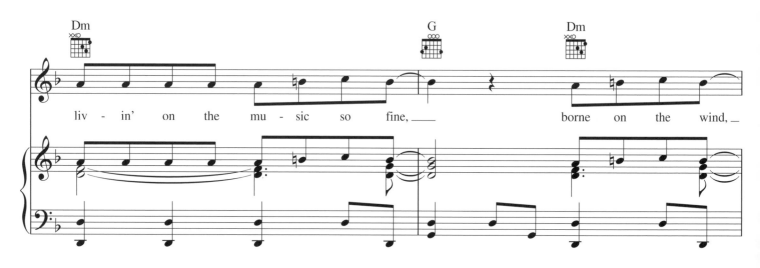

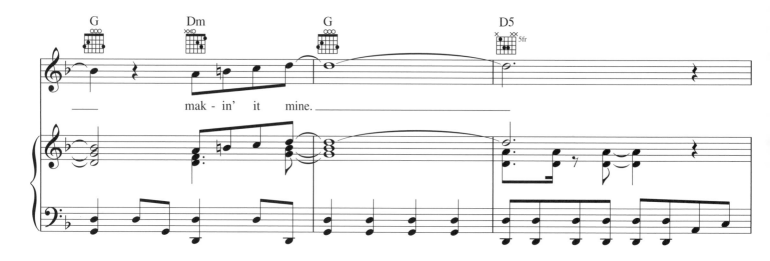

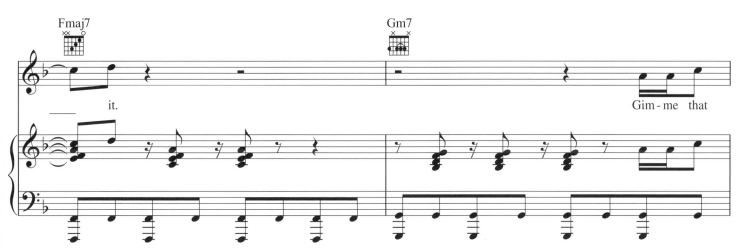

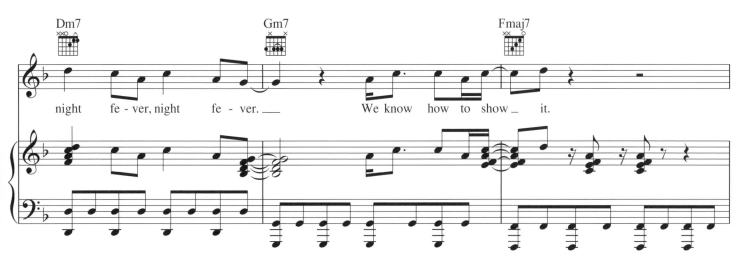

OH, PRETTY WOMAN

Words and Music by ROY ORBISON
and BILL DEES

Moderate Rock

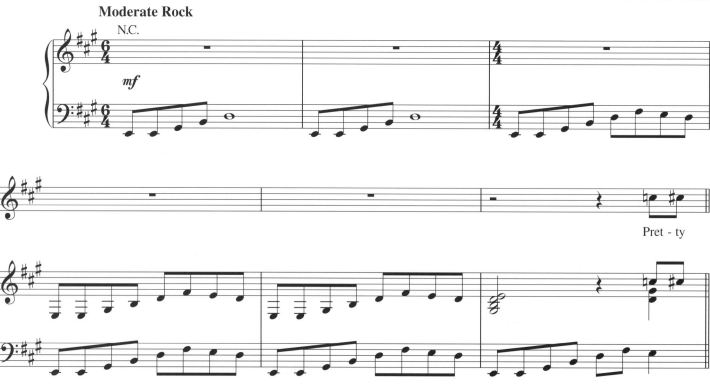

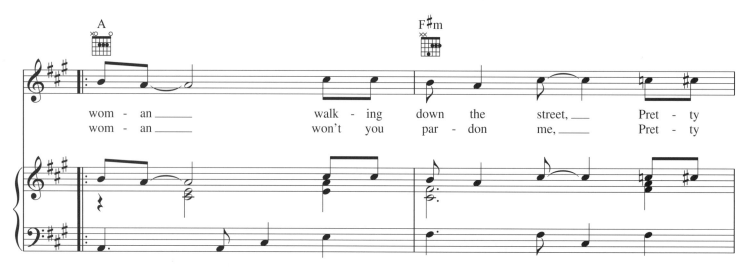

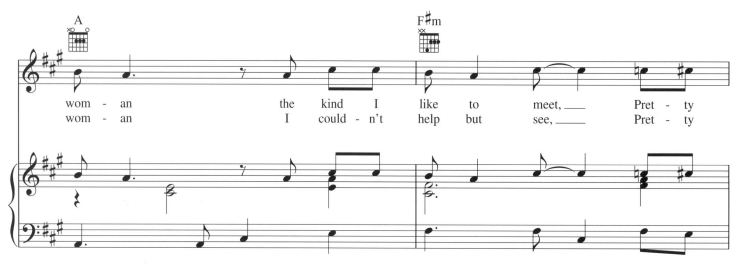

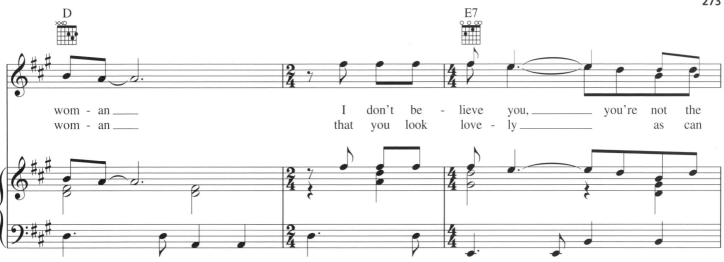

wom - an ____ I don't be - lieve you, _____ you're not the
wom - an ____ that you look love - ly _____ as can

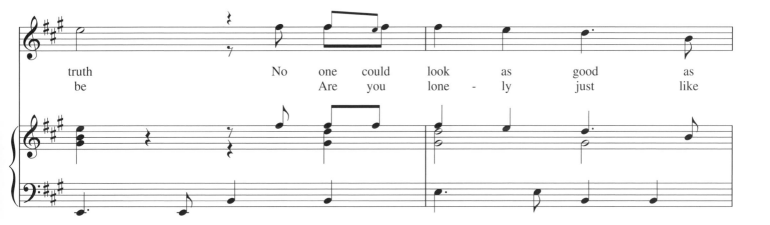

truth No one could look as good as
be Are you lone - ly just like

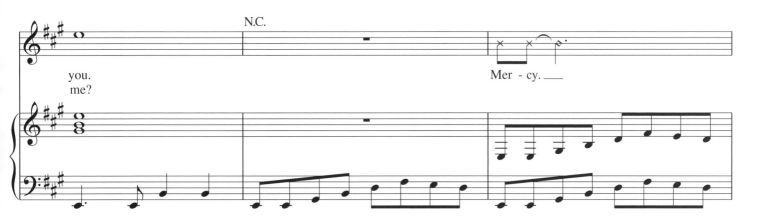

you. Mer - cy. ___
me?

Pret - ty

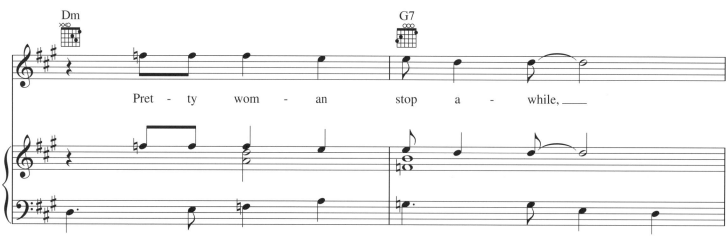

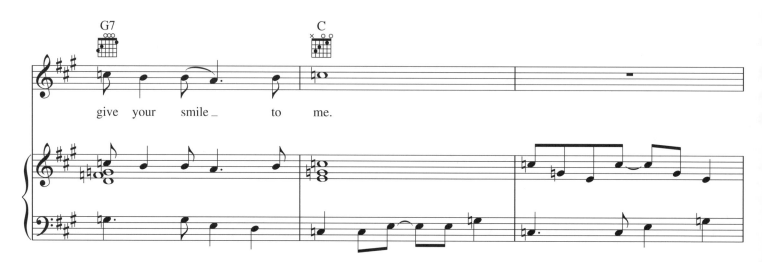

look my way, _____ Pret - ty wom - an

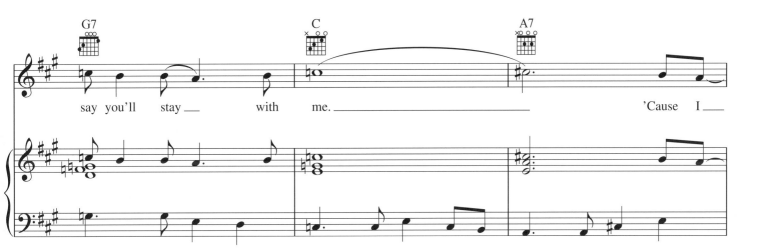

say you'll stay ___ with me. _____ 'Cause I ___

___ need you ___ I'll treat you right.

Come with me ba - by. ___ Be mine to -

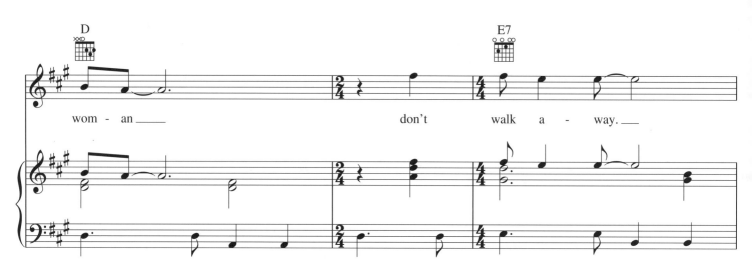

Hey,   O.   K.

If that's the way it must be ___ O.   K.

I guess I'll go on home, ___ it's late ___ There'll be to-

mor - row night but wait!   What do I   see? ___

Is she walk - ing back to me? _____ Yeah, _____ she's walk - ing back to me! _____ Oh, _____ Pret - ty wom - an.

ON MY OWN
from LES MISÉRABLES

Music by CLAUDE-MICHEL SCHÖNBERG
Lyrics by ALAIN BOUBLIL, JEAN-MARC NATEL,
HERBERT KRETZMER, JOHN CAIRD
and TREVOR NUNN

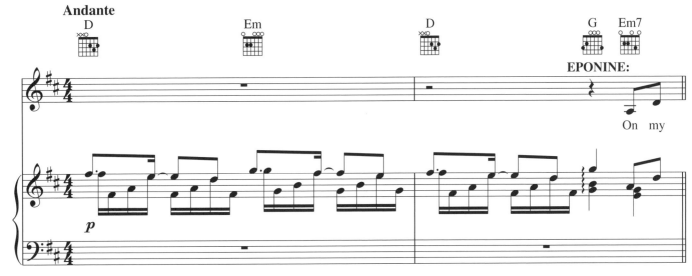

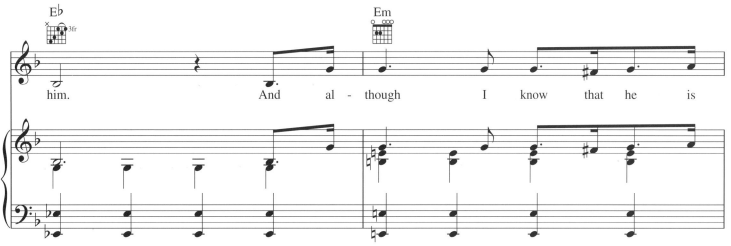

him. And al - though I know that he is

blind, Still I say there's a way for us. I

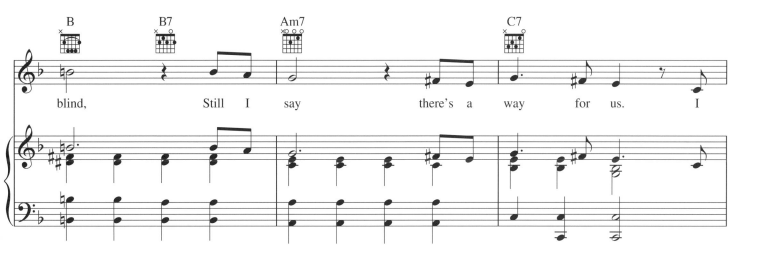

love him, _____ but when the night is o - ver, _____ he is

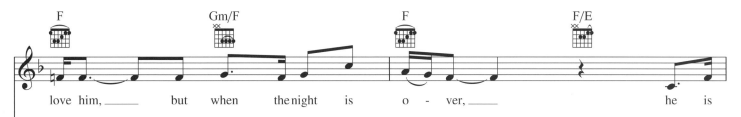

gone, the riv - er's just a riv - er. With -

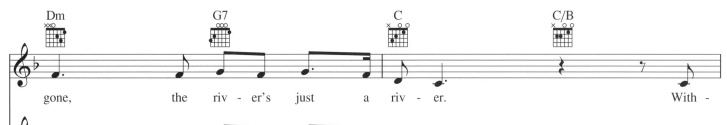

out me his world will go on turn - ing. _____ The

world is full of hap - pi - ness that I have nev - er known. I

love him, _____ I love him, _____ I

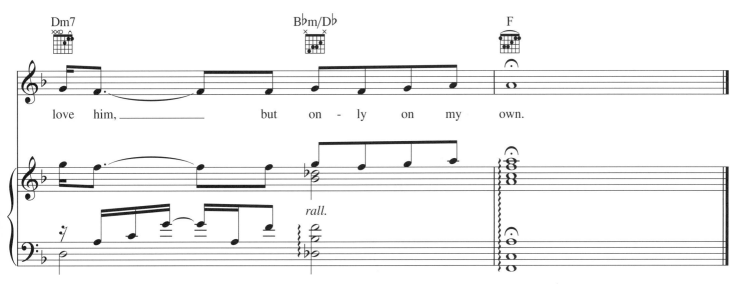

love him, _____ but on - ly on my own.

PARADISE BY THE DASHBOARD LIGHT

Words and Music by
JIM STEINMAN

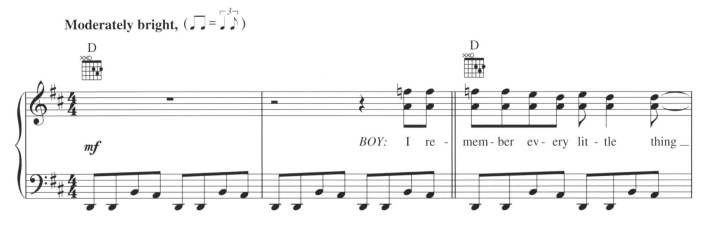

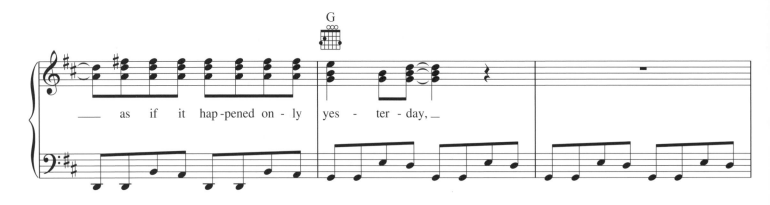

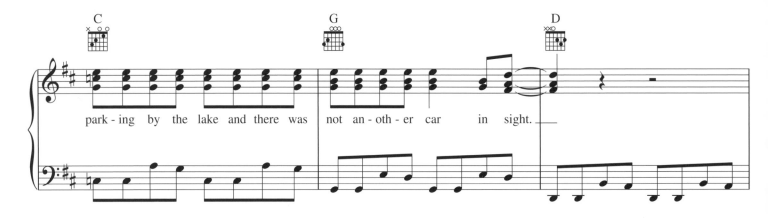

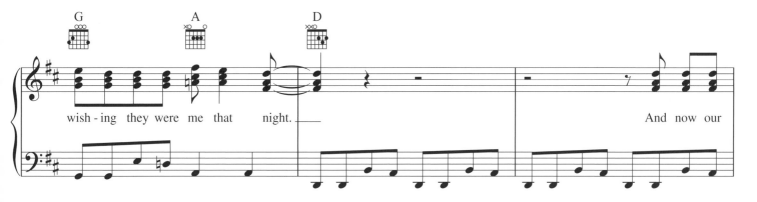

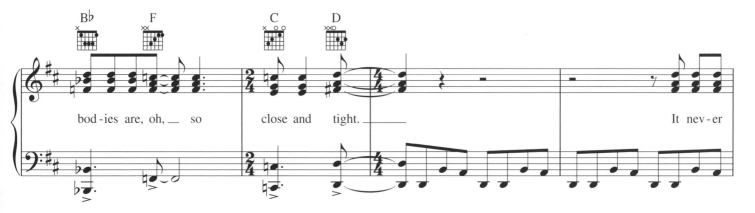

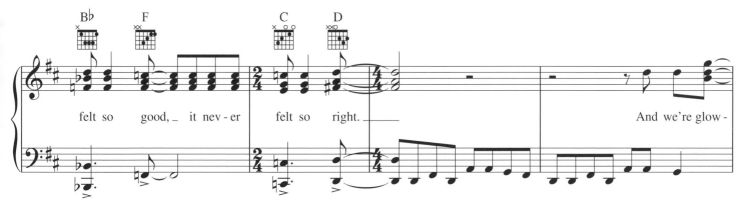

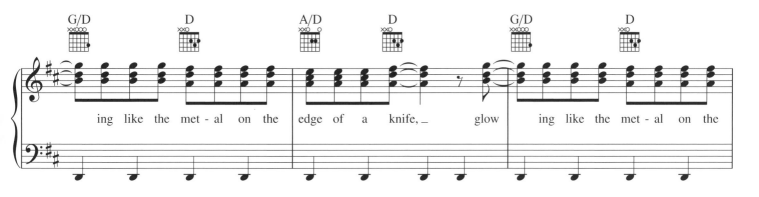

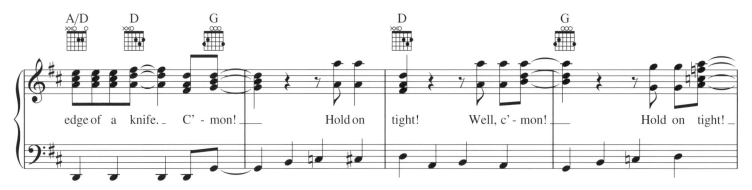

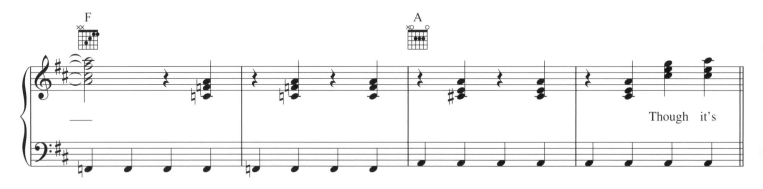

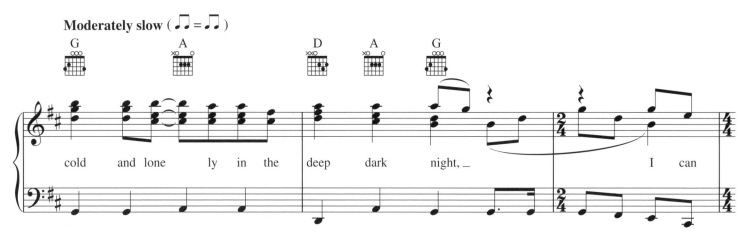

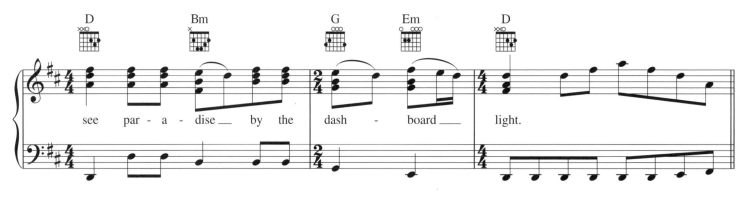

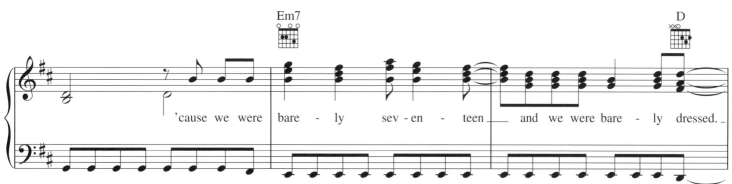

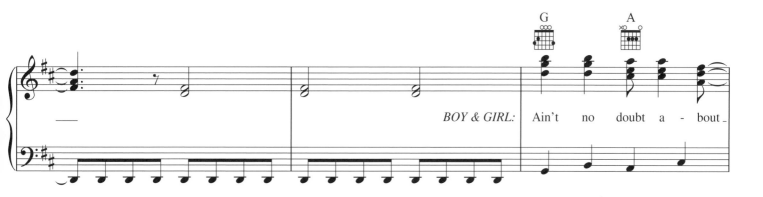

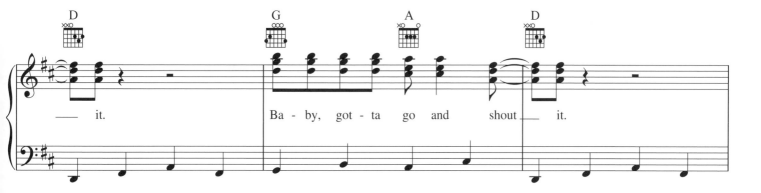

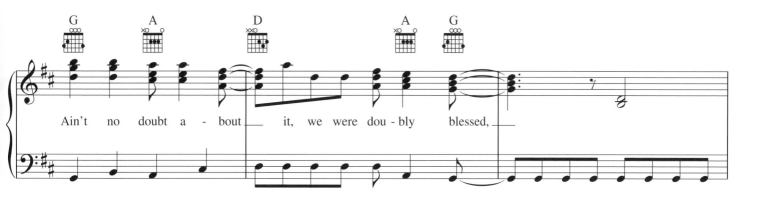

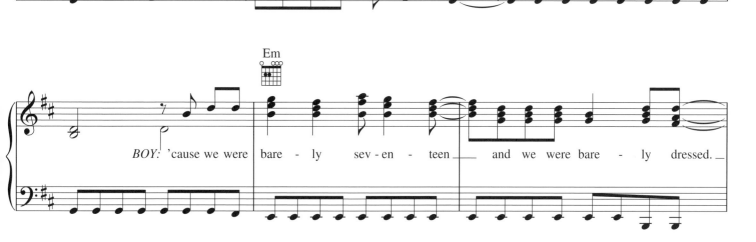

Ba - by, don't-cha hear my heart, ___ you got it drown-ing out the ra - di - o. ___

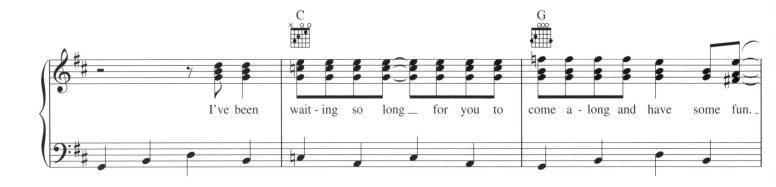

I've been wait - ing so long ___ for you to come a - long and have some fun. ___

And I got - ta let ya know, no, ___

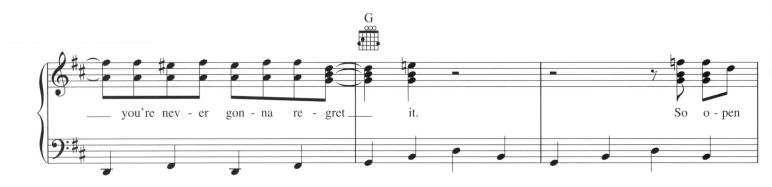

___ you're nev - er gon - na re - gret ___ it. So o - pen

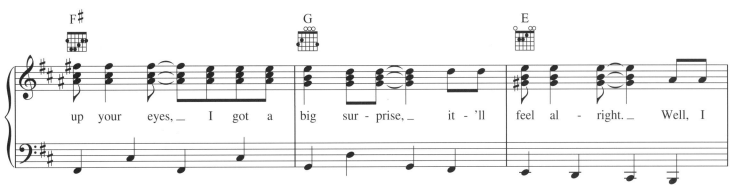

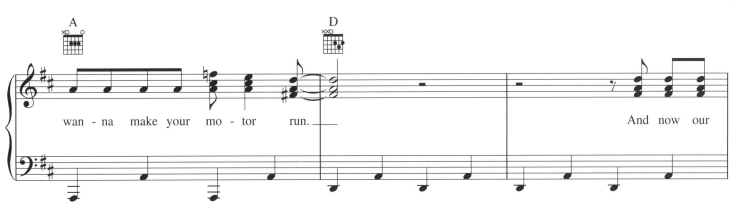

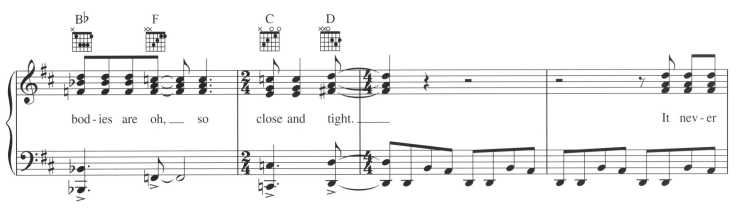

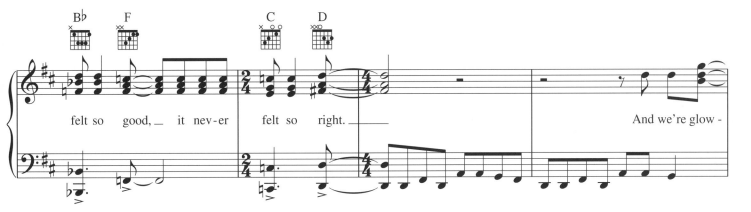

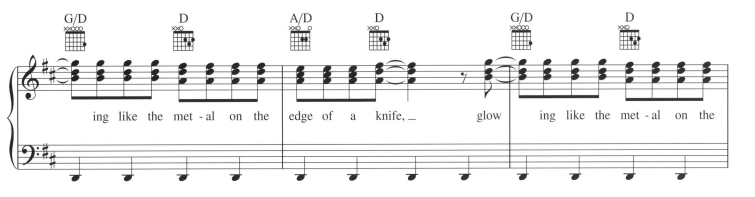

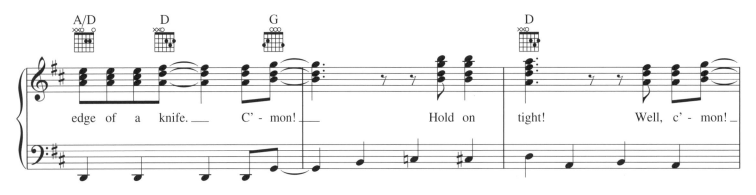

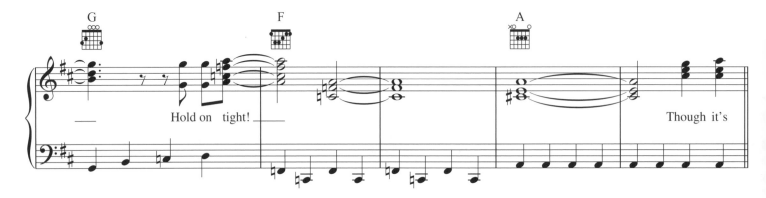

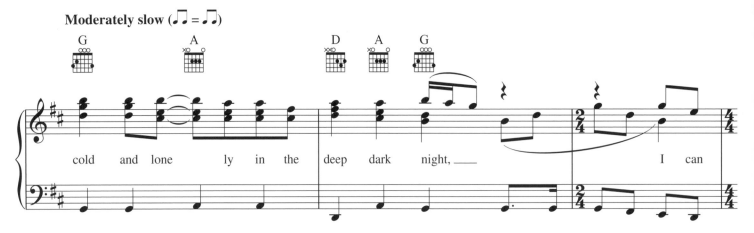

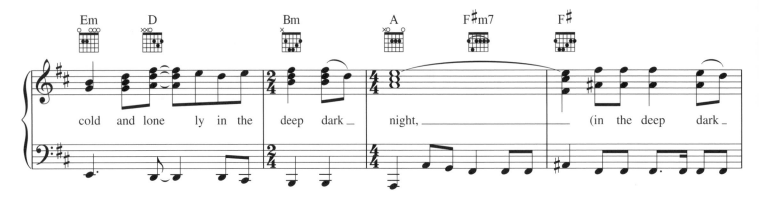

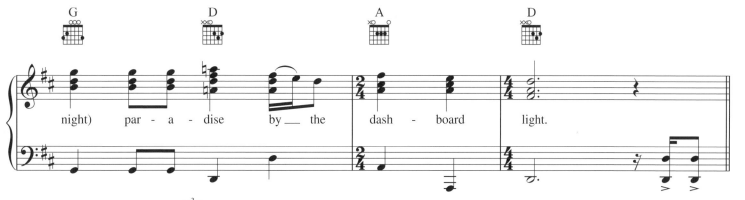

night) par - a - dise by __ the dash - board light.

Tempo Primo (♩♩ = ♩ ♪)

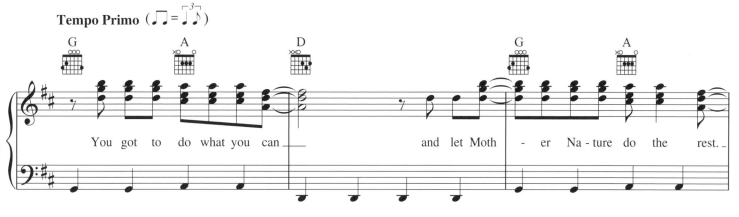

You got to do what you can __ and let Moth - er Na - ture do the rest. __

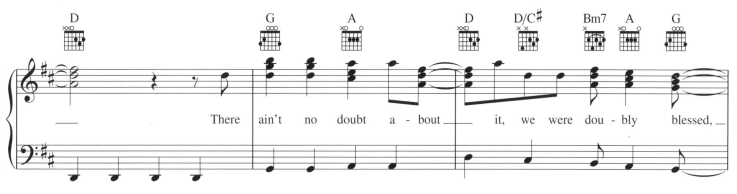

__ There ain't no doubt a - bout __ it, we were dou - bly blessed, __

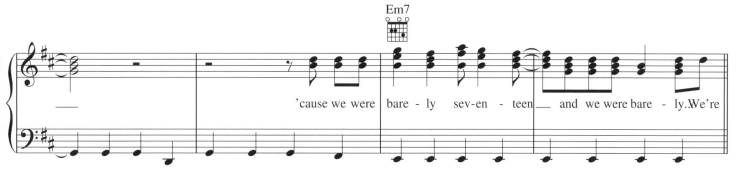

__ 'cause we were bare - ly sev - en - teen __ and we were bare - ly. We're

Somewhat slower, with a beat (♩♩ = ♩♩)

gon - na go all __ the way to - night, we're gon - na go all the way and to - night's the night. We're
gon - na go all __ the way to - night, we're gon - na go all the way and to - night's the night.

(Funky background for Dialogue)

mp

Repeat as necessary

BASEBALL PLAY-BY-PLAY ON THE CAR RADIO

O.K., here we go, we got a real pressure cooker going here, two down, nobody on, no score, bottom of the ninth, there's the wind up, and there it is, a line shot up the middle, look at him go. This boy can really fly!

He's rounding first and really turning it on now, he's not letting up at all, he's gonna try for second; the ball is bobbled out in center, and here comes the throw, and what a throw! He's gonna slide in head first, here he comes, he's out! No, wait safe-safe at second base, this kid really makes things happen out there.

Batter steps up to the plate, here's the pitch–he's going, and what a jump he's got, he's trying for third, here's the throw, it's in the dirt–safe at third! Holy cow, stolen base!

He's taking a pretty big lead out there, almost daring him to try and pick him off. The pitcher glances over, winds up, and it's bunted, bunted down the third base line, the suicide squeeze is on! Here he comes, squeeze play, it's gonna be close, here's the throw, here's the play at the plate, holy cow, I think he's gonna make it!

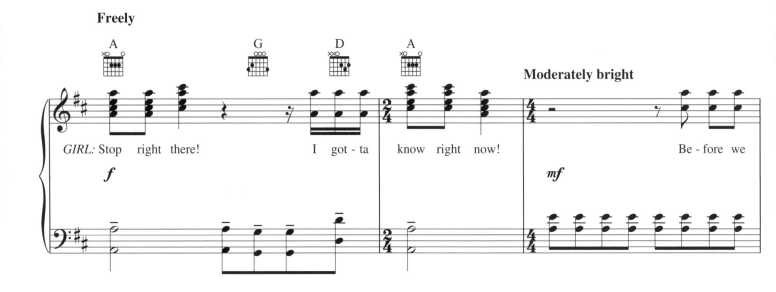

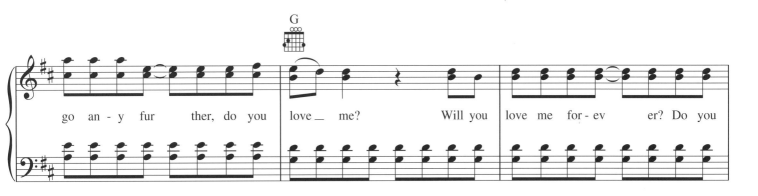

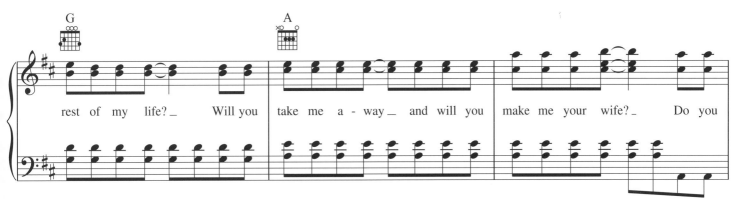

take me a - way __ and will you make me your wife? __ I got - ta know right now.

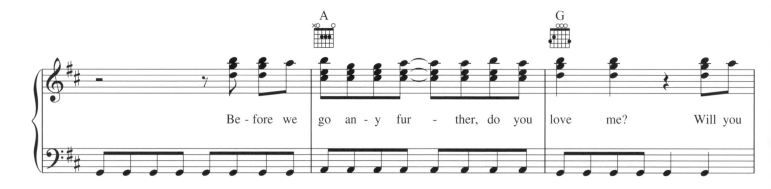

Be - fore we go an - y fur - ther, do you love me? Will you

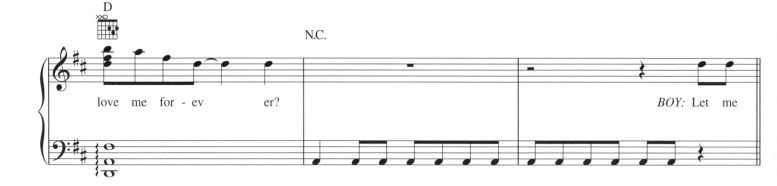

love me for - ev - er? *BOY:* Let me

sleep on __ it. __ Ba - by, ba - by, let me sleep on it. __

Let me sleep on it, __ and I'll give you an an - swer in the

morn - ing. Let me sleep on ___ it. ___

Ba - by, ba - by, let me sleep on it. ___ Let me sleep on it. ___ I'll

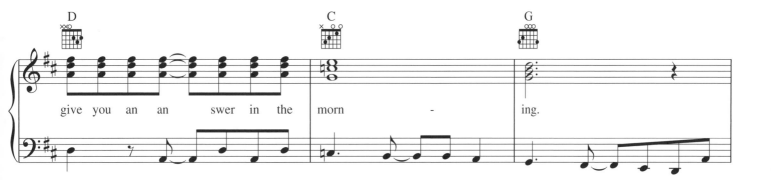

give you an an - swer in the morn - ing.

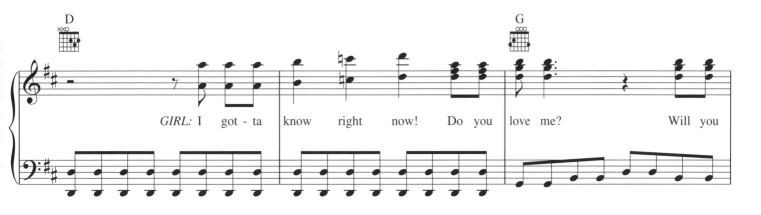

GIRL: I got - ta know right now! Do you love me? Will you

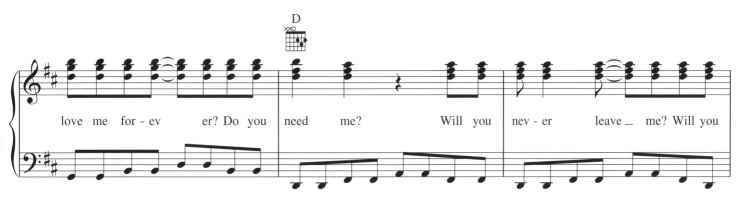

love me for - ev er? Do you need me? Will you nev - er leave ___ me? Will you

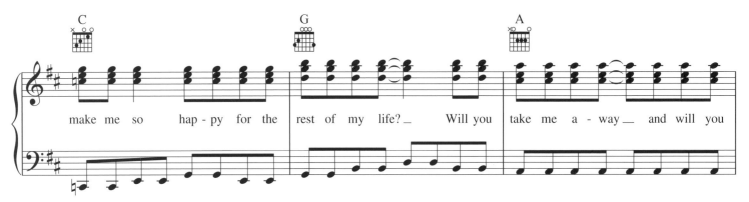

make me so hap-py for the rest of my life?_ Will you take me a-way_ and will you

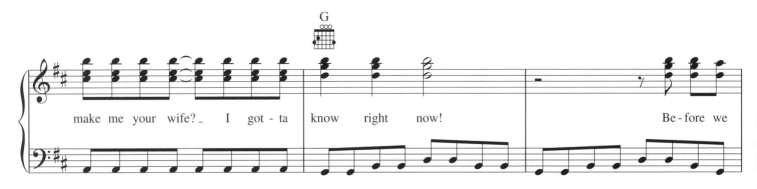

make me your wife?_ I got-ta know right now! Be-fore we

go an-y fur ther, do you love me? Will you love me for-ev er?

(Spoken:) What's it gonna be, boy? Come on! I can wait all night!

What's it gonna be, boy... yes or no? What's it gonna be, boy? Yes...

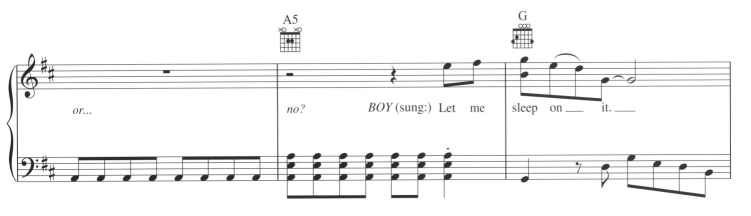

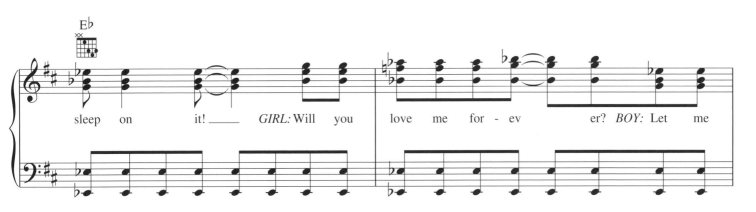

sleep on it! _____ *GIRL:* Will you love me for - ev er? *BOY:* Let me

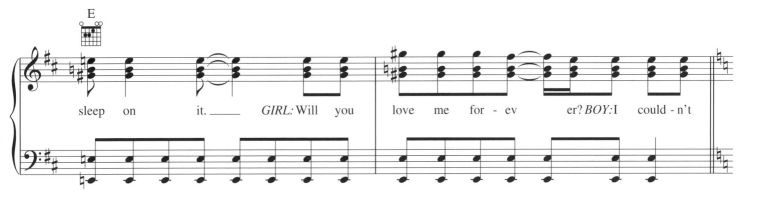

sleep on it. _____ *GIRL:* Will you love me for - ev er? *BOY:* I could - n't

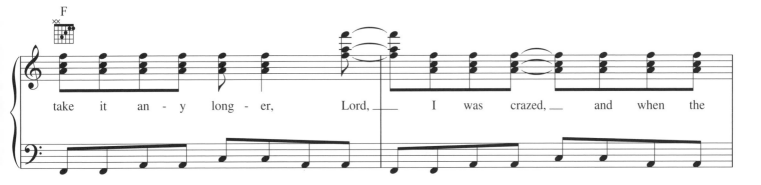

take it an - y long - er, Lord, _____ I was crazed, _____ and when the

feel - ing came up - on me like a ti - dal wave, _____ I start - ed

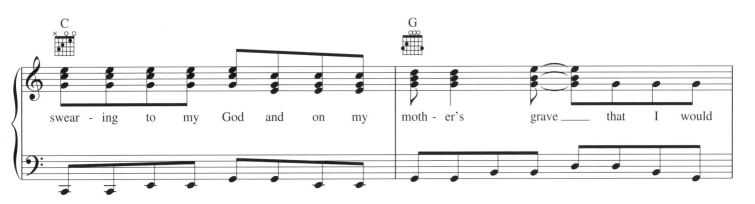

swear - ing to my God and on my moth - er's grave _____ that I would

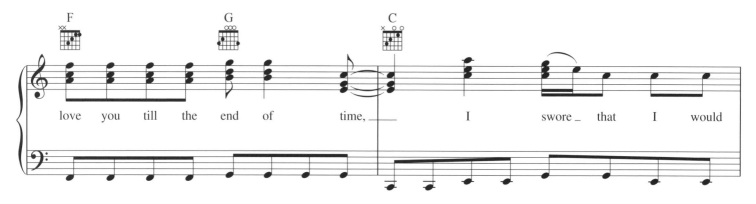

love you till the end of time, ___ I swore ___ that I would

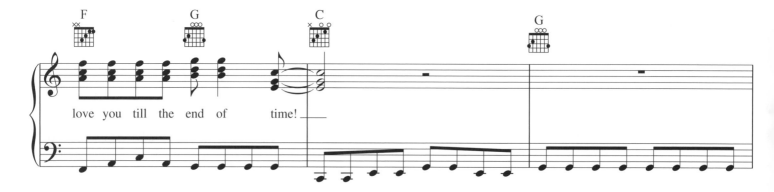

love you till the end of time! ___

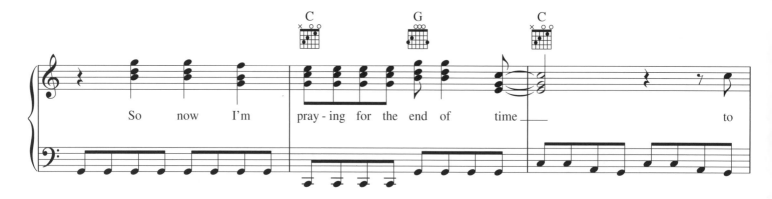

So now I'm pray-ing for the end of time ___ to

hur-ry up and ar-rive. ___ 'Cause

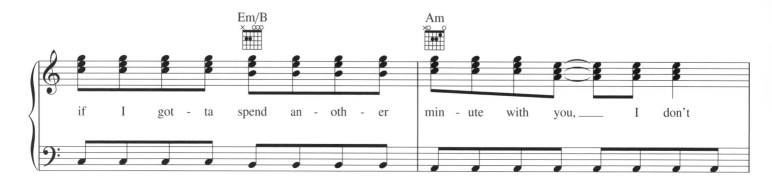

if I got-ta spend an-oth-er min-ute with you, ___ I don't

think that I can real - ly sur - vive. I'll nev - er

break my prom - ise or for - get my vow, ___ but

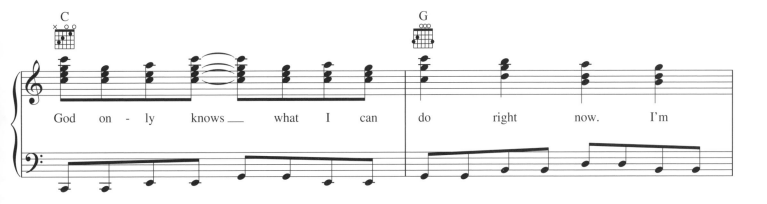

God on - ly knows ___ what I can do right now. I'm

pray - ing for the end of time, ___ it's all that I can do. ___

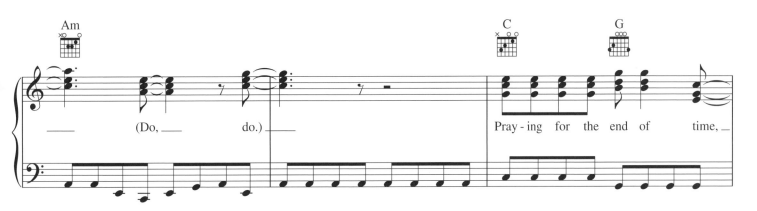

___ (Do, ___ do.) ___ Pray - ing for the end of time, ___

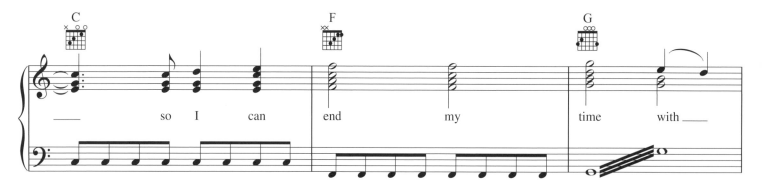

so I can end my time with ___

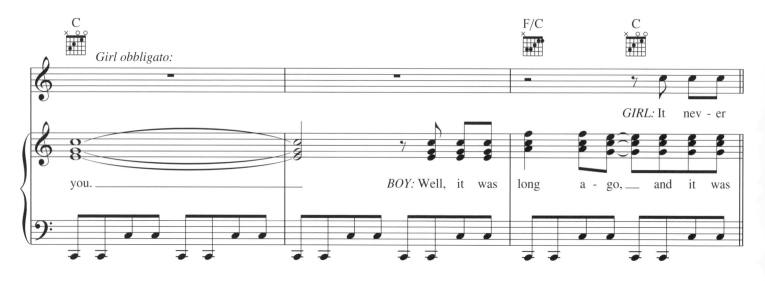

Girl obbligato:

you. ___

GIRL: It nev-er

BOY: Well, it was long a-go, ___ and it was

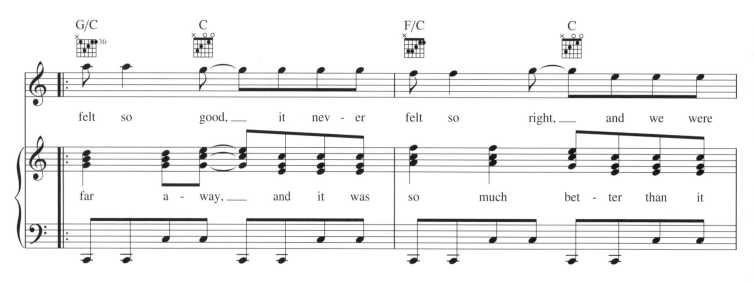

felt so good, ___ it nev-er felt so right, ___ and we were

far a-way, ___ and it was so much bet-ter than it

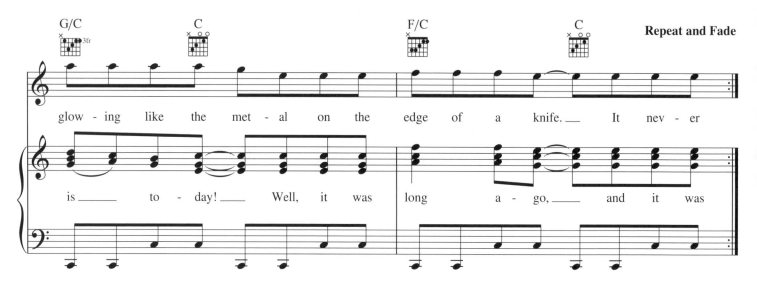

Repeat and Fade

glow-ing like the met-al on the edge of a knife. ___ It nev-er

is ___ to-day! ___ Well, it was long a-go, ___ and it was

POPULAR
from the Broadway Musical WICKED

Music and Lyrics by
STEPHEN SCHWARTZ

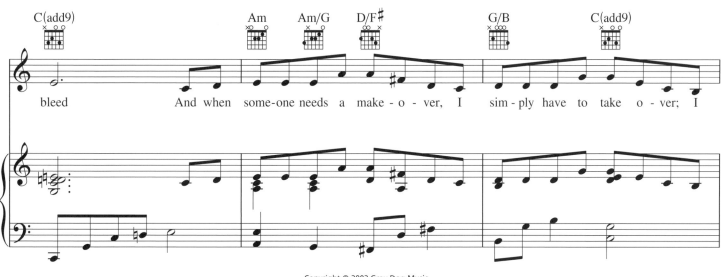

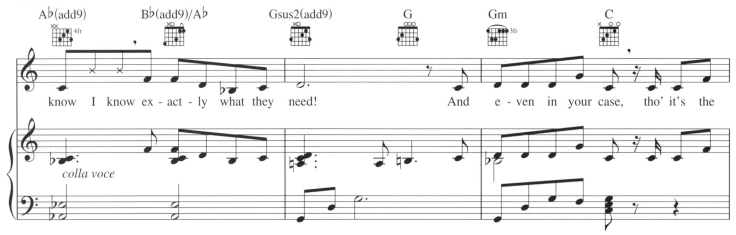

know I know ex-act-ly what they need! And e-ven in your case, tho' it's the

colla voce

tough-est case I've yet to face,___ don't wor-ry, I'm de-ter-mined to suc-

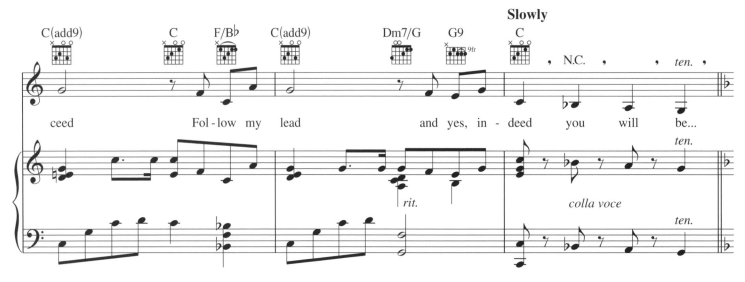

ceed Fol-low my lead and yes, in-deed you will be...

rit. *colla voce*

Pop-u-lar,___ You're gon-na be pop-u-lar! I'll teach ___ you the

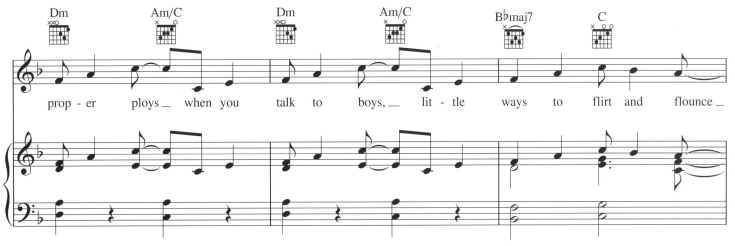

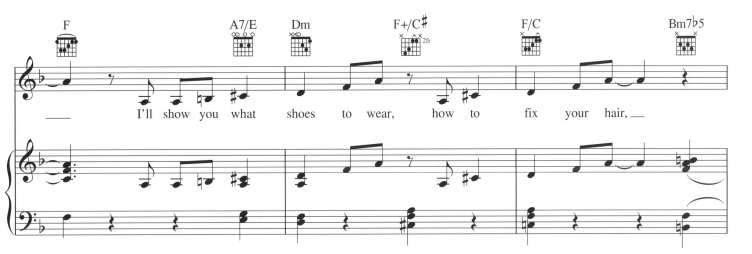

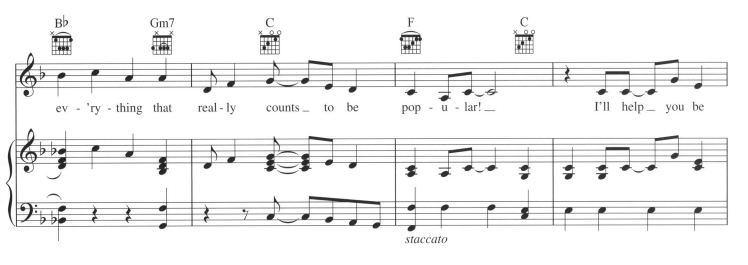

be - com - ing pop - u - ler... lar...

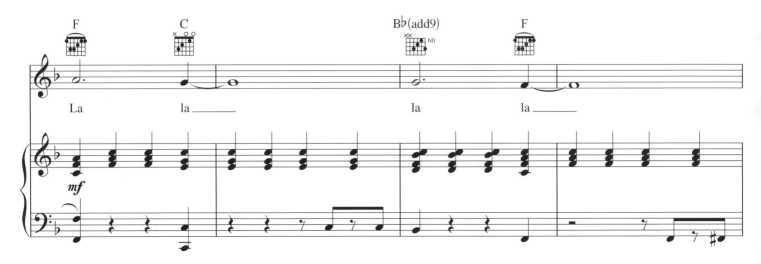

La la la la

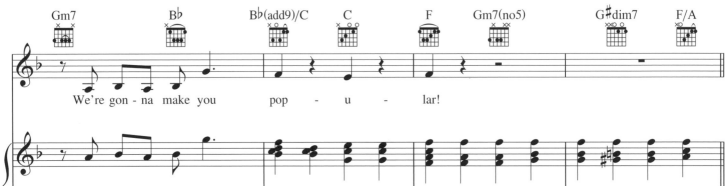

We're gon - na make you pop - u - lar!

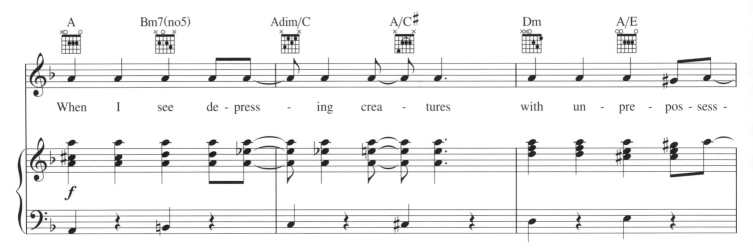

When I see de - press - ing crea - tures with un - pre - pos - sess -

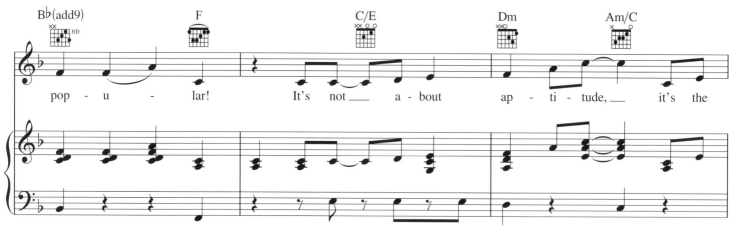

pop - u - lar! It's not ___ a - bout ap - ti - tude, ___ it's the

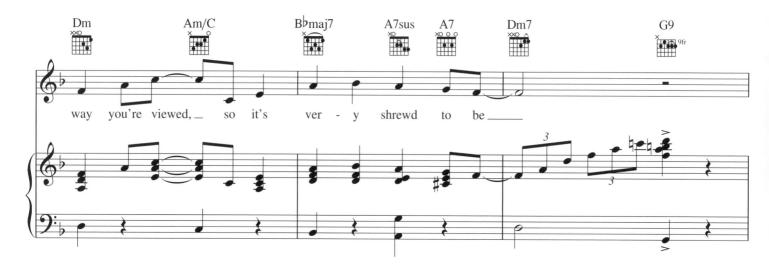

way you're viewed, ___ so it's ver - y shrewd to be _____

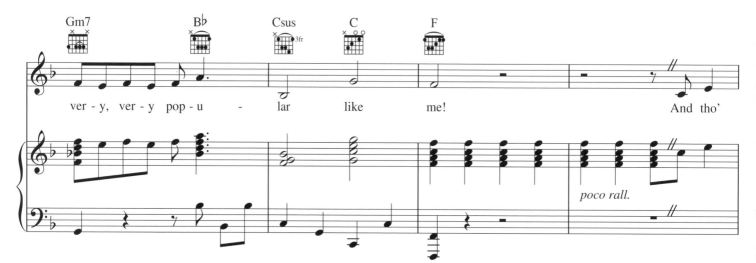

ver - y, ver - y pop - u - lar like me! And tho'

poco rall.

Freely

you pro - test ___ your dis - in - ter - est, ___ I know clan - des - tine -

mp *colla voce*

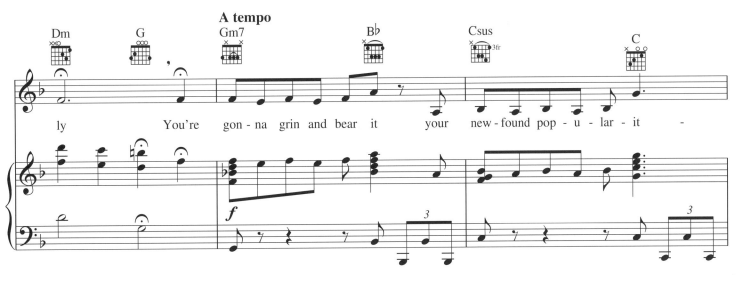

A tempo

ly You're gon-na grin and bear it your new-found pop-u-lar-it -

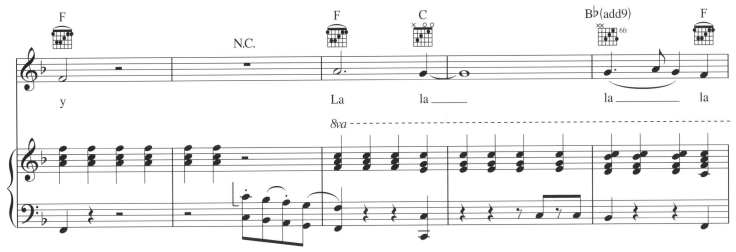

y La la _____ la _____ la

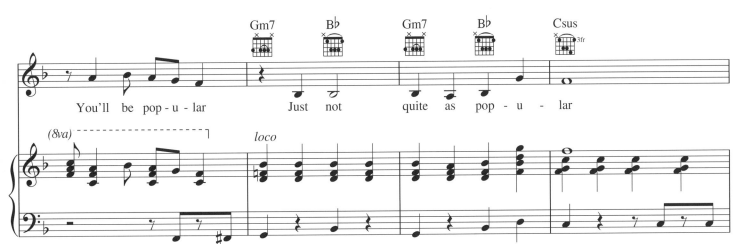

You'll be pop-u-lar Just not quite as pop-u-lar

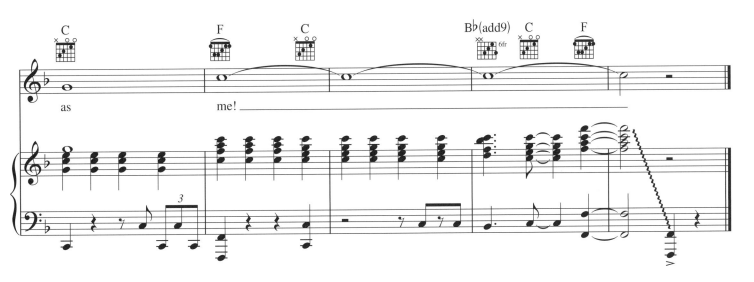

as me! _____

POKER FACE

Words and Music by STEFANI GERMANOTTA
and RedOne

Dance Pop

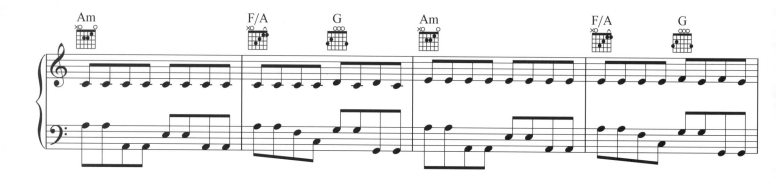

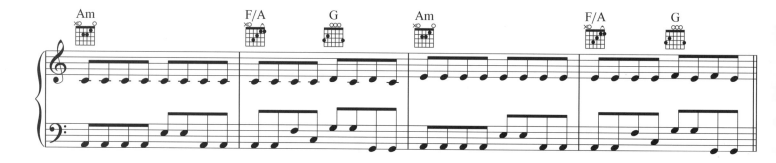

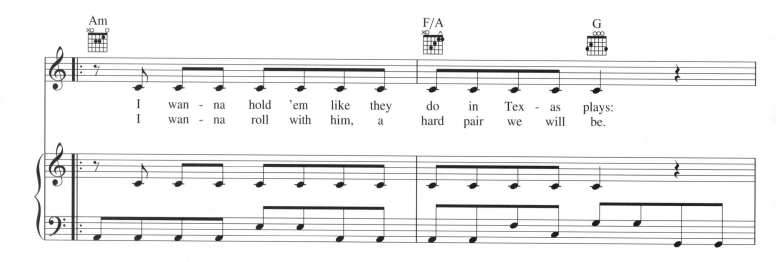

I wan-na hold 'em like they do in Tex-as plays:
I wan-na roll with him, a hard pair we will be.

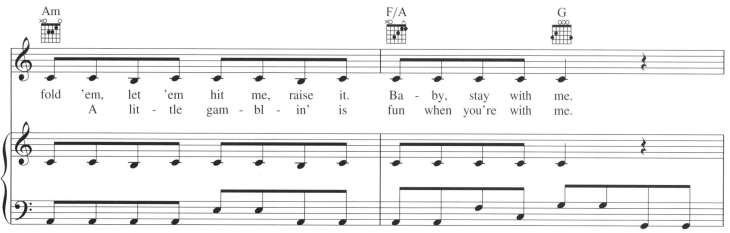

fold 'em, let 'em hit me, raise it. Ba - by, stay with me.
A lit - tle gam - bl - in' is fun when you're with me.

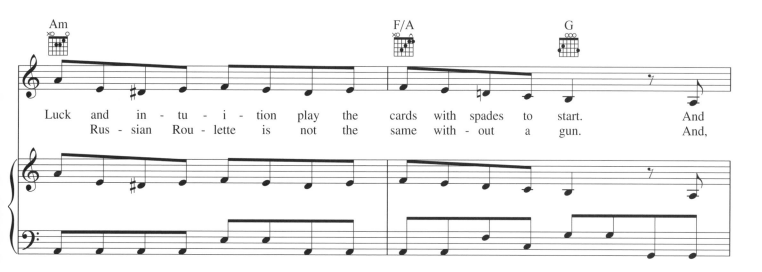

Luck and in - tu - i - tion play the cards with spades to start. And
Rus - sian Rou - lette is not the same with - out a gun. And,

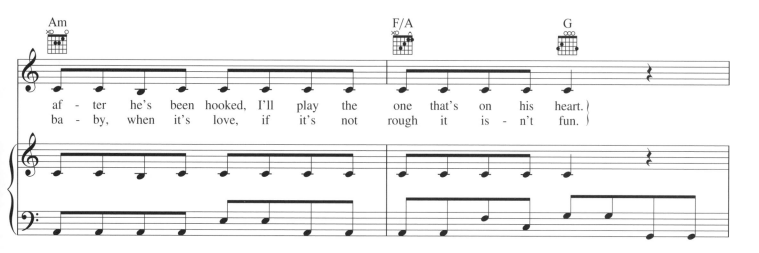

af - ter he's been hooked, I'll play the one that's on his heart.
ba - by, when it's love, if it's not rough it is - n't fun.

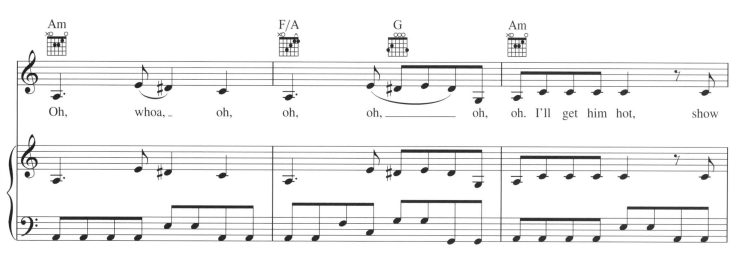

Oh, whoa, __ oh, oh, oh, _____ oh, oh. I'll get him hot, show

him what I got. __ Oh, whoa, _ oh, oh, oh, _____ oh,

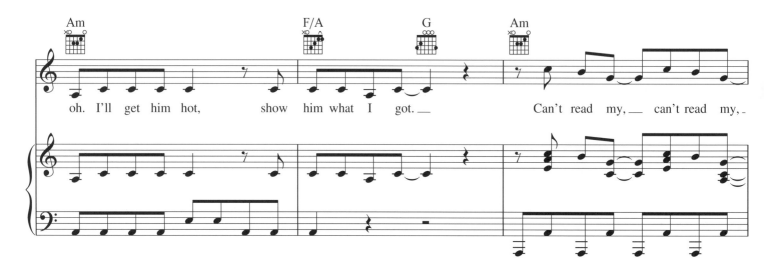

oh. I'll get him hot, show him what I got. __ Can't read my, __ can't read my, _

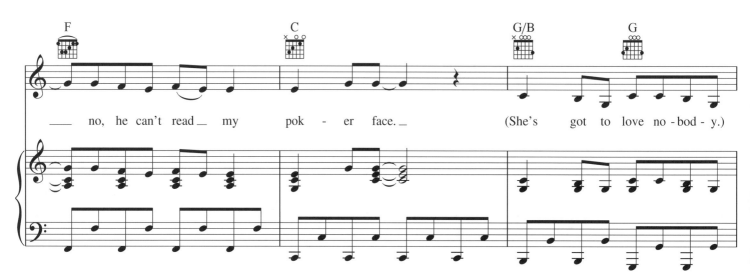

__ no, he can't read __ my pok - er face. _ (She's got to love no - bod - y.)

Can't read my, __ can't read my, ___ no, he can't read __ my pok - er face. _

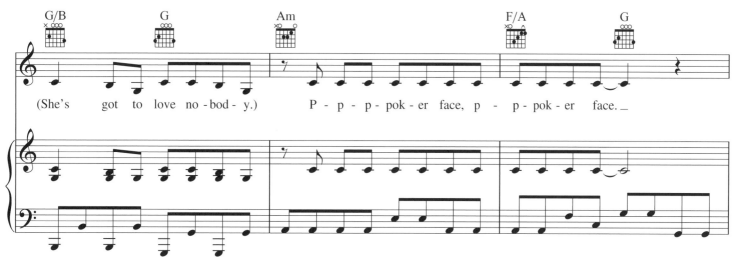

(She's got to love no-bod-y.) P - p - p - pok-er face, p - p-pok-er face. _

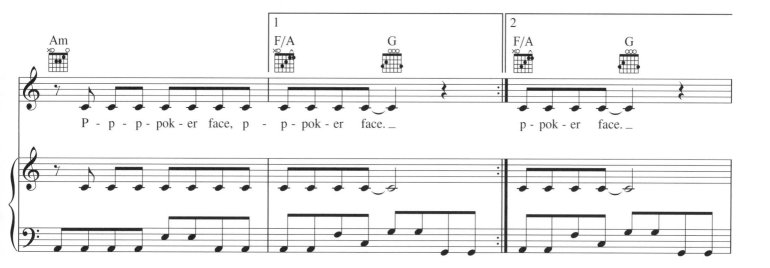

P - p - p-pok-er face, p - p-pok-er face. _ p-pok-er face. _

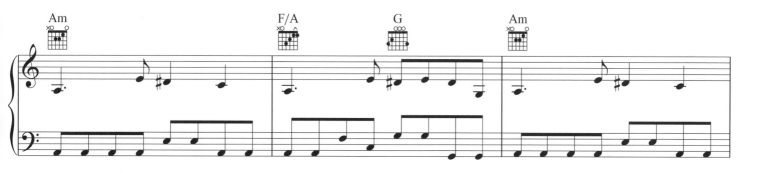

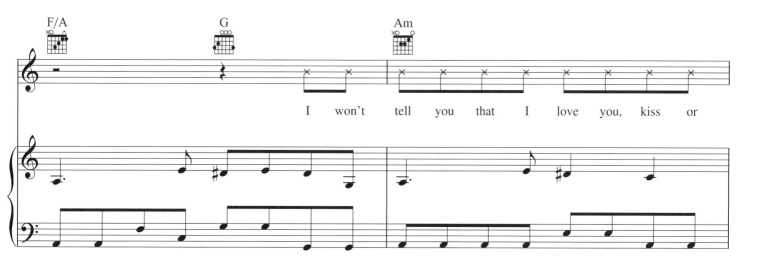

I won't tell you that I love you, kiss or

hug you 'cause I'm bluff - in' with my muf - fin. I'm not ly - in', I'm just

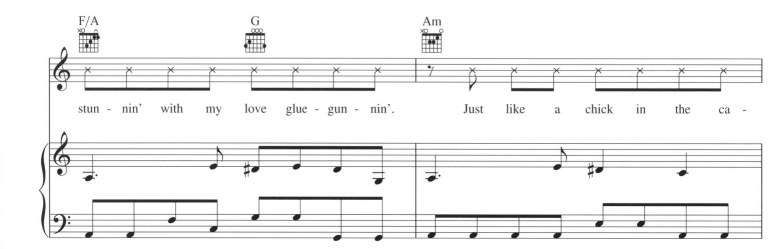

stun - nin' with my love glue - gun - nin'. Just like a chick in the ca -

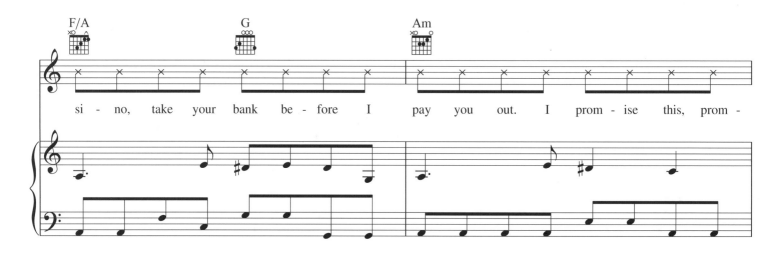

si - no, take your bank be - fore I pay you out. I prom - ise this, prom -

ise this. Check this hand, 'cause I'm mar - vel - ous.
Can't read my,___ can't read my,___

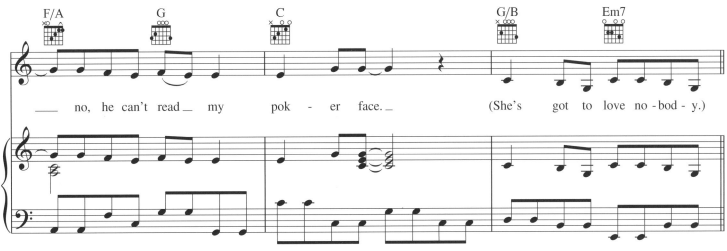

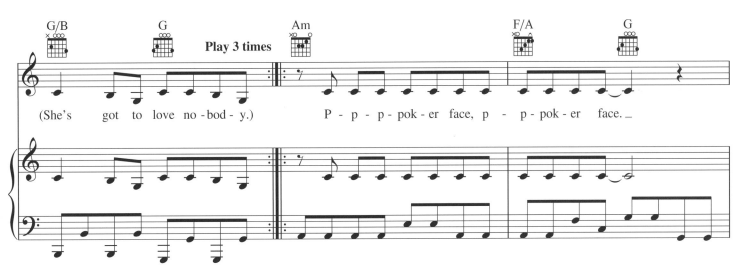

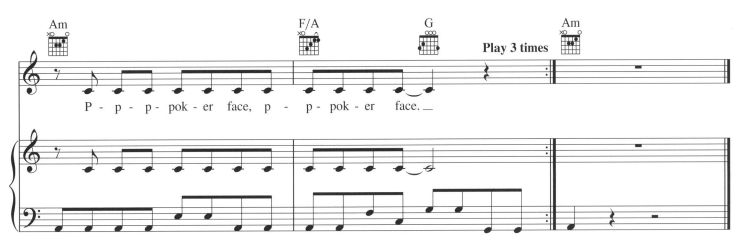

RED, RED WINE

Words and Music by
NEIL DIAMOND

Slow Country beat

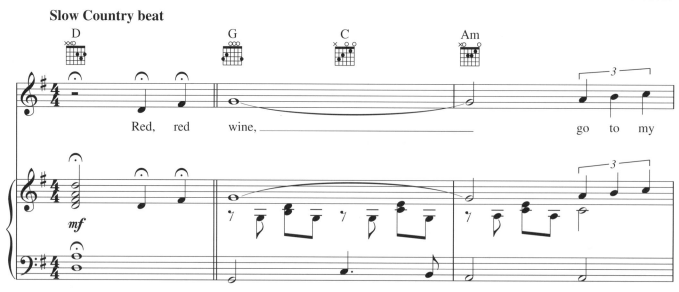

Red, red wine, _____ go to my head,

make me for- get that I

still need her so.

Red, red

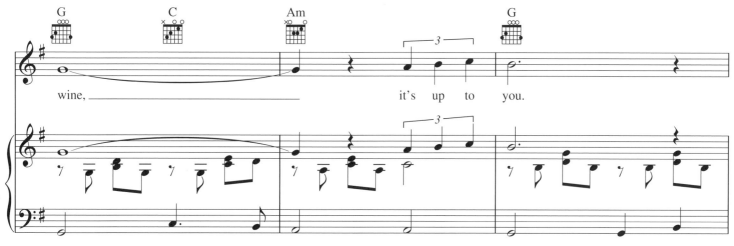

wine, _____ it's up to you.

All I can do, I've done; but mem-'ries won't

go. No, mem-'ries won't go. _____

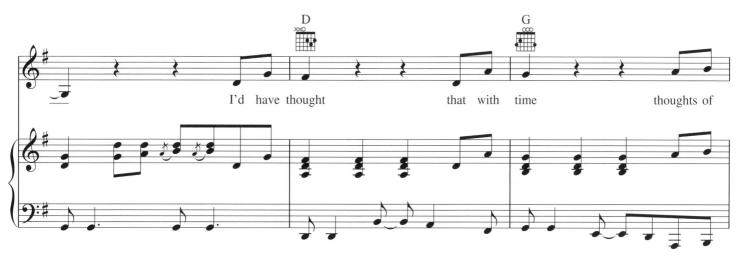

I'd have thought that with time thoughts of

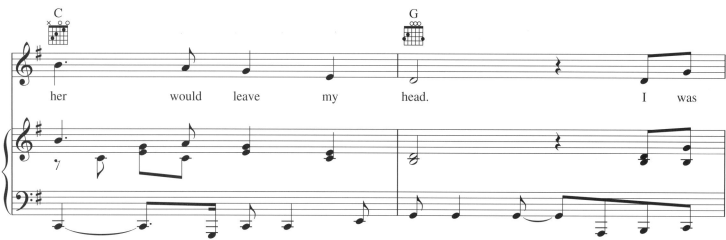

her would leave my head. I was

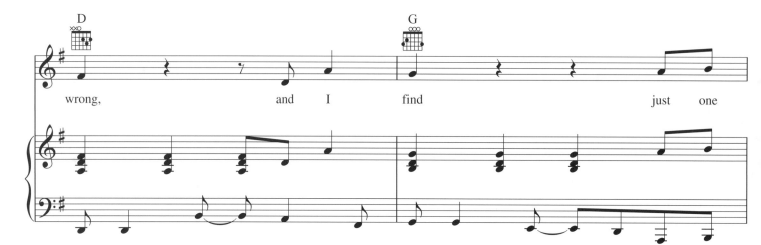

wrong, and I find just one

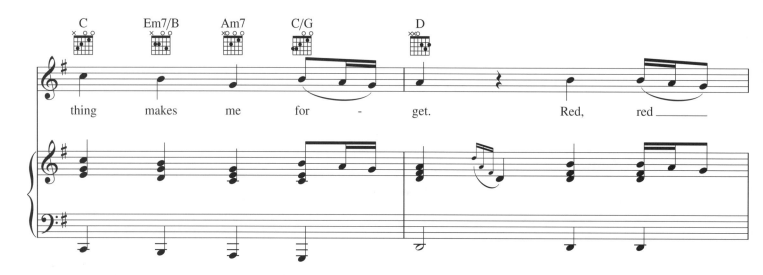

thing makes me for - get. Red, red

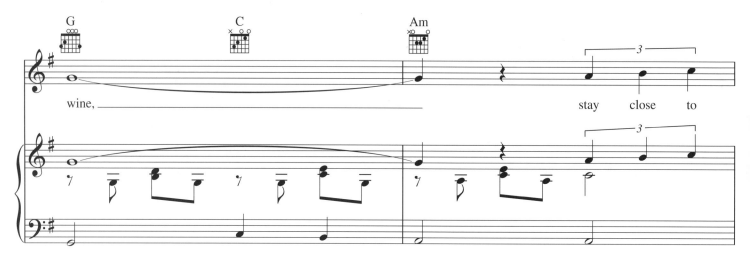

wine, stay close to

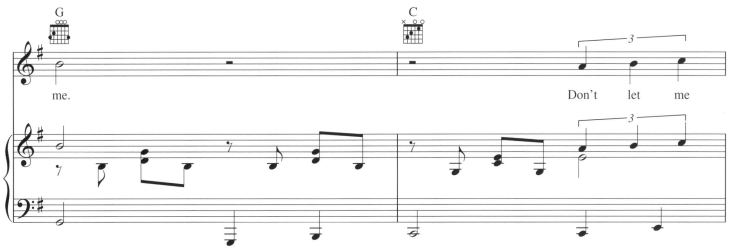

me.   Don't let me

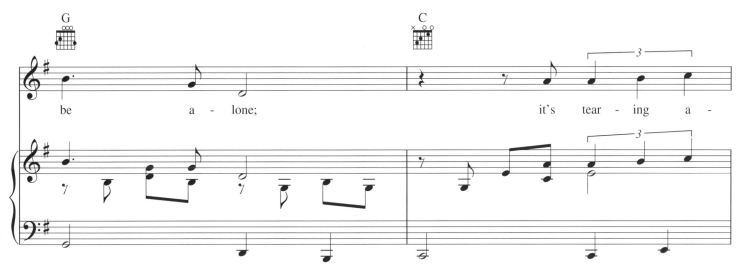

be   a - lone;   it's   tear - ing   a -

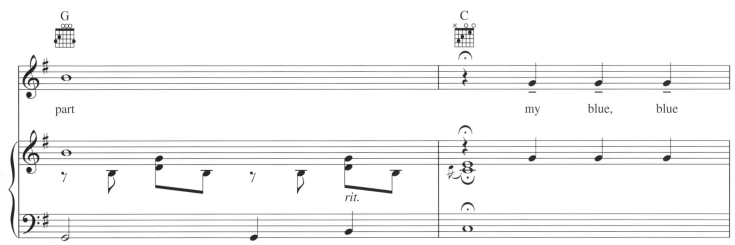

part   my   blue,   blue

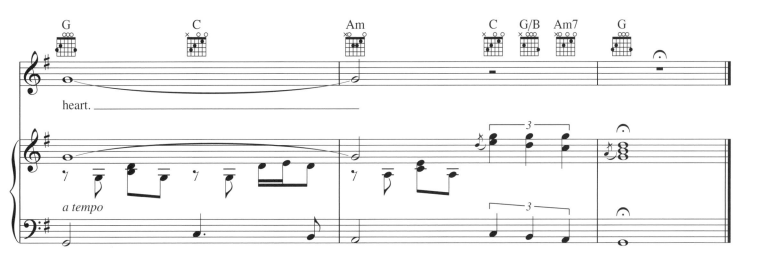

heart.

REHAB

Words and Music by
AMY WINEHOUSE

Retro Blues

Lyrics:

They tried to make me go to re-hab, I said, "No, no, no."

Yes, I been black, but when I come back, you won't know, know, know.

I ain't got the time,

and if my dad - dy ___ thinks ___ I'm fine, _____ he's

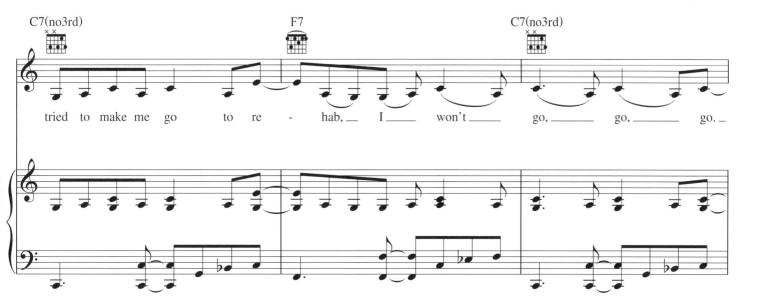

tried to make me go to re - hab, ___ I ___ won't ___ go, ___ go, ___ go. ___

I'd rath - er be   at home _____
The man   said, "Why   you think _____
I won't   ev - er   want to ___ drink _____

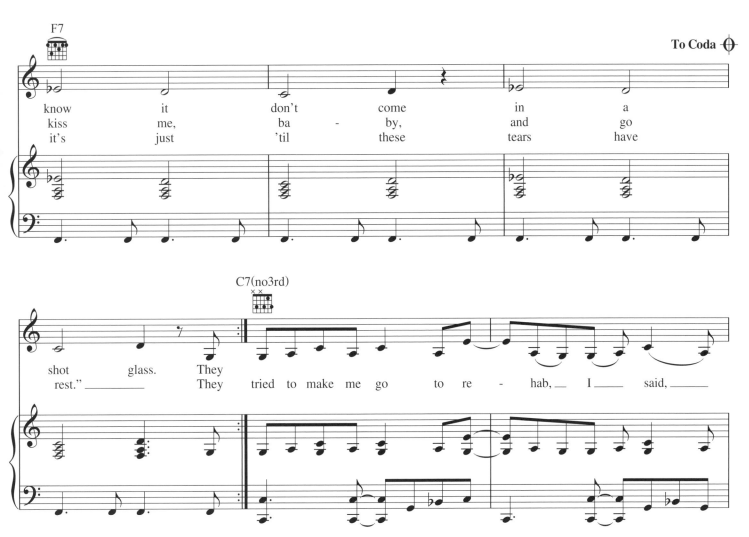

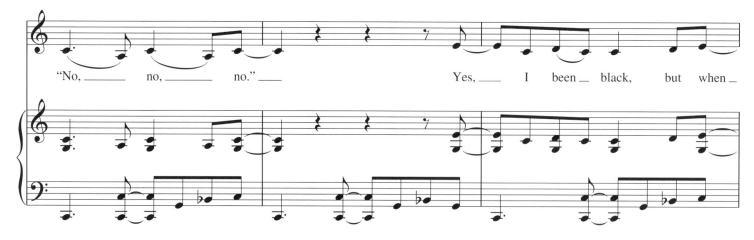

"No, ____ no, ____ no." ____ Yes, ____ I been ____ black, but when ____

D.S. al Coda

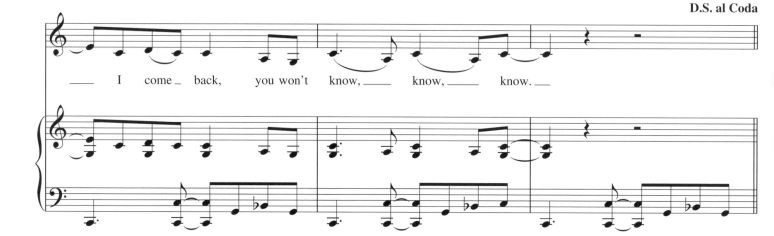

____ I come ____ back, you won't know, ____ know, ____ know. ____

CODA

C7(no3rd)

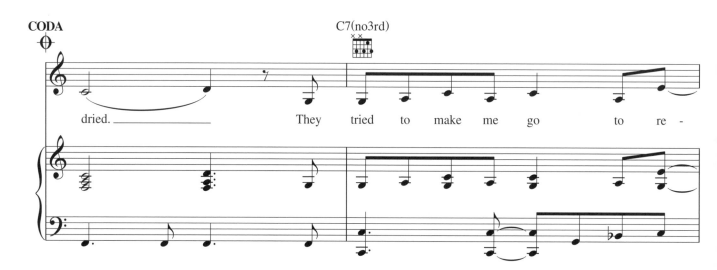

dried. _____ They tried to make me go to re-

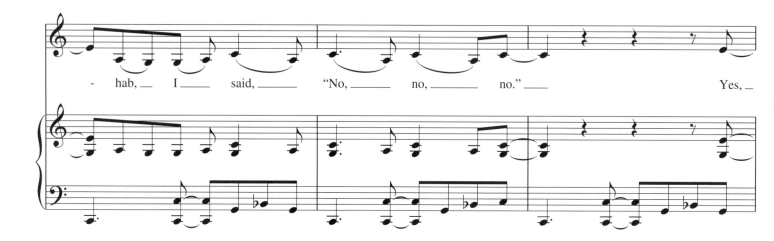

- hab, I ____ said, ____ "No, ____ no, ____ no." ____ Yes,

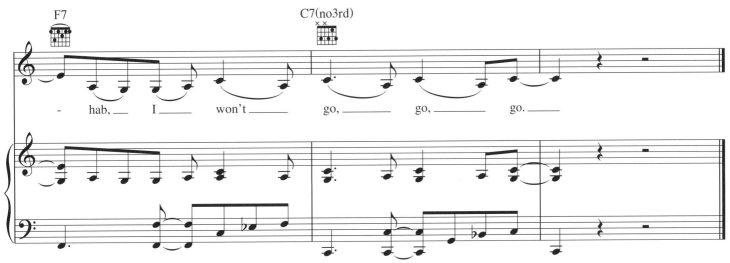

RELEASE ME

Words and Music by ROBERT YOUNT,
EDDIE MILLER and DUB WILLIAMS

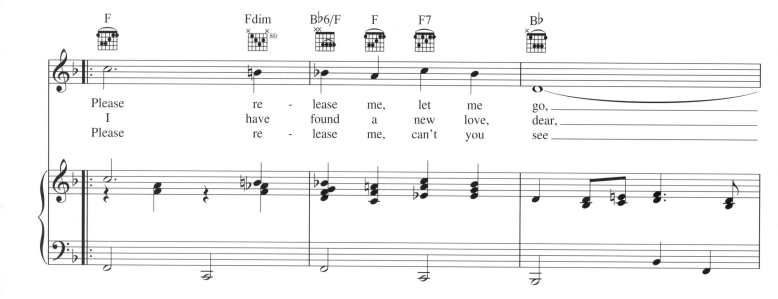

Please   re - lease me,   let   me   go, _____
I   have   found   a   new   love,   dear, _____
Please   re - lease me,   can't   you   see _____

_____   for   I   don't   love   you   an - y -
_____   and   I   will   al - ways   want   her
_____   you'd   be   a   fool   to   cling   to

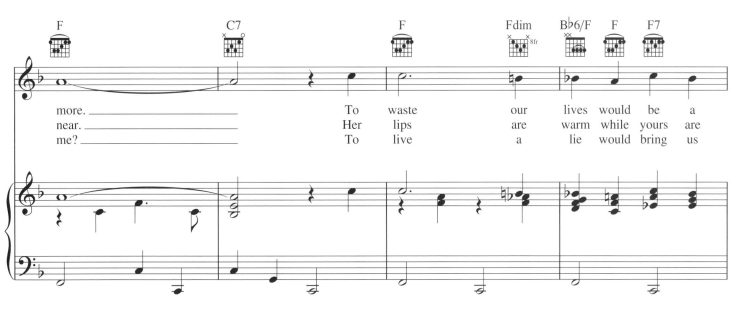

more. _____ To waste our lives would be a
near. _____ Her lips are warm while yours are
me? _____ To live a lie would bring us

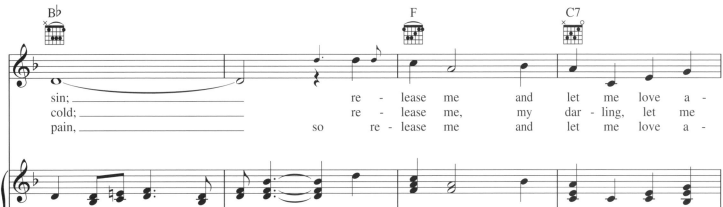

sin; _____ re - lease me and let me love a -
cold; _____ re - lease me, my dar - ling, let me
pain, _____ so re - lease me and let me love a -

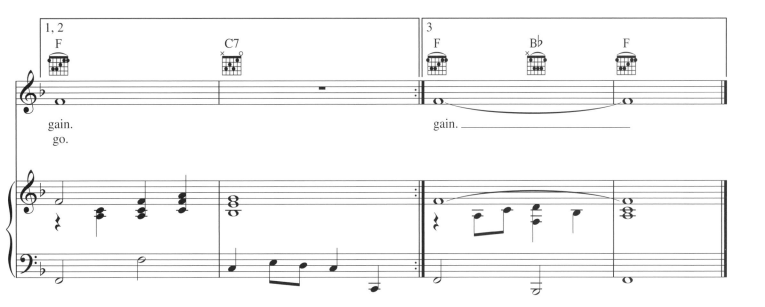

1, 2
gain.
go.

3
gain. _____

RESPECT

Words and Music by
OTIS REDDING

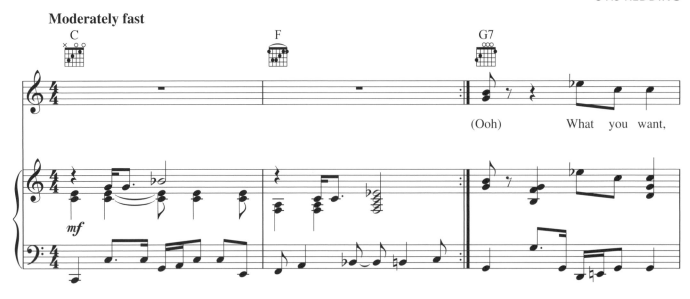

Moderately fast

(Ooh)   What you want,

(ooh)   ba - by, I got.   (Ooh)   What you need, (ooh)   do you know I got it?

(Ooh)   All I'm ask - in' (ooh)   is for a lit - tle re - spect when you come home.   Hey, __
(Just a lit - tle bit,)

ba - by. When you get home, mis - ter.
(just a lit - tle bit,) (just a lit - tle bit,) (just a lit - tle bit.)

I ain't gon' do you wrong while _ you're gone. Ain't gon' do you wrong _

_ 'cause I ___ don't wan - na. All I'm ask - in' is for a lit - tle re -

spect when you come home, ba - by, when you get home, yeah.
(Just a lit - tle bit,) (just a lit - tle bit,) (just a lit - tle bit,)

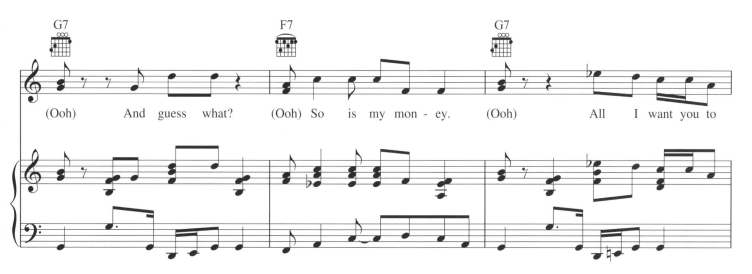

Ooh, __ your kiss - es, (ooh) sweet-er than hon - ey.

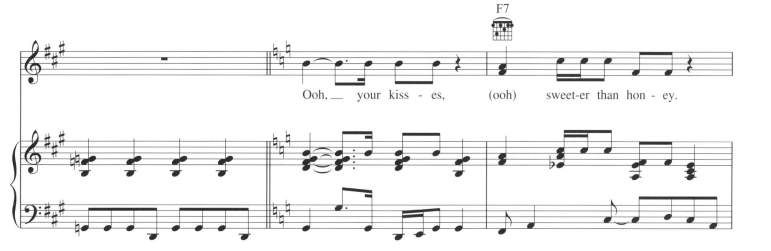

(Ooh) And guess what? (Ooh) So is my mon - ey. (Ooh) All I want you to

do for me is give it to me when you get home, yeah, ba - by, whip it to me
(Ooh) (Re - re - re - re - re - re - re - re - re - re -

when you get home.
spect, just a lit - tle bit,) (just a lit - tle bit.) R - E - S - P - E - C - T,

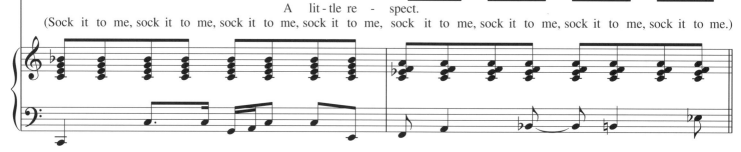

find out what it means to me. R - E - S - P - E - C - T, take care of T - C - B.

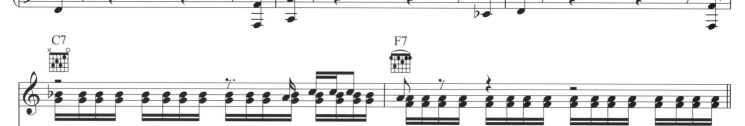

A lit - tle re - spect.
(Sock it to me, sock it to me, sock it to me, sock it to me, sock it to me, sock it to me, sock it to me, sock it to me.)

Repeat and Fade
(vocal ad lib.)

Optional Ending

Whoa, ___ yeah, a lit - tle re - spect.
(Just a lit - tle bit,) (just a lit - tle bit.)

SINGLE LADIES
(Put a Ring on It)

Words and Music by BEYONCÉ KNOWLES,
THADDIS HARRELL, CHRISTOPHER STEWART
and TERIUS NASH

do - in' my own lit - tle thing. You de - cid - ed to dip and now you wan-na trip 'cause an -
tight - er than my De - re - on __ jeans. Act - in' __ up, __ drink __ in my cup, __

oth - er broth - er no - ticed me. I'm up on him, he up on me. Don't
I can care __ less what you think. I need no per - mis - sion. Did I men - tion? Don't

pay him an - y at - ten - tion. __ Just cried my tears for three good years, you
pay him an - y at - ten - tion. __ 'Cause you had your turn and now you gon' learn what it

E5

can't be mad at me.
real-ly feels __ like to miss __ me. __ 'Cause if you like it then you should have put a ring on it. __ If you

RING OF FIRE

Words and Music by MERLE KILGORE
and JUNE CARTER

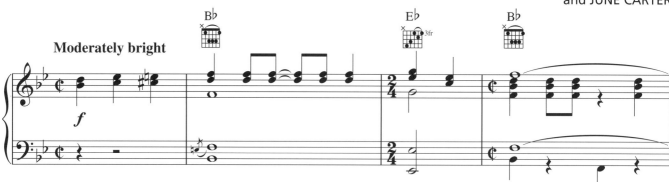

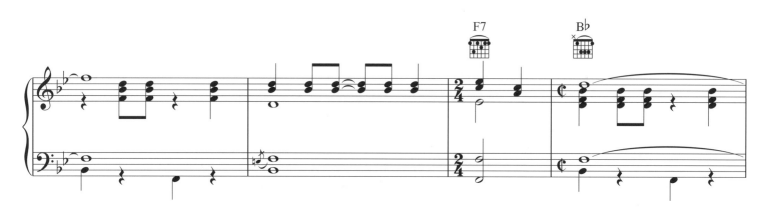

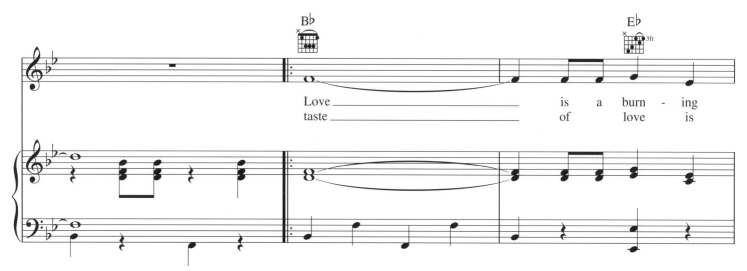

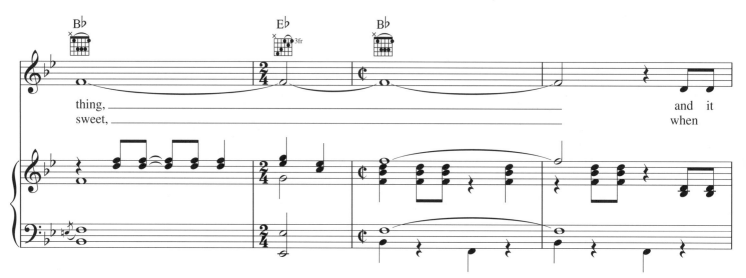

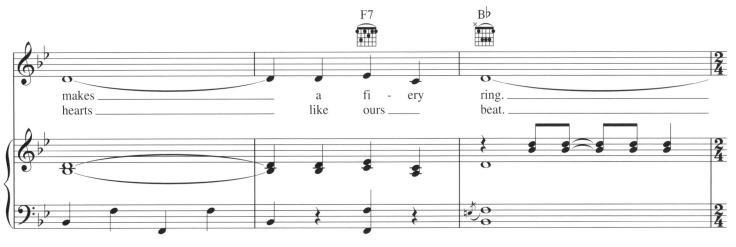

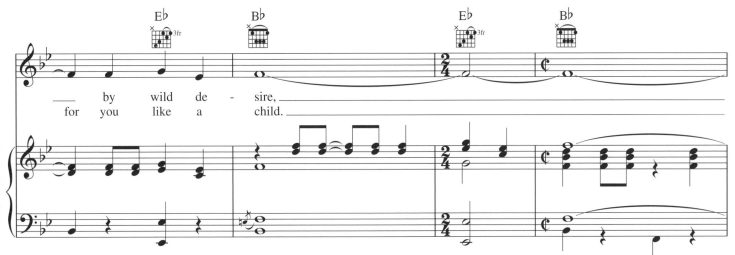

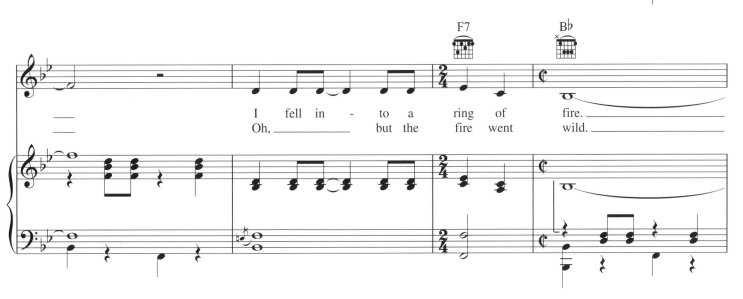

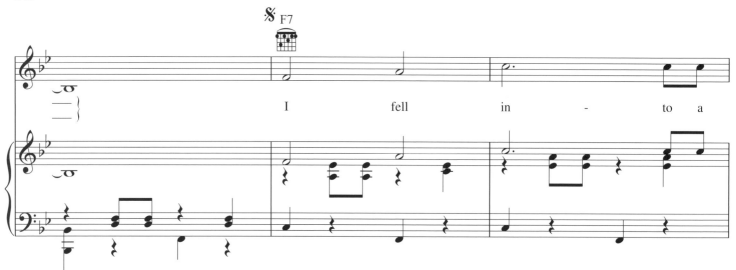

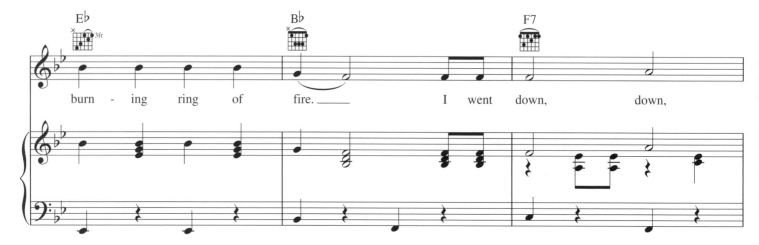

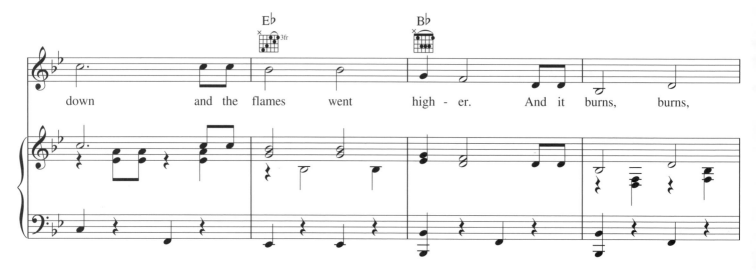

ROCK AND ROLL ALL NITE

Words and Music by PAUL STANLEY
and GENE SIMMONS

Moderately fast Rock

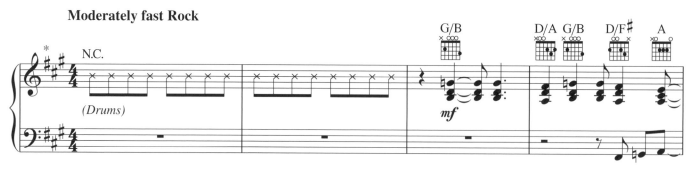

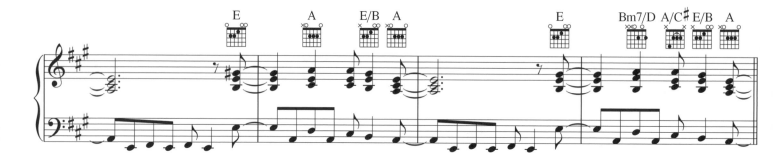

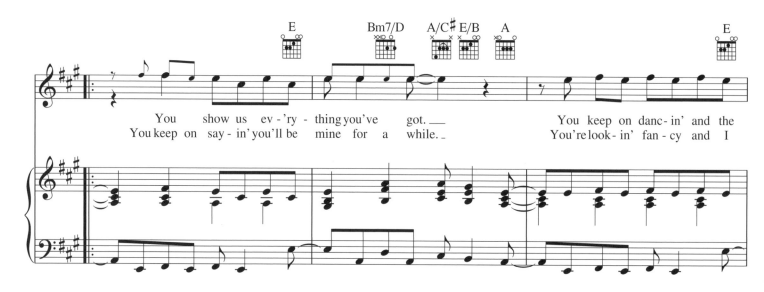

You show us ev-'ry-thing you've got. ___ You keep on danc-in' and the
You keep on say-in' you'll be mine for a while. ___ You're look-in' fan-cy and I

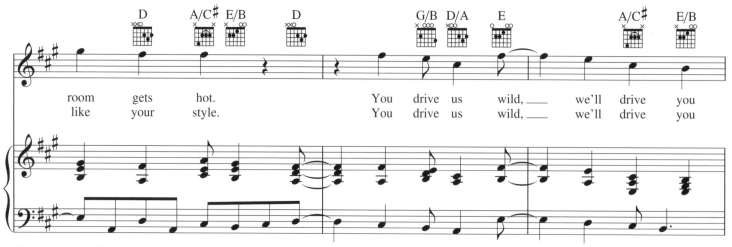

room gets hot. You drive us wild, ___ we'll drive you
like your style. You drive us wild, ___ we'll drive you

*Recorded a half step lower.

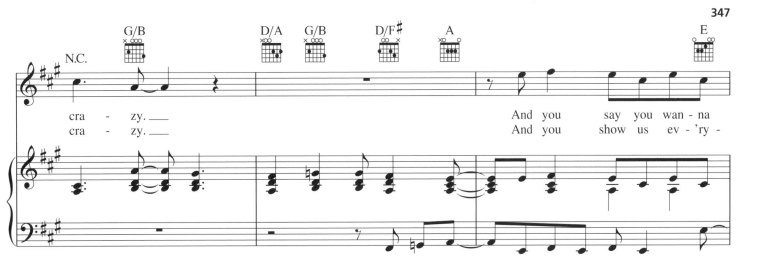

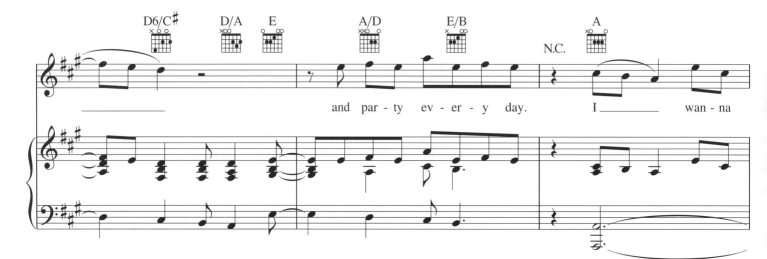

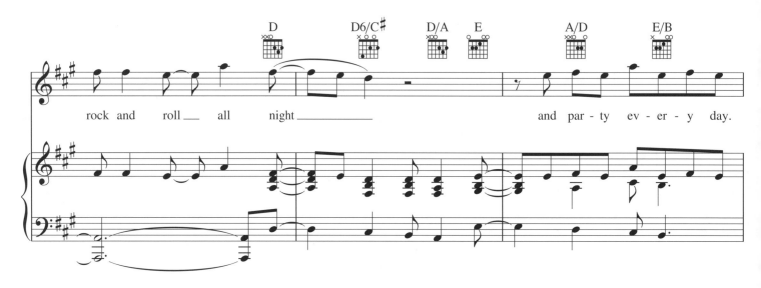

and par-ty ev-er-y day. I wan-na rock and roll ___ all night ___

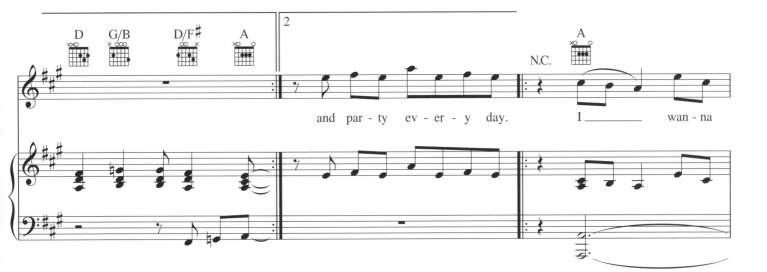

and par-ty ev-er-y day.

and par-ty ev-er-y day. I ___ wan-na

Repeat ad lib. and Fade

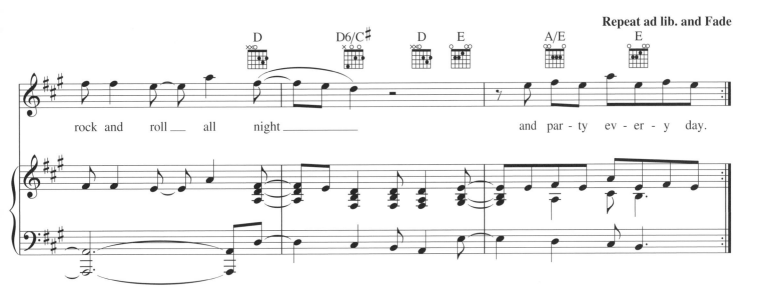

rock and roll ___ all night _____ and par-ty ev-er-y day.

THE SHOOP SHOOP SONG
(It's in His Kiss)

Words and Music by
RUDY CLARK

wan - na know _ if he loves you so, ___ it's in his kiss. _____ (That's where it is.) _
wan - na know _ if he loves you so, ___ it's in his kiss. _____

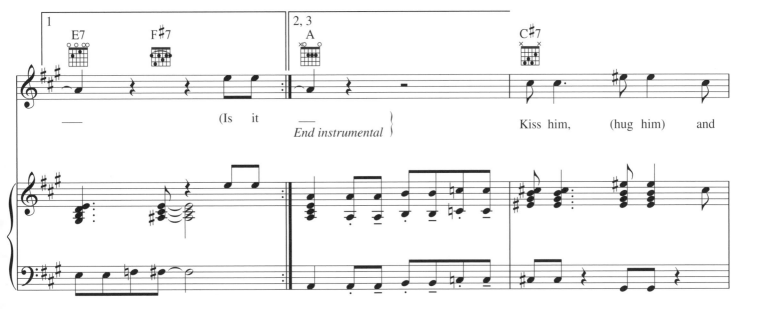

___ (Is it ___) *End instrumental*   Kiss him, (hug him) and

squeeze him tight, _ and find out what you wan - na know. _____

If it's love, __ if it real-ly __ is, __ it's there in his

kiss. _____ (How 'bout the way he acts?) _ Oh, __ no, ___ that's not the way, _ and

you're not lis-t'nin' to all ____ that I say. _____ If you wan-na know _ if he

loves you so, ____ it's in his kiss. ____

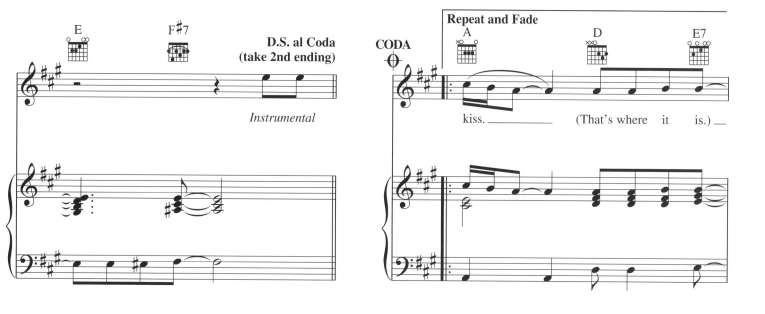

Instrumental

D.S. al Coda
(take 2nd ending)

CODA

Repeat and Fade

kiss. ____ (That's where it is.) ____

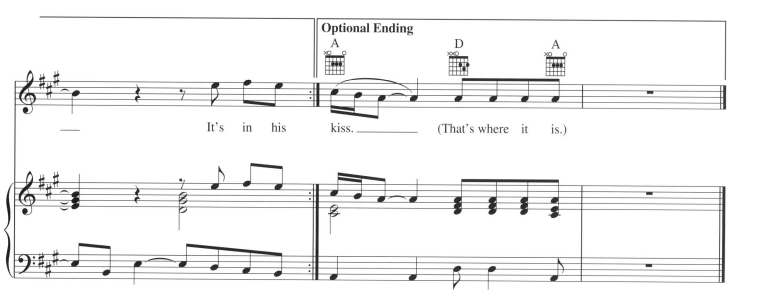

____ It's in his kiss. ____ (That's where it is.)

Optional Ending

STAND BY ME

Words and Music by JERRY LEIBER,
MIKE STOLLER and BEN E. KING

Moderately, with a beat

When the

night has come ___ and the land is
sky that we look up - on ___ should tum - ble and

dark and the moon ___ is the on - ly light we
fall and the moun - tains ___ should crumble in - to the

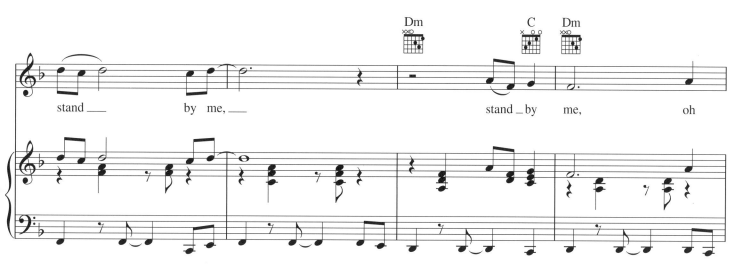

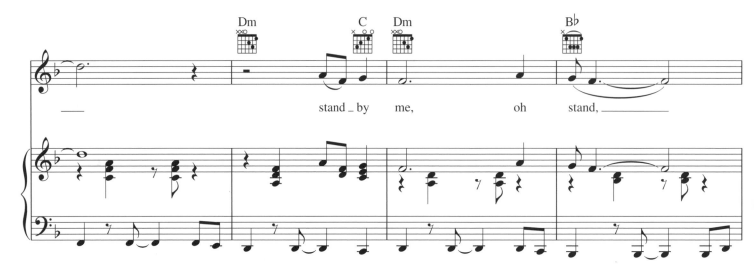

SURFIN' U.S.A.

Words and Music by
CHUCK BERRY

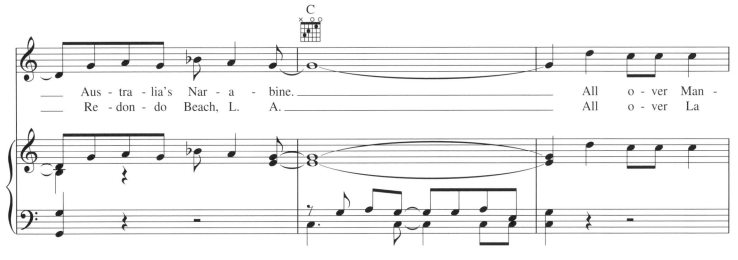

Aus - tra - lia's Nar - a - bine. _____ All o - ver Man -
Re - don - do Beach, L. A. _____ All o - ver La

hat - tan _____ and down Do - he - ny way. _____
Jol - la, _____ at Wai - a - me - a Bay. _____

Ev - 'ry - bod - y's gone surf - in', _____ surf - in' U. S. A. _____

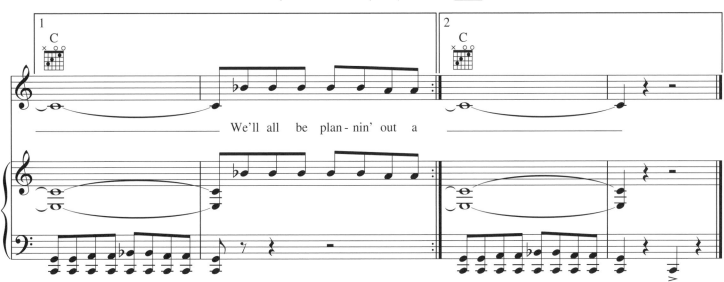

We'll all be plan - nin' out a

SUMMER NIGHTS
from GREASE

Lyric and Music by WARREN CASEY
and JIM JACOBS

SWAY
(Quien será)

English Words by NORMAN GIMBEL
Spanish Words and Music by PABLO BELTRAN RUIZ

When ma-rim-ba rhy-thms start to play, dance with me,
Quien se-rá la que me quie-ra a mi Quien se-rá

make me sway.___ Like the la-zy o-cean hugs the shore,
Quien se-rá___ Quien se-rá la que me dé su a-mor

hold me close, sway me more._____ Like a flow-er bend-ing
Quien se-rá Quien se-rá _____ Yo no sé si la po-

SWEET CHILD O' MINE

Words and Music by W. AXL ROSE,
SLASH, IZZY STRADLIN',
DUFF McKAGAN and STEVEN ADLER

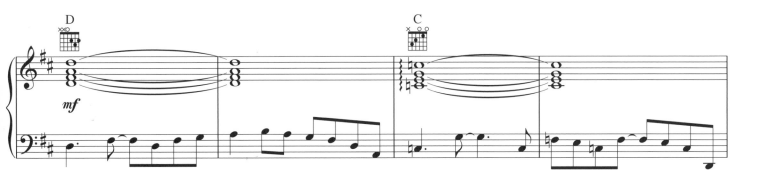

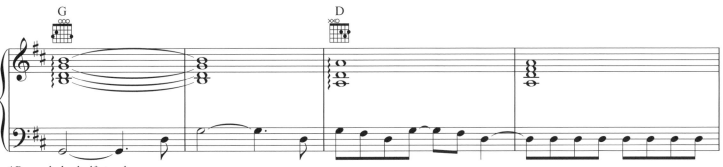

Recorded a half step lower.

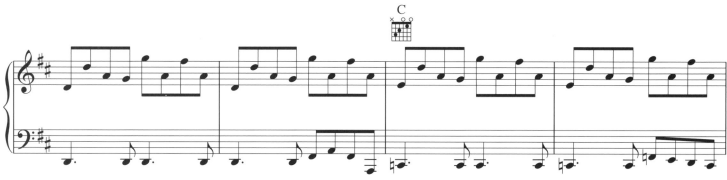

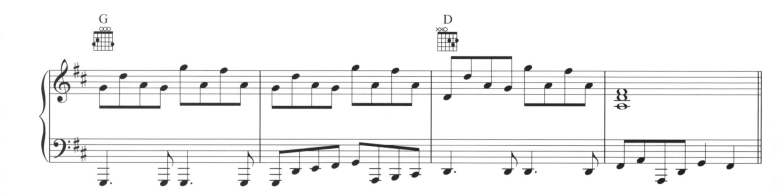

She's got a smile __ that it seems to me __ re - minds __ me of child - hood
She's got eyes __ of the blu - est skies, __ as if _____ they __

mem - o - ries, __ where ev - 'ry - thing __ was as fresh __ as the bright __ blue sky. __
thought of rain. __ I hate __ to look __ in - to _____ those eyes and see an ounce __

Whoa, oh, __ oh, oh, __

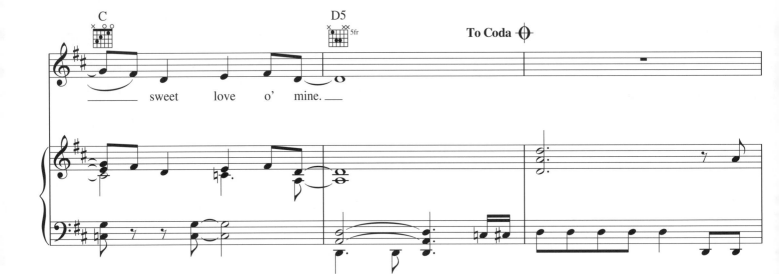

__ sweet love o' mine. __

To Coda

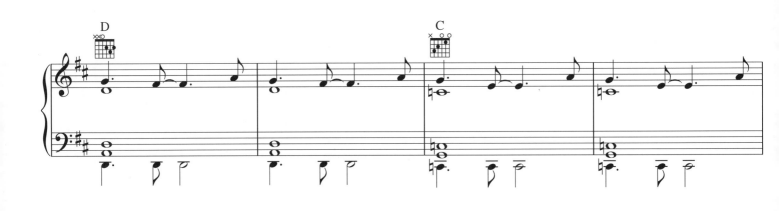

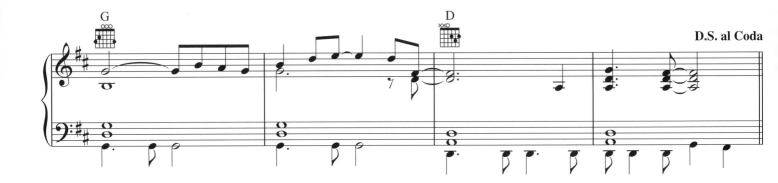

D.S. al Coda

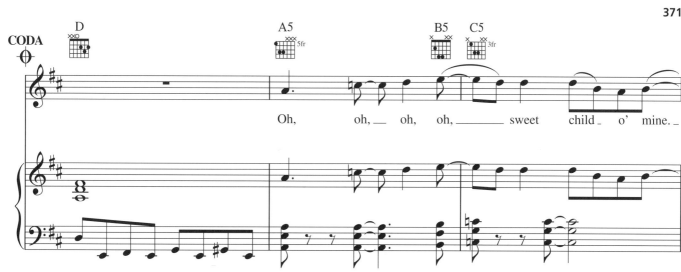

Oh, oh, _ oh, oh, _____ sweet child _ o' mine. _

Woo, _____ yeah, _ yeah! Ooh, _____

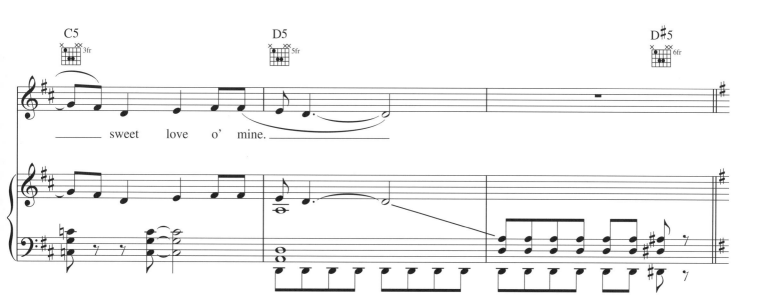

_____ sweet love o' mine. _____

(Guitar solo ad lib.)

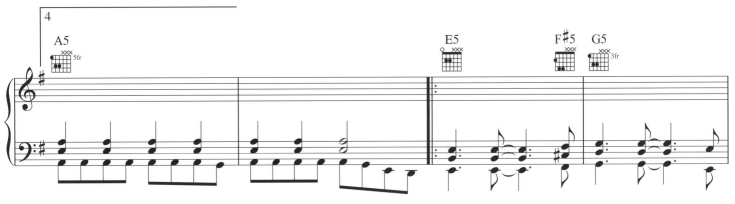

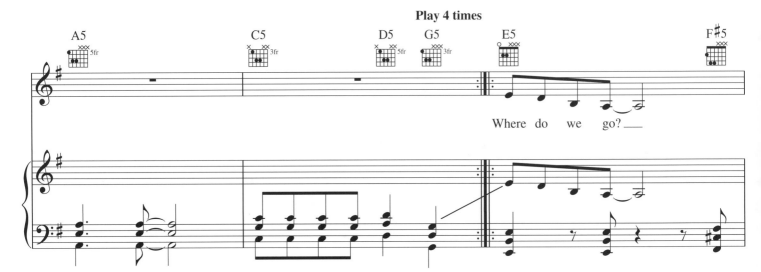

SWEET CAROLINE

Words and Music by
NEIL DIAMOND

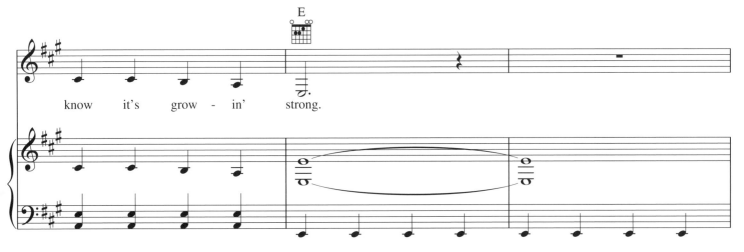

know it's grow - in' strong.

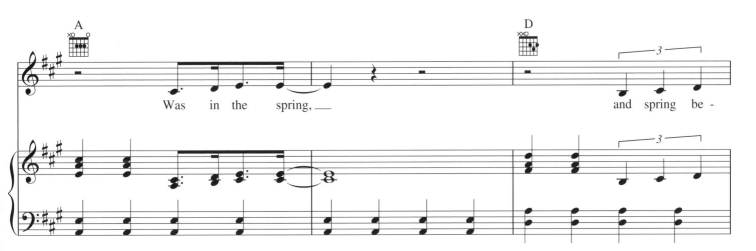

Was in the spring, ___ and spring be -

came the sum - mer. Who'd have be - lieved ___ you'd come a -

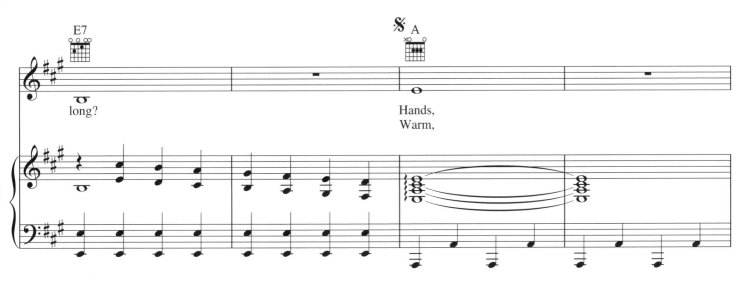

long?
Hands,
Warm,

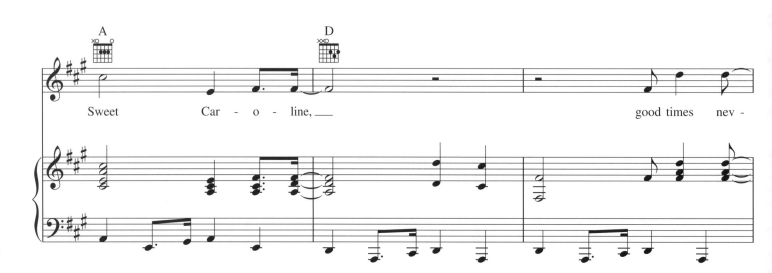

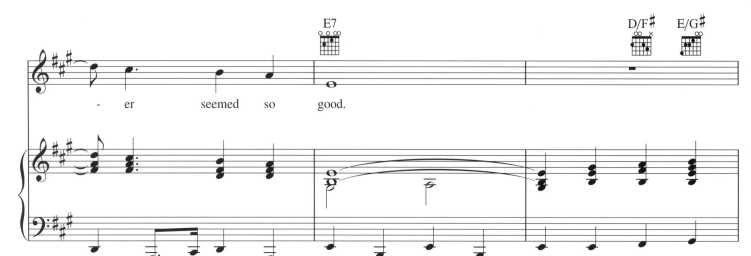

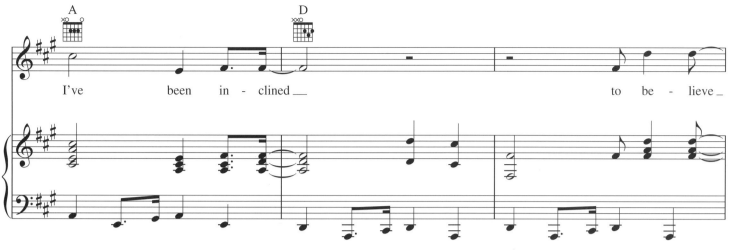

I've been in-clined ___ to be-lieve ___

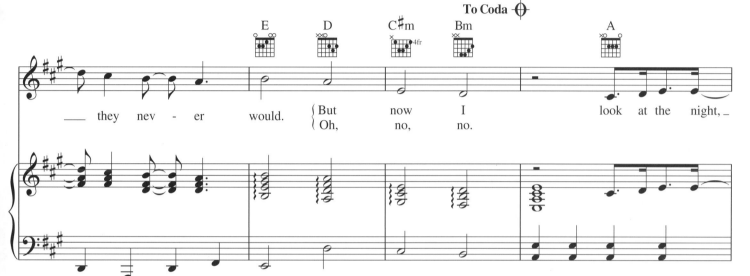

To Coda ⊕

___ they nev-er would. But now I look at the night, ___
Oh, now no, no.

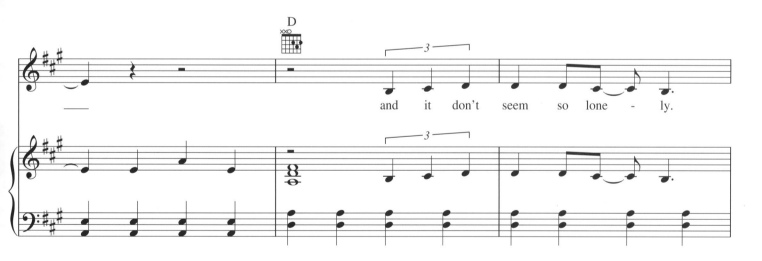

and it don't seem so lone-ly.

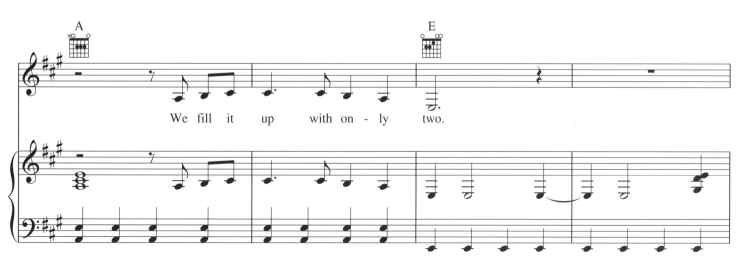

We fill it up with on-ly two.

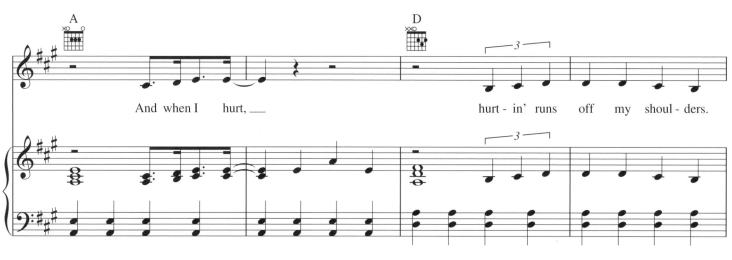

And when I hurt, ___ hurt - in' runs off my shoul - ders.

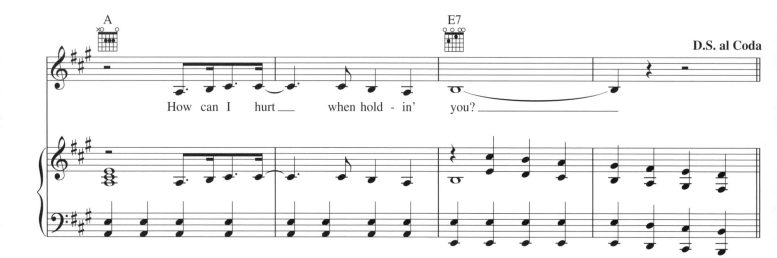

How can I hurt ___ when hold - in' you? ___

CODA

THREE TIMES A LADY

Words and Music by
LIONEL RICHIE

Slowly

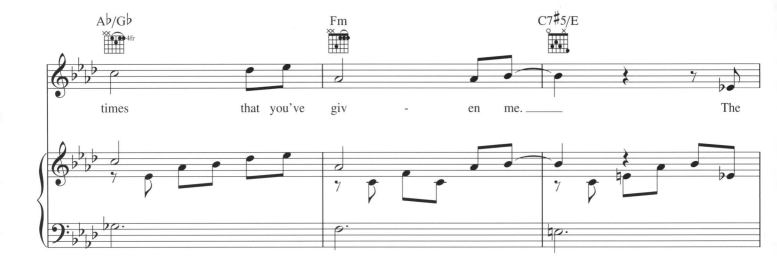

Thanks for the times that you've giv - en me. The mem - 'ries are all in my mind. The

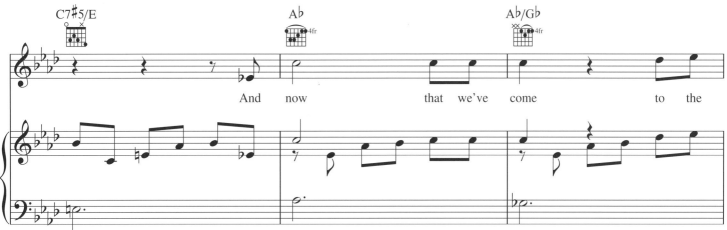

And now that we've come to the

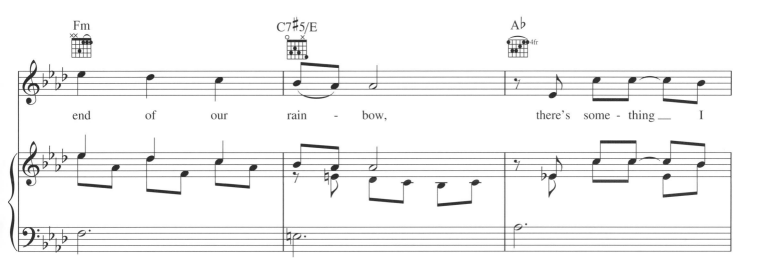

end of our rain - bow, there's some - thing ___ I

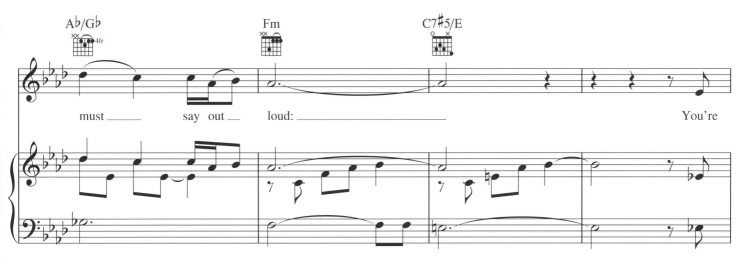

must ___ say out ___ loud: ___ You're

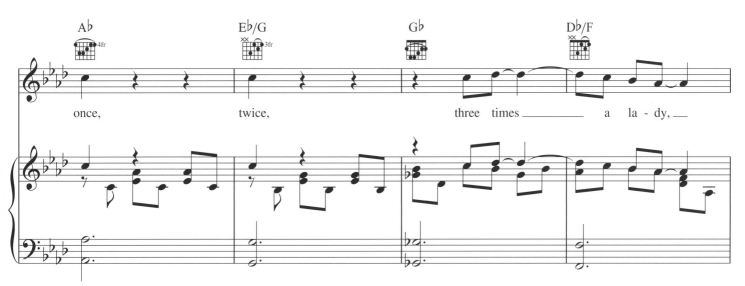

once, twice, three times ___ a la - dy, ___

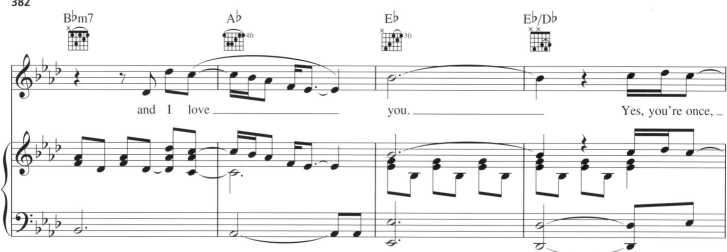

and I love _____ you. _____ Yes, you're once, __

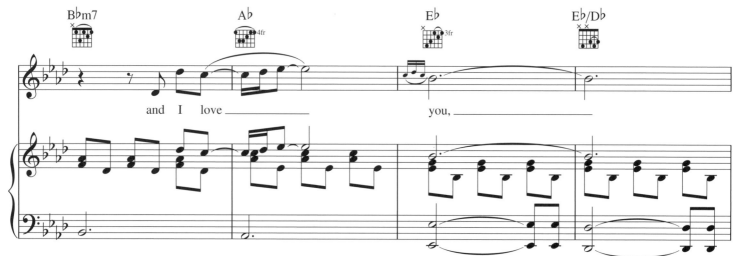

__ twice, __ three times a la - dy,

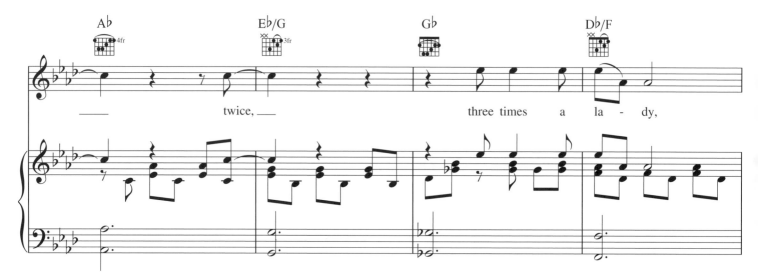

and I love _____ you, _____

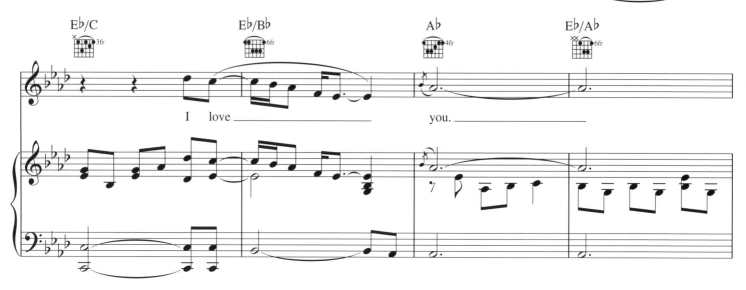

I love _____ you. _____

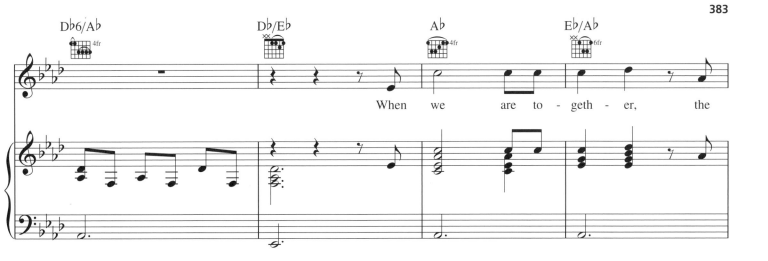

When we are to-geth-er, the

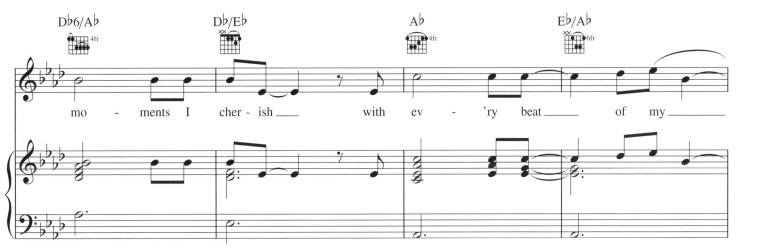

mo-ments I cher-ish ___ with ev-'ry beat ___ of my ___

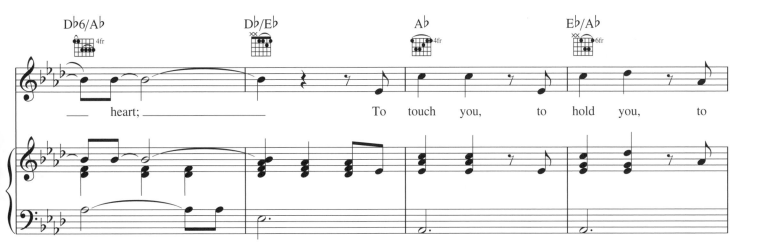

___ heart; ___ To touch you, to hold you, to

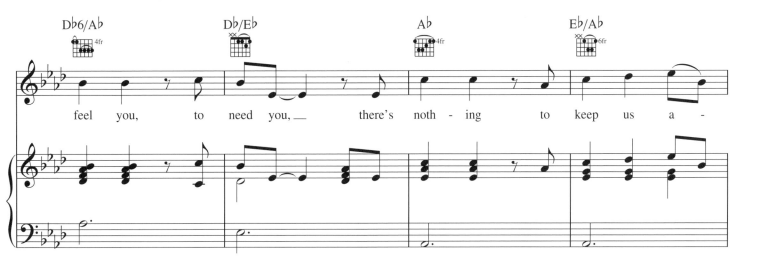

feel you, to need you, ___ there's noth-ing to keep us a-

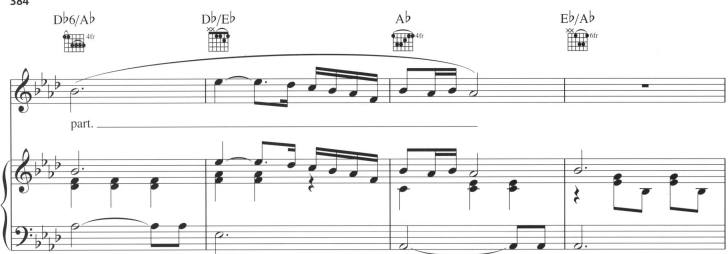

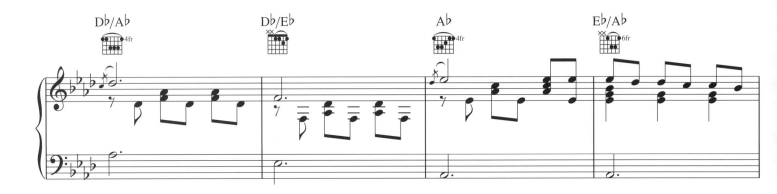

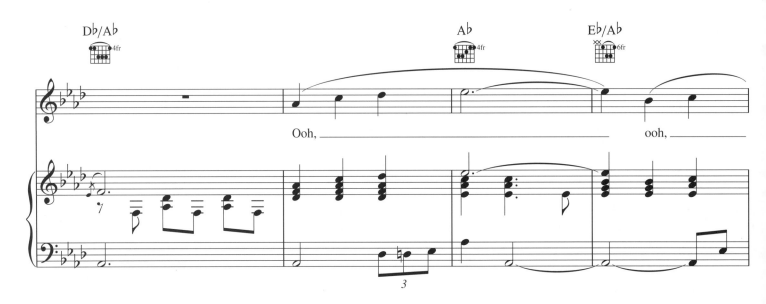

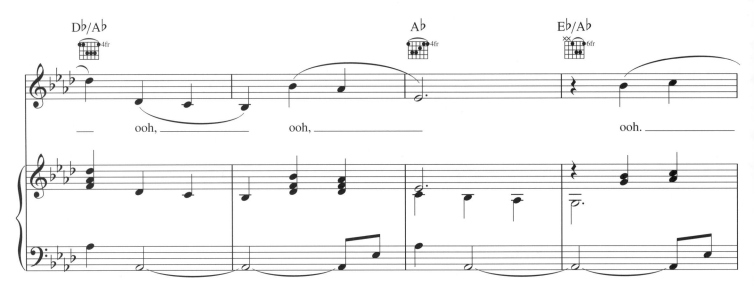

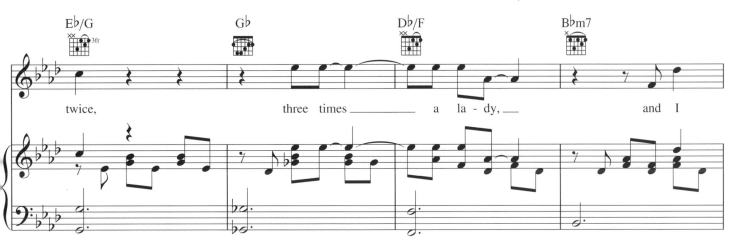

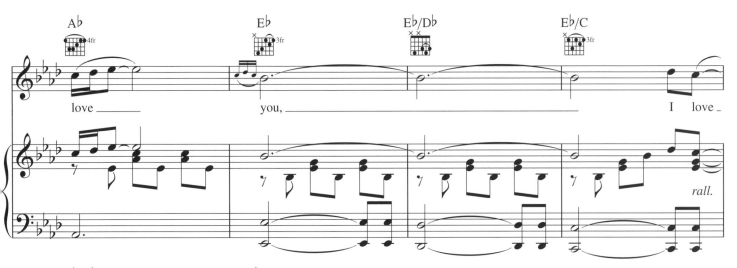

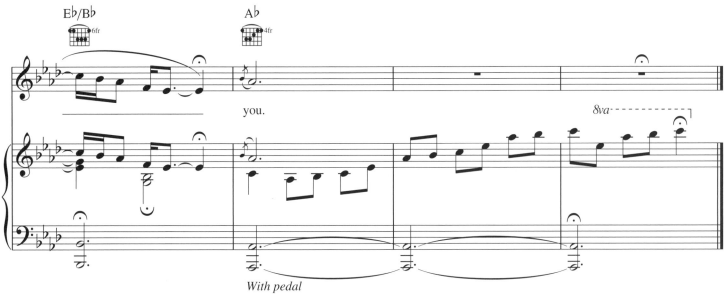

(I've Had)
THE TIME OF MY LIFE
from DIRTY DANCING

Words and Music by FRANKE PREVITE,
JOHN DeNICOLA and DONALD MARKOWITZ

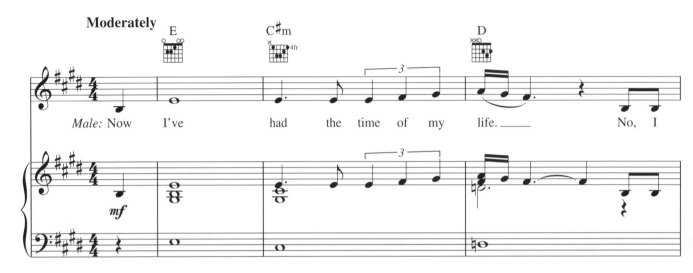

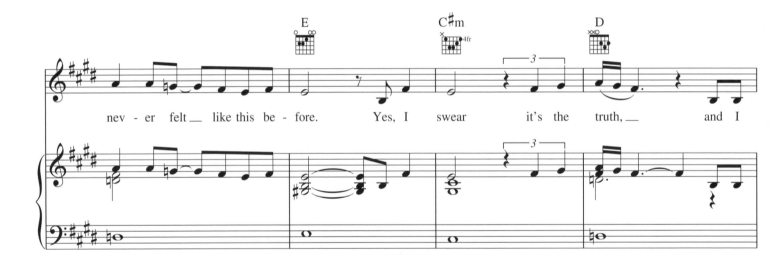

sy. _____

Both: Now with

pas - sion in our eyes _____ there's no way we could _ dis - guise _ it se - cret -

ly. _____

So we

take each oth -er's hand _____ 'cause we seem to un - der - stand _ the ur - gen -

fore. Yes, I swear it's the truth,_____ and I owe it all to you._____

Male: Hey, ba - by.

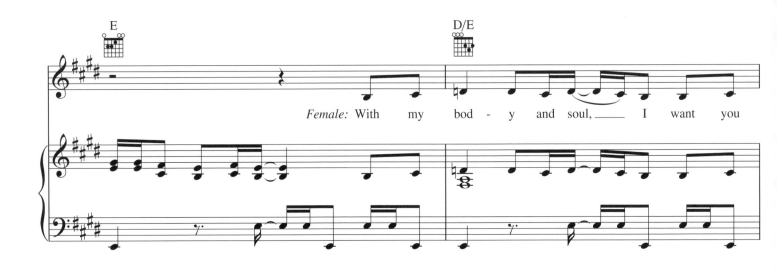

Female: With my bod - y and soul,____ I want you

more than you'll ev - er know._ *Male:* So we'll

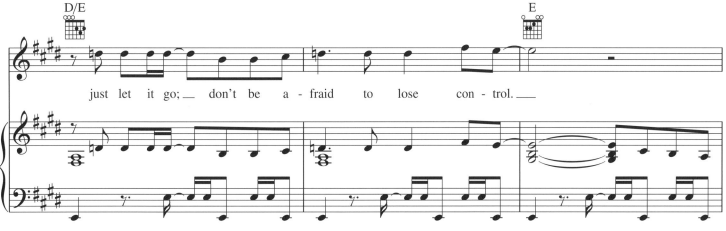

just let it go; __ don't be a-fraid to lose con - trol. __

Female: Yes, I know what's on __ your mind when you say stay with me to-

night. _____ *Male:* Stay __ with me. Just re-mem - ber, you're the

one thing __ *Female:* I _____ can't get e - nough of. *Male:* So I'll tell you

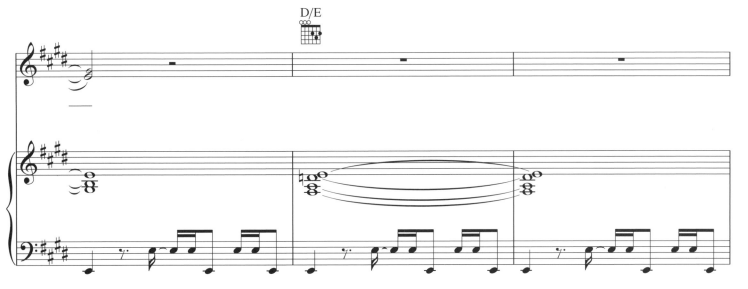

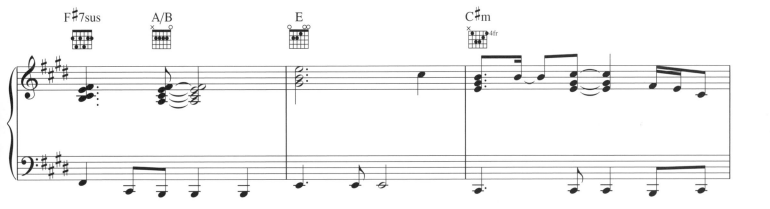

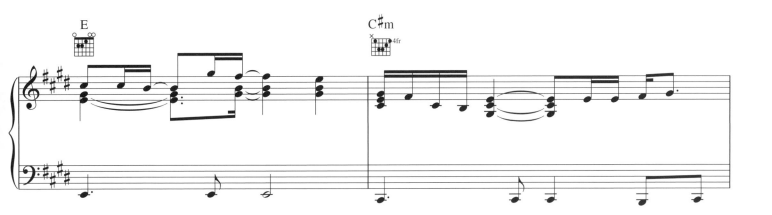

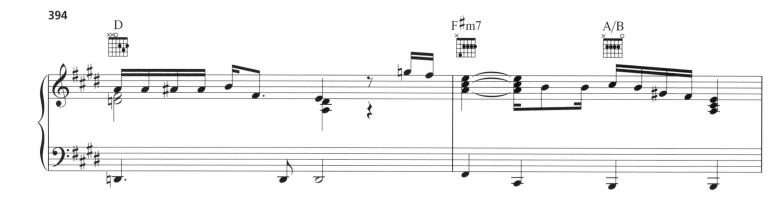

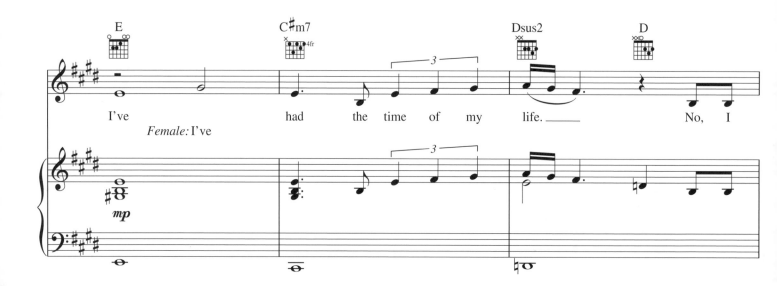

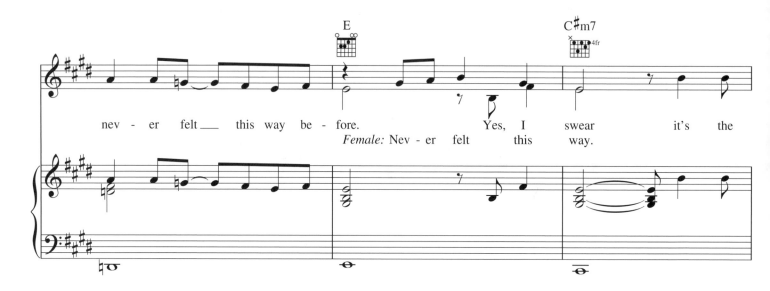

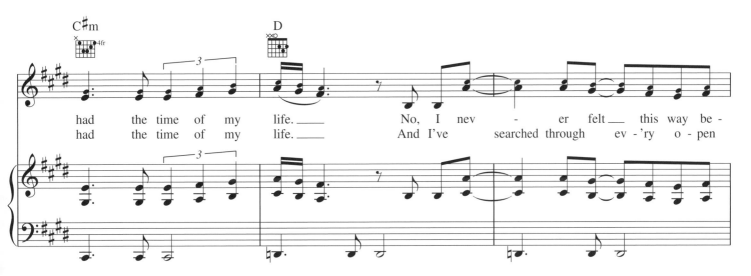

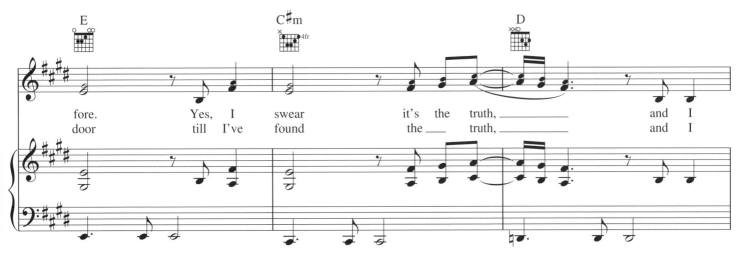

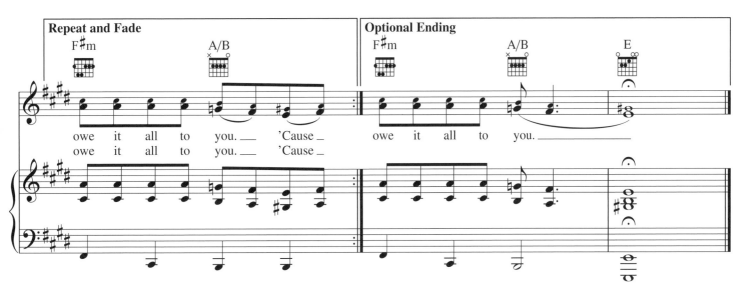

TRUE COLORS

Words and Music by BILLY STEINBERG
and TOM KELLY

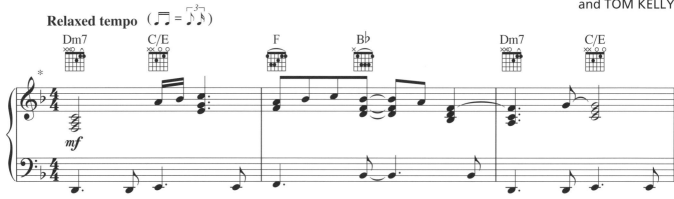

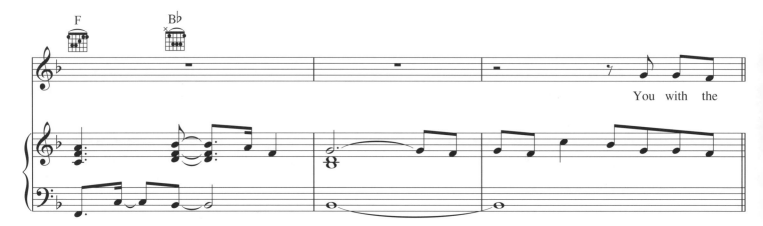

You with the

sad eyes, don't be dis-cour-aged. Oh, I re-al-ize it's
smile then, don't be un-hap-py. Can't re-mem-ber when I

hard to take cour-age. In a world full of peo-ple
last saw you laugh-ing. If this world makes you cra-zy and you're

Recorded a half step higher.

you can lose sight of it and the dark-ness in-side you makes you
tak-in' all you can bear, just call me up be-cause you

feel so small. But I
know I'll be there. And I'll see your true col-ors shin-

-in' through. I see your true col-ors and that's why I love___ you. So,

don't be a-fraid___ to let them show.___ Your true col-ors,

To Coda

true col - ors are beau -ti -ful, ooh, _ like a rain - bow.

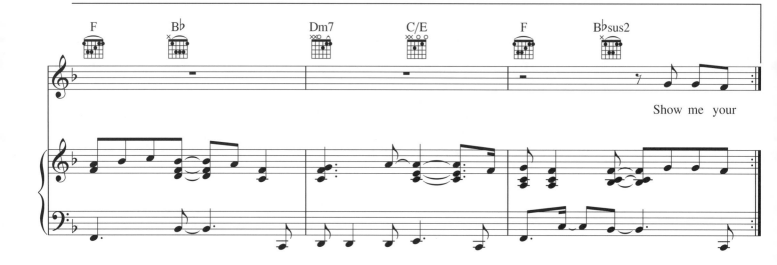

Show me your

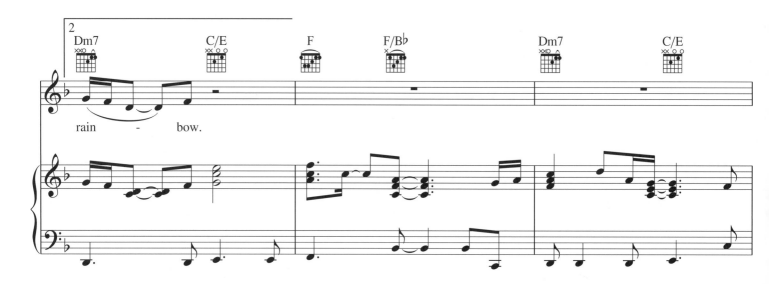

rain - bow.

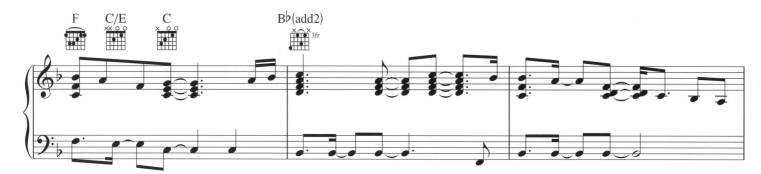

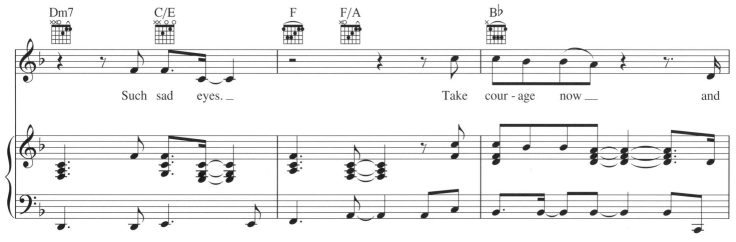

Such sad eyes. _ Take cour-age now _ and

re-al-ize, when this world makes you cra-zy and you're

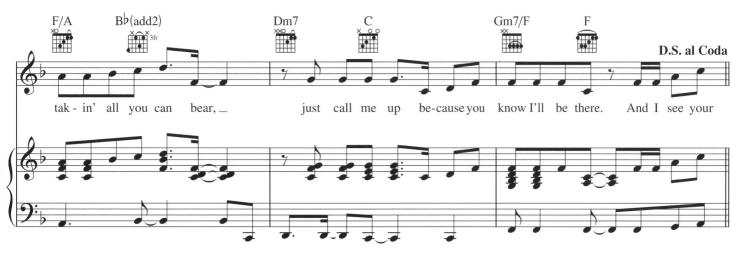

tak-in' all you can bear, _ just call me up be-cause you know I'll be there. And I see your

D.S. al Coda

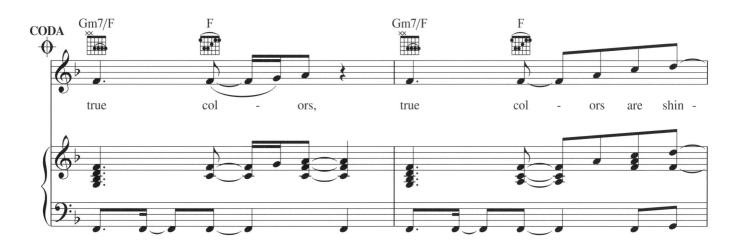

CODA

true col - ors, true col - ors are shin -

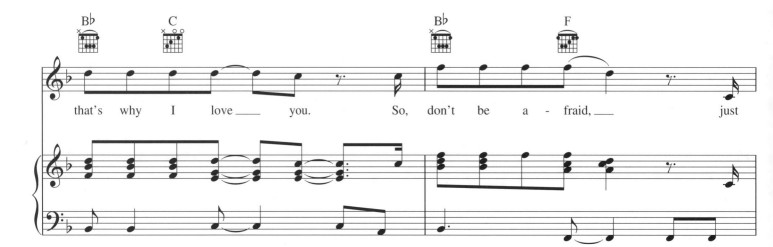

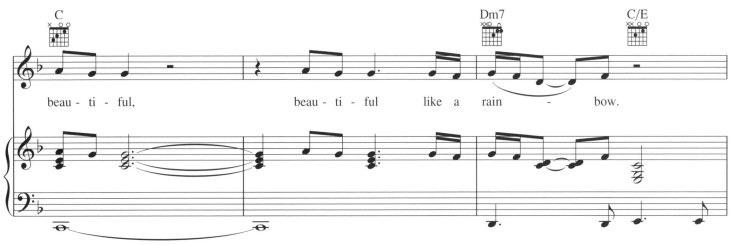

beau - ti - ful, beau - ti - ful like a rain - bow.

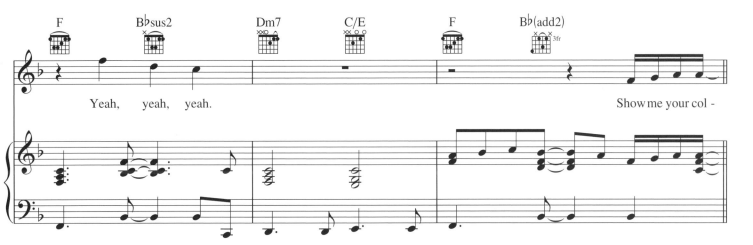

Yeah, yeah, yeah. Show me your col -

- ors. Show me your rain - bow.

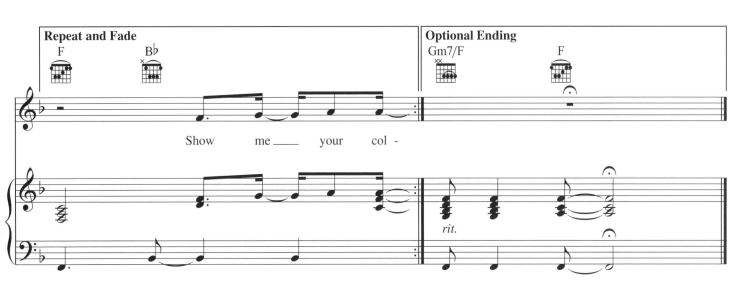

Repeat and Fade

Show me___ your col -

Optional Ending

rit.

UNCHAINED MELODY

from the Motion Picture UNCHAINED

Lyric by HY ZARET
Music by ALEX NORTH

Moderately slow

Whoa, _____ my _____ love, __ my

dar - lin', _____ I've hun - gered for _____ your __

_____ touch a long, lone - ly

VIVA LA VIDA

Words and Music by GUY BERRYMAN, JON BUCKLAND,
WILL CHAMPION and CHRIS MARTIN

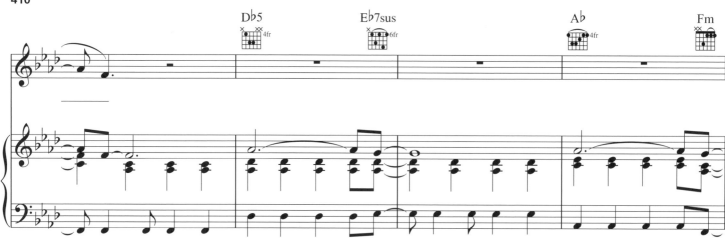

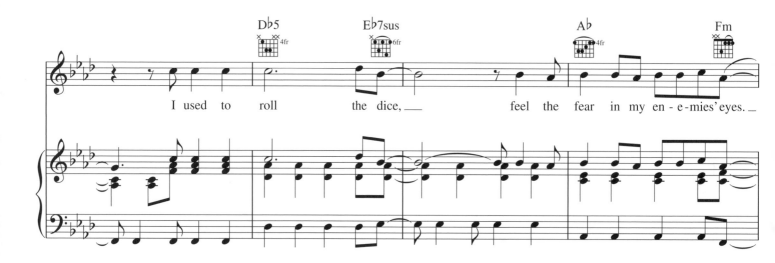

I used to roll the dice, ___ feel the fear in my en - e -mies' eyes. ___

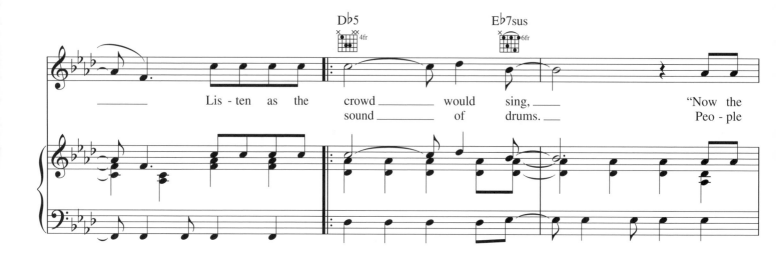

Lis - ten as the crowd _____ would sing, ___ "Now the
sound _____ of drums. ___ Peo - ple

Ro - man Cath - o - lic choirs ___ are sing - ing. Be my mir - ror, my sword ___

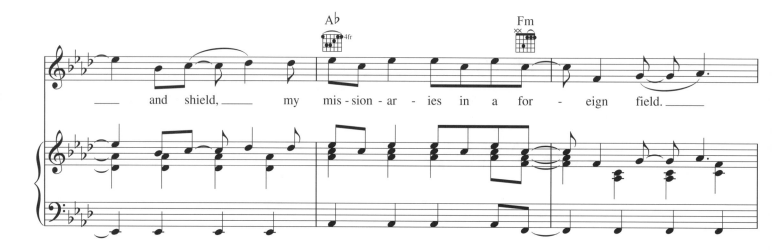

___ and shield, ___ my mis - sion - ar - ies in a for - eign field. ___

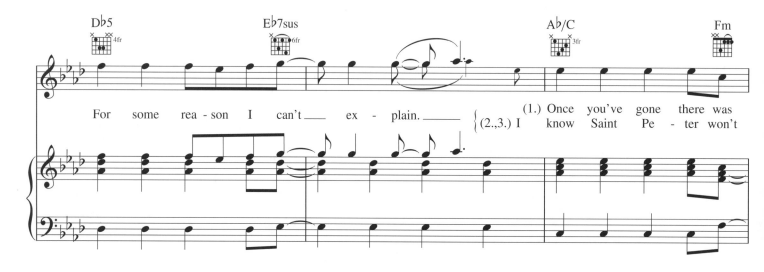

For some rea - son I can't ___ ex - plain. ___ {(2.,3.) I know Saint Pe - ter won't
{(1.) Once you've gone there was

To Coda ⊕

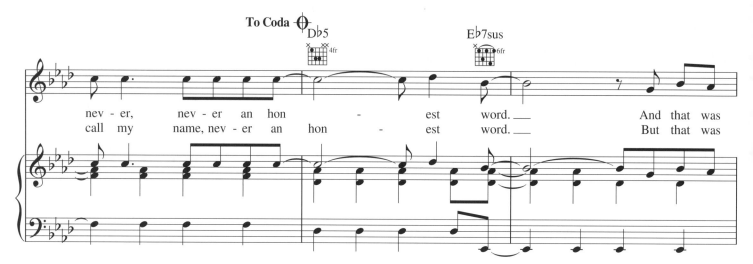

nev - er, nev - er an hon - est word. ___ And that was
call my name, nev - er an hon - est word. ___ But that was

when I   ruled   the   world. _____
when I   ruled   the   world. _

It was a wick-ed and wild _____ wind _

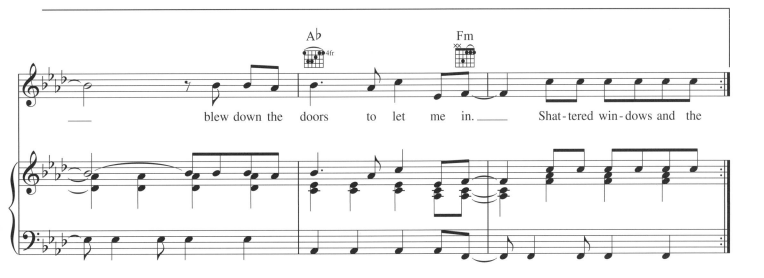

_____   blew down the   doors   to   let   me   in. _____   Shat-tered win-dows and the

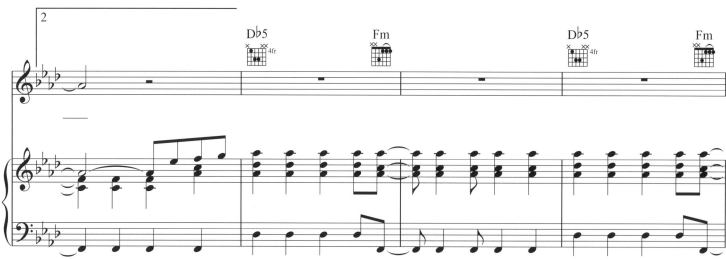

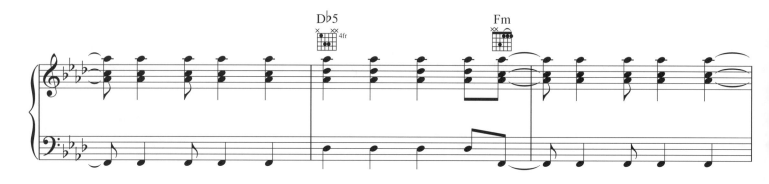

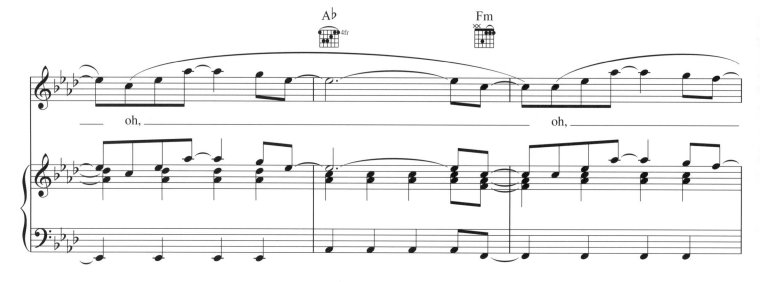

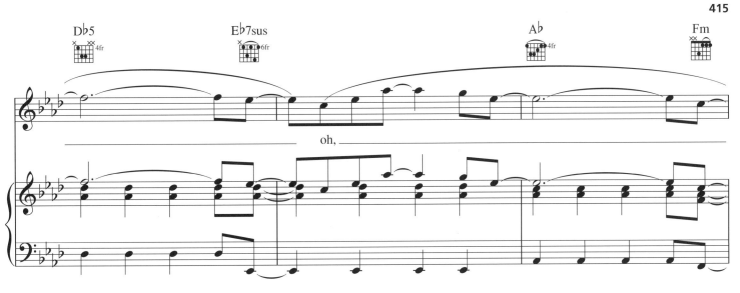

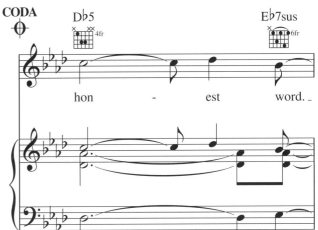

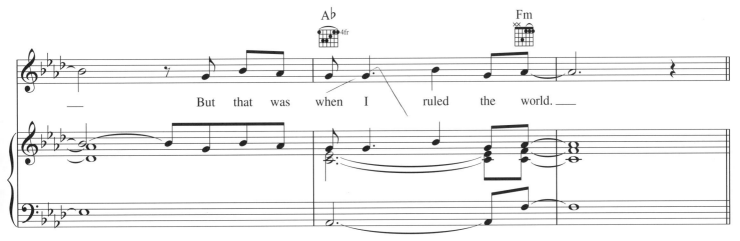

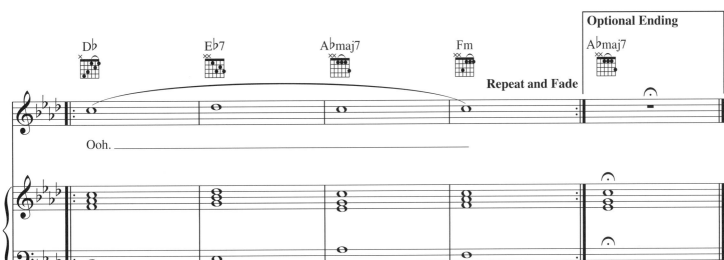

WALKING ON SUNSHINE

Words and Music by
KIMBERLEY REW

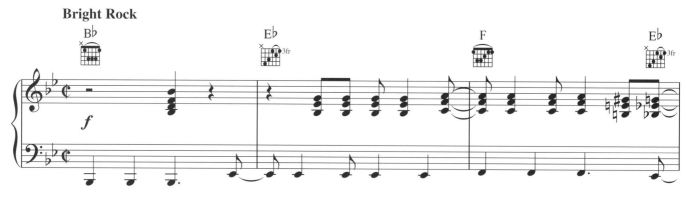

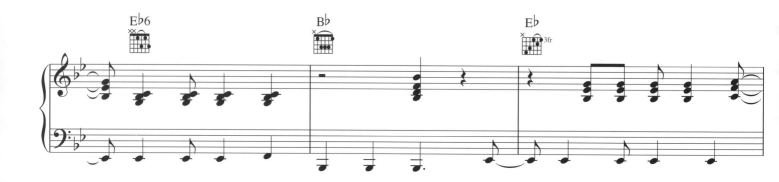

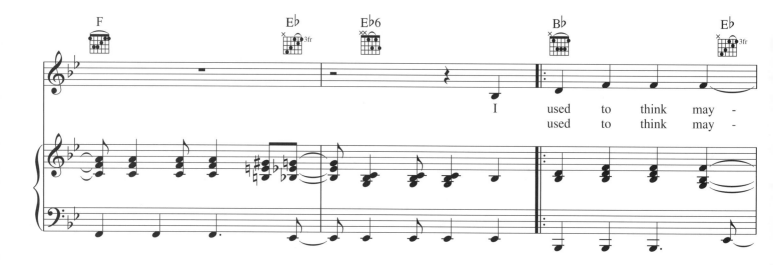

I used to think may-
used to think may-

-be you loved _____ me, now ba-by, I'm _____ sure. _____
-be you loved _____ me, now I know that it's true. _____

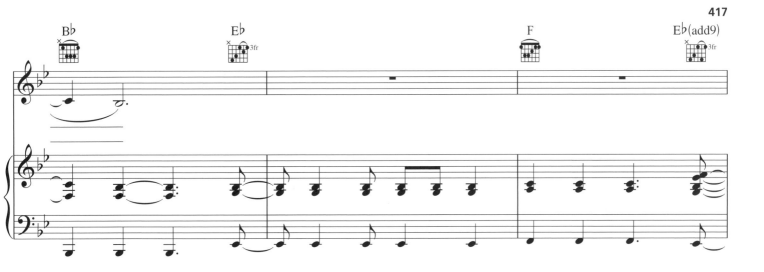

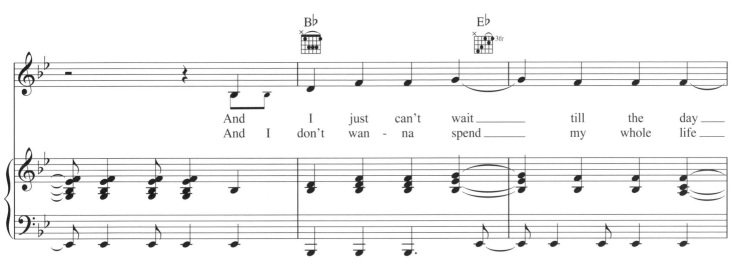

And I just can't wait _____ till the day ___
And I don't wan - na spend _____ my whole life ___

_____ when you knock _____ on my door. _____
_____ just a - wait - ing for you. _____

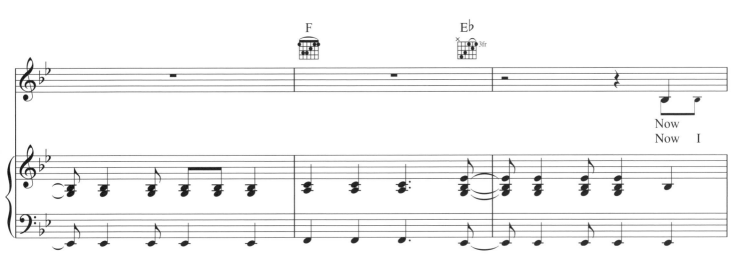

Now
Now I

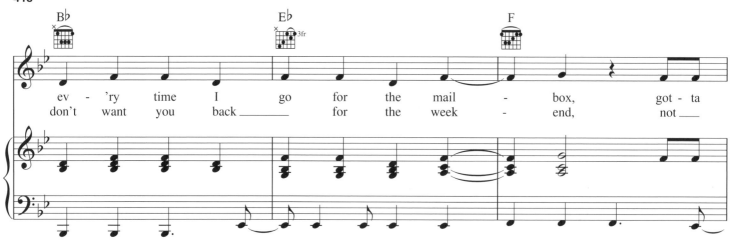

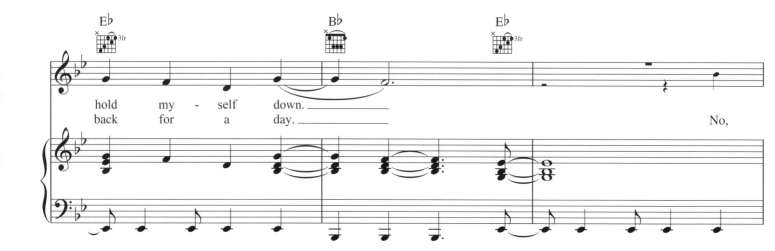

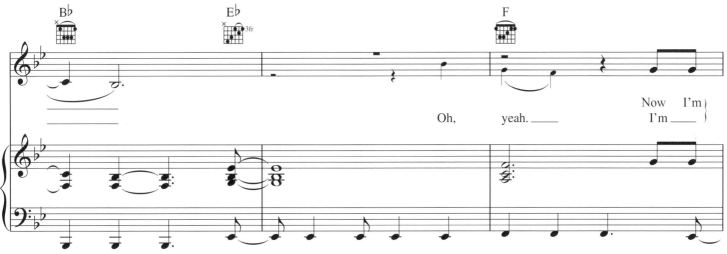

Oh, yeah.____ Now I'm
I'm____

walk - ing on ____ sun - shine. Whoa. ____

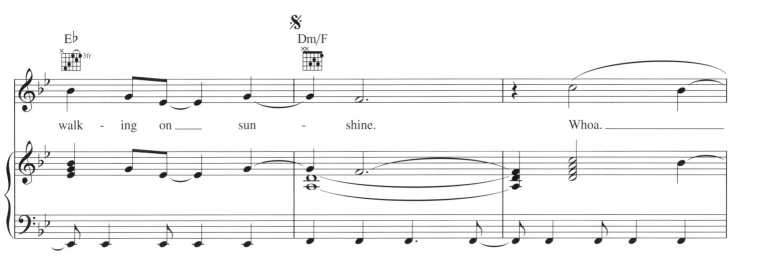

____ I'm walk - ing on ____ sun - shine.

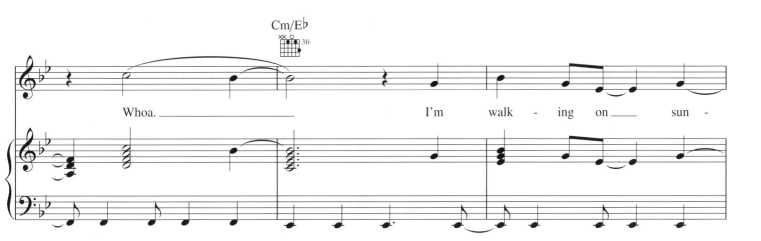

Whoa. ____ I'm walk - ing on ____ sun -

-shine. Whoa, _____ and

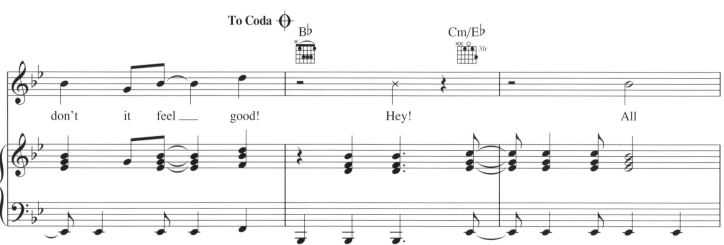

To Coda ⊕

don't it feel ___ good! Hey! All

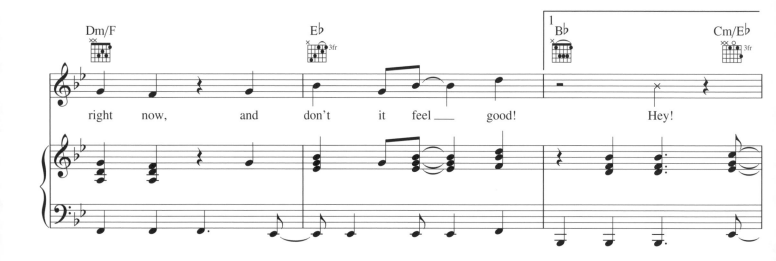

right now, and don't it feel ___ good! Hey!

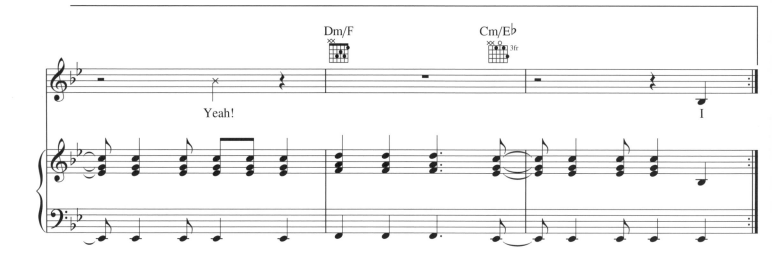

Yeah! I

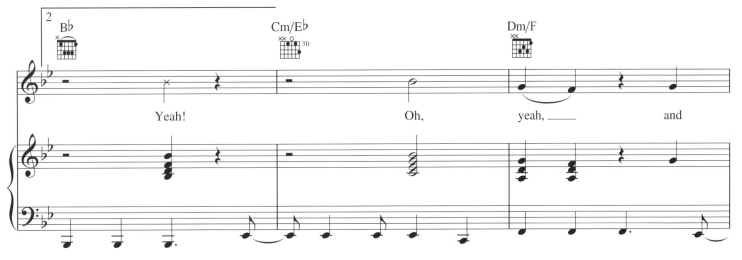

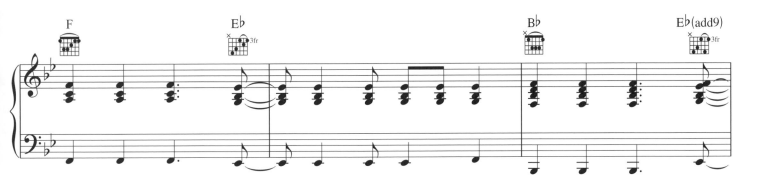

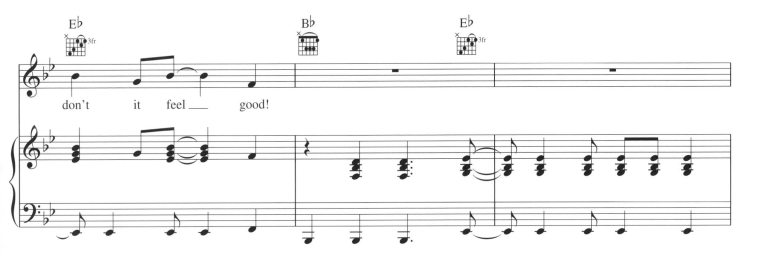

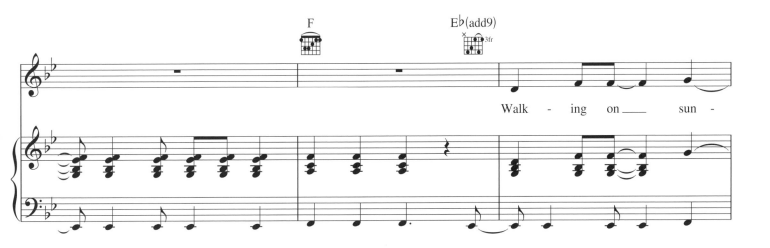

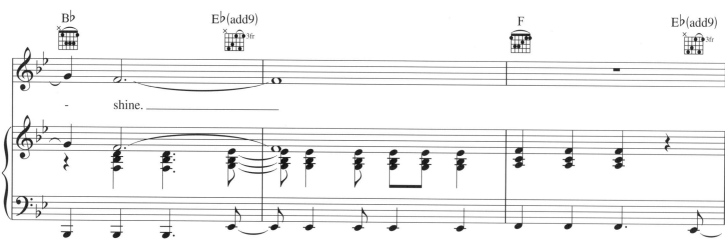

-shine. _____

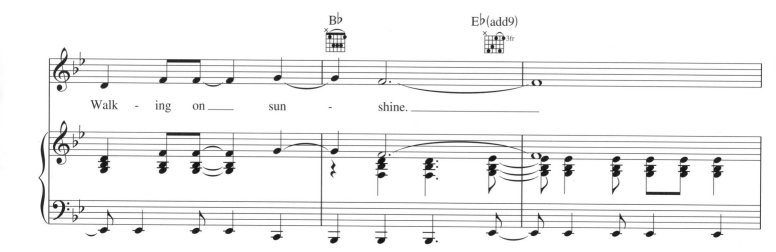

Walk - ing on ____ sun - shine. _____

I feel a - live, ____ I feel a love, _

____ I feel a love ____ that's real - ly real. I feel a - live, _

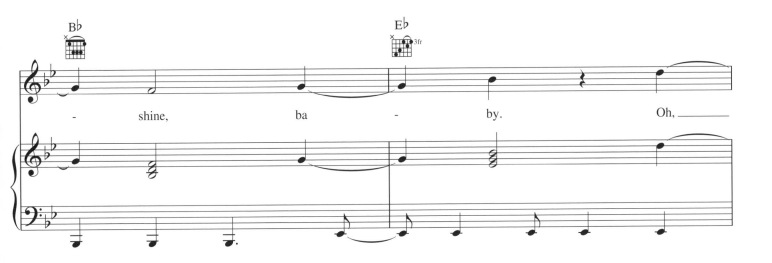

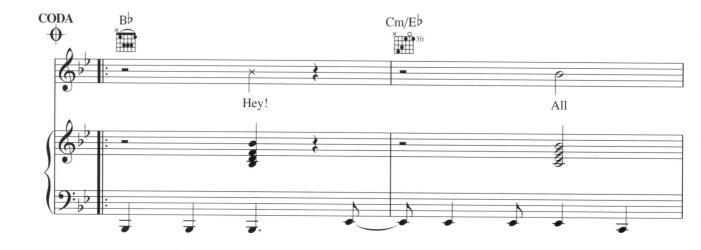

THE WAY WE WERE

Words by ALAN and MARILYN BERGMAN
Music by MARVIN HAMLISCH

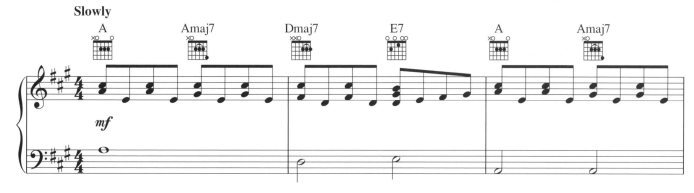

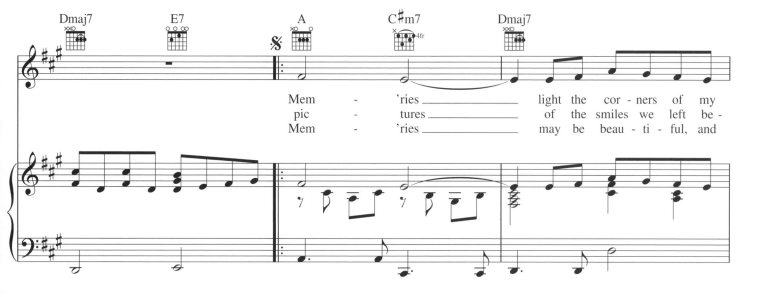

Mem - 'ries _____ light the cor - ners of my
pic - tures _____ of the smiles we left be -
Mem - 'ries _____ may be beau - ti - ful, and

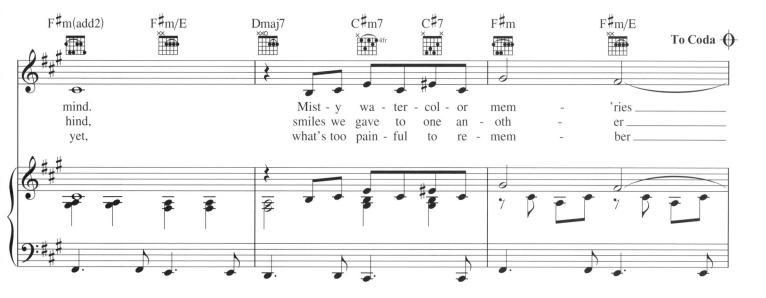

mind.
hind,   smiles we gave to one an - oth - er _____
yet,   what's too pain - ful to re - mem - ber _____

Mist - y wa - ter - col - or mem - 'ries _____

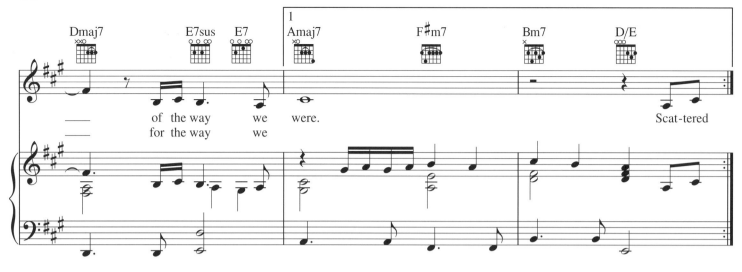

of the way we were.
for the way we

Scat-tered

were. Can it be that it was all so sim-ple then,

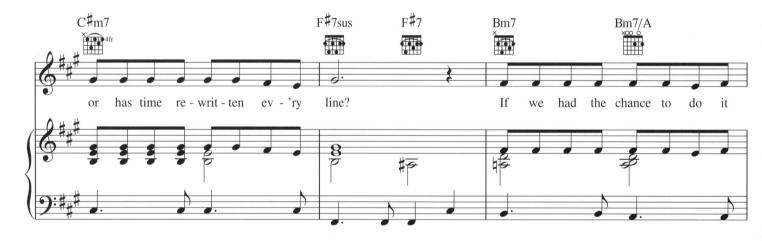

or has time re-writ-ten ev-'ry line? If we had the chance to do it

all a-gain, tell me would we? Could we?

D.S. al Coda

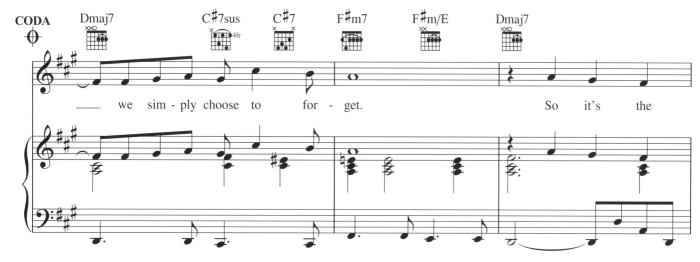

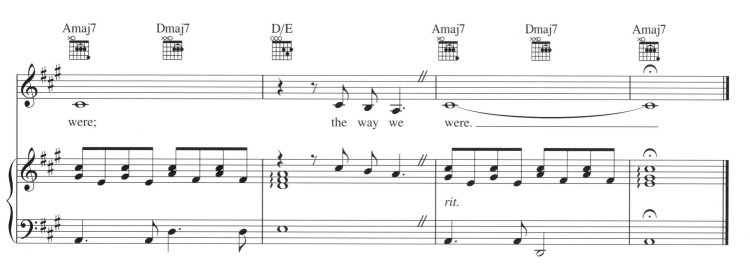

WE ARE THE WORLD

Words and Music by LIONEL RICHIE
and MICHAEL JACKSON

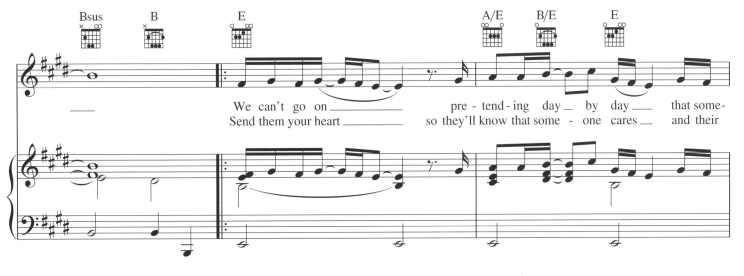

We can't go on _____ pre-tend-ing day __ by day ___ that some-
Send them your heart _____ so they'll know that some - one cares ___ and their

one, some-where will soon make a change. We are all a part __ of ___ God's
lives will be strong-er and free. As God has shown __ us ____ by

great big fam-i - ly ____ and the truth, you know, love is all we need. __
turn-ing stone _ to bread, _ so we all must lend a help-ing hand. __

We are the world, ___ we are the chil - dren, we are the ones _

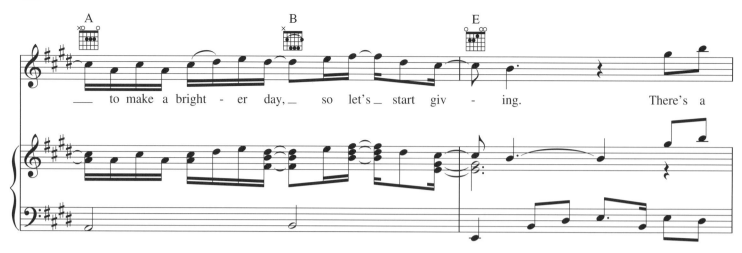

to make a bright - er day,__ so let's__ start giv - ing. There's a

choice we're mak - ing,_____ we're sav - ing our__ own lives.__ It's true__

__ we make__ bet - ter days,__ just you__ and me.__

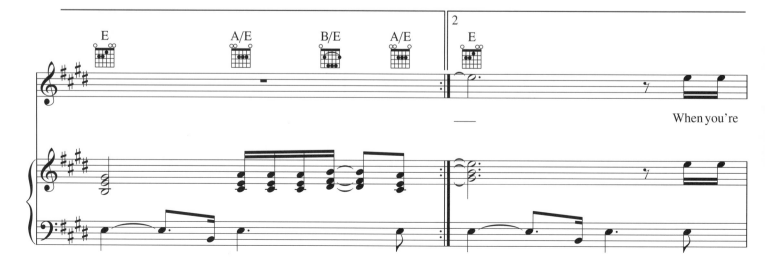

__ When you're

we are the chil - dren, we are the ones _

_ to make a bright - er day, _ so let's _ start giv - ing. There's a

choice we're mak - ing, _ we're sav - ing our _ own lives. _ It's true _

_ we make bet - ter days, just you _ and me. _ We are the world, _

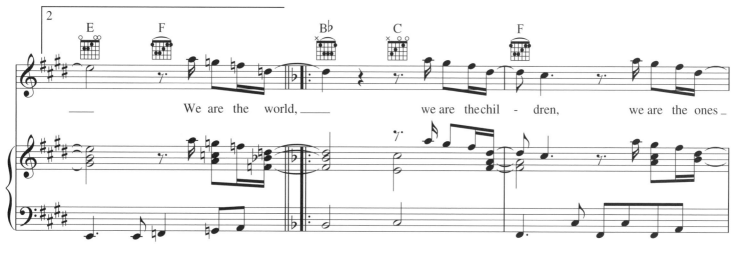

We are the world, _____ we are the chil - dren, we are the ones _

_____ to make a bright - er day, _ so let's _ start giv - ing. There's a

choice we're mak - ing, _____ we're sav - ing our _ own lives. _ It's true _

_____ we make bet - ter days, _ just you _ and me. _ We are the world, _

Y.M.C.A.

Words and Music by JACQUES MORALI,
HENRI BELOLO and VICTOR WILLIS

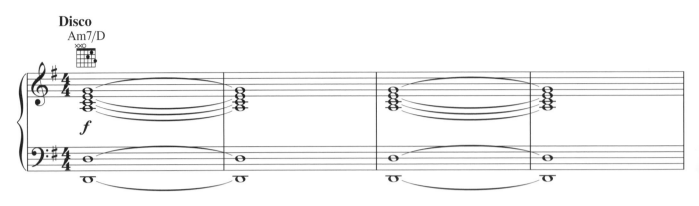

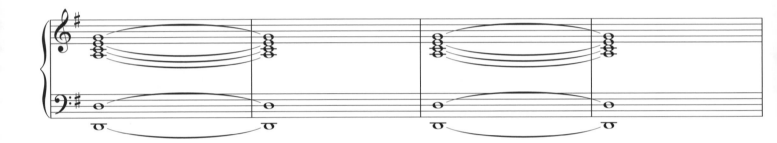

1. Young man, there's no
2., 3. (See additional lyrics)

young man, when you're short on your dough. You can stay there and I'm

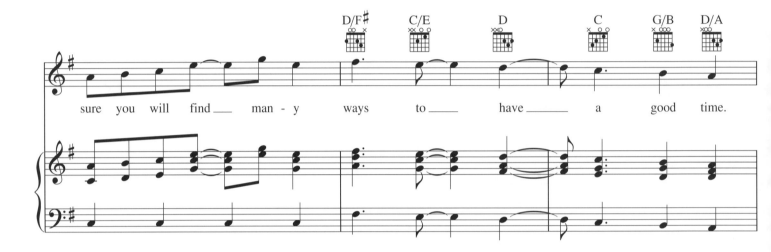

sure you will find ___ man - y ways to ___ have ___ a good time.

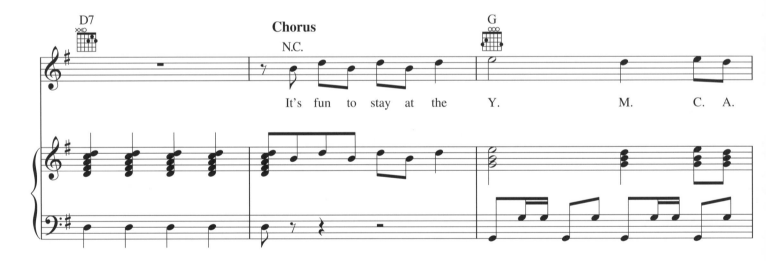

Chorus

N.C.

It's fun to stay at the Y. M. C. A.

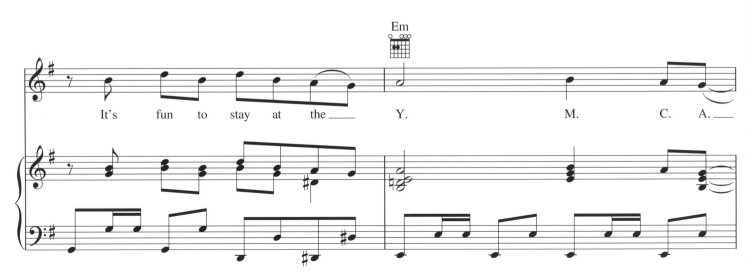

It's fun to stay at the ___ Y. M. C. A. ___

They have ev-er-y-thing ___ for young

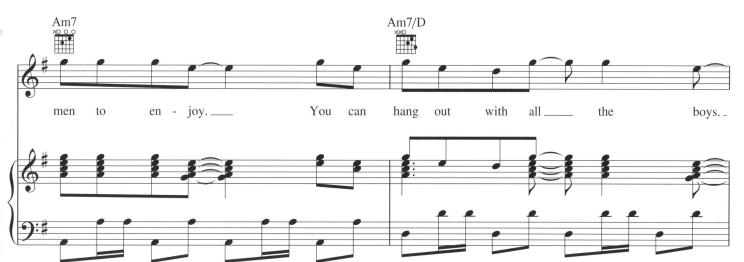

men to en-joy. ___ You can hang out with all ___ the boys. _

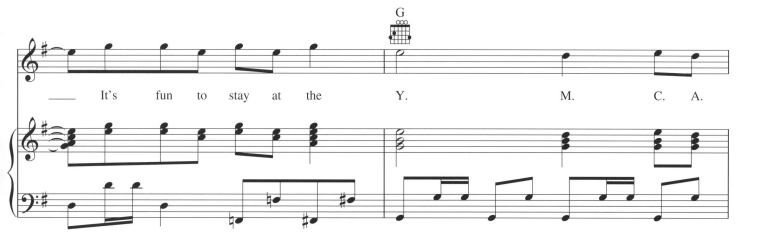

___ It's fun to stay at the Y. M. C. A.

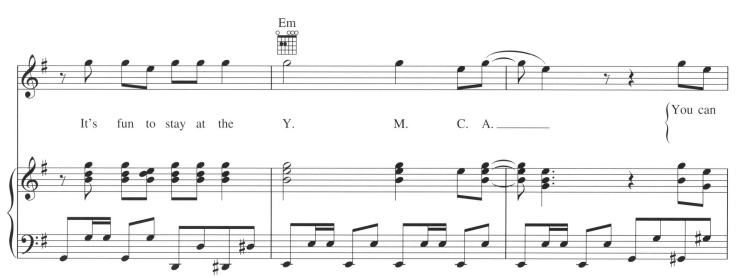

It's fun to stay at the Y. M. C. A. ___ You can

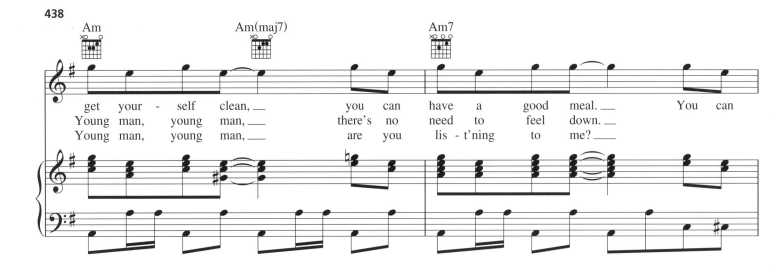

get your-self clean, ___ you can have a good meal. ___ You can
Young man, young man, ___ there's no need to feel down. ___ You can
Young man, young man, ___ are you lis - t'ning to me? ___

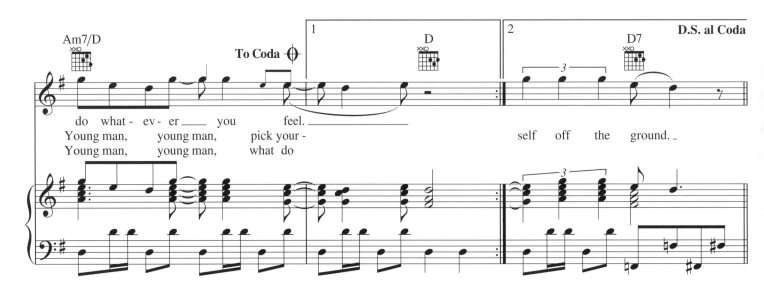

D.S. al Coda

do what - ev - er ___ you feel. ___
Young man, young man, pick your - self off the ground. ___
Young man, young man, what do

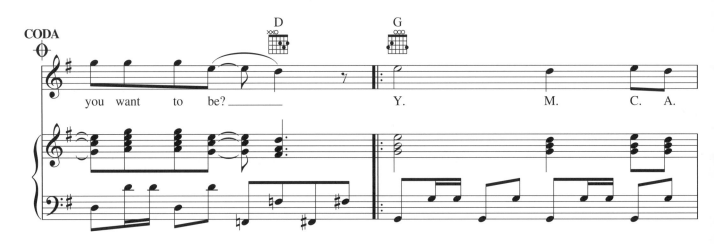

you want to be? _____ Y. M. C. A.

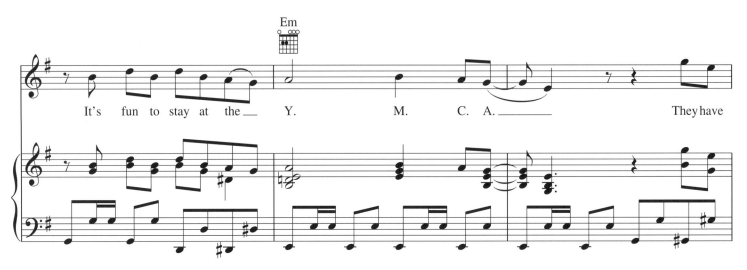

It's fun to stay at the ___ Y. M. C. A. ___ They have

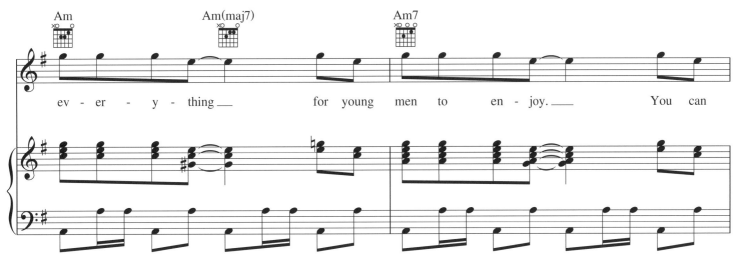

ev - er - y - thing ___ for young men to en - joy. ___ You can

hang out with all ___ the boys. ___ It's fun to stay at the

Additional Lyrics

2. Young man, are you listening to me?
   I said, young man, what do you want to be?
   I said, young man, you can make real your dreams
   But you've got to know this one thing.

   No man does it all by himself.
   I said, young man, put your pride on the shelf.
   And just go there to the Y.M.C.A.
   I'm sure they can help you today.
   Chorus

3. Young man, I was once in your shoes.
   I said, I was down and out and with the blues.
   I felt no man cared if I were alive.
   I felt the whole world was so jive.

   That's when someone come up to me
   And said, "Young man, take a walk up the street.
   It's a place there called the Y.M.C.A.
   They can start you back on your way."
   Chorus

YOU BELONG WITH ME

Words and Music by TAYLOR SWIFT
and LIZ ROSE

Recorded a half step lower.

I'm in the room, it's a typ-i-cal Tues-day night.___ I'm lis-t'nin' to the kind of

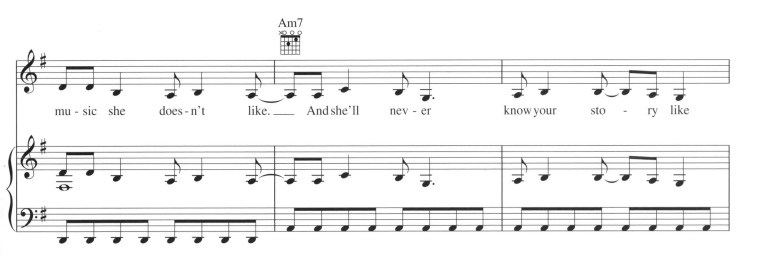

mu-sic she does-n't like.___ And she'll nev-er know your sto-ry like

I do.

But she wears short skirts,
She wears high heels,

I wear T-shirts.
I wear sneak-ers.

She's cheer cap-tain and I'm on the bleach-ers,

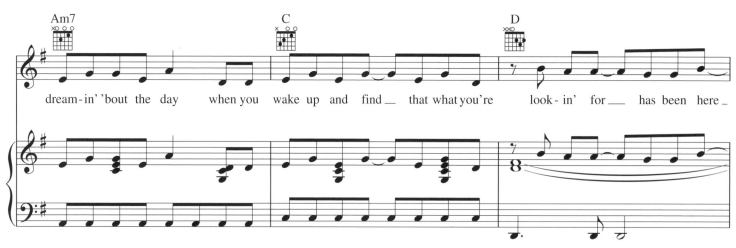

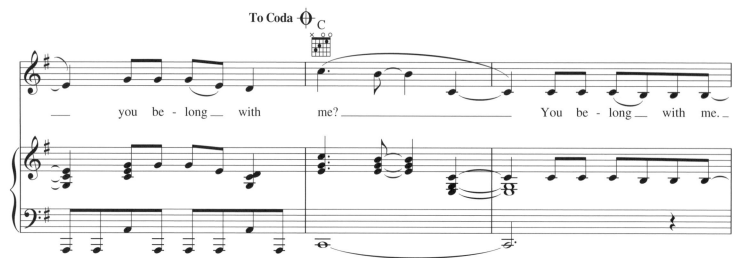

Walk - in' the streets with you __

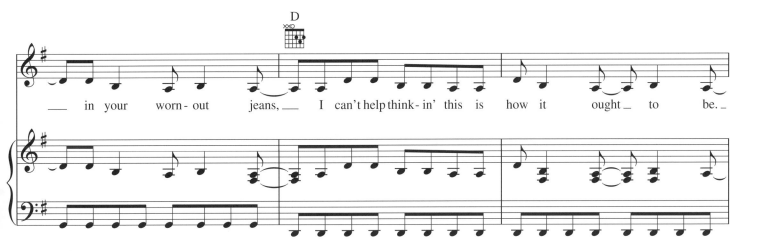

__ in your worn - out jeans, __ I can't help think-in' this is how it ought __ to be. __

Laugh-in' on a park bench, think-in' to my - self, __ "Hey, is - n't this

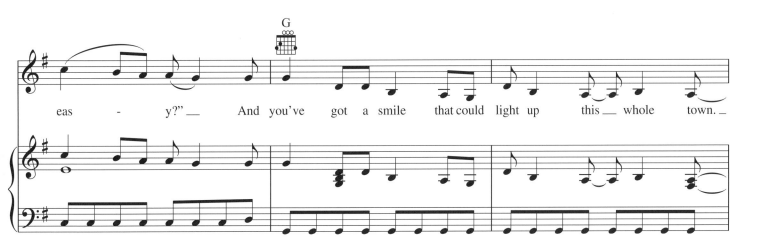

eas - y?" __ And you've got a smile that could light up this __ whole town. __

I have-n't seen it in a while since she brought you down. You say you're fine. I know you

D.S. al Coda

bet - ter than that. Hey, what you do - in' with a girl like that?

CODA

me? Stand - in' by and wait-

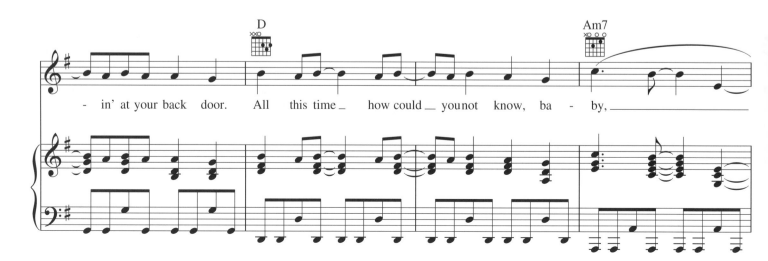

- in' at your back door. All this time how could you not know, ba - by,

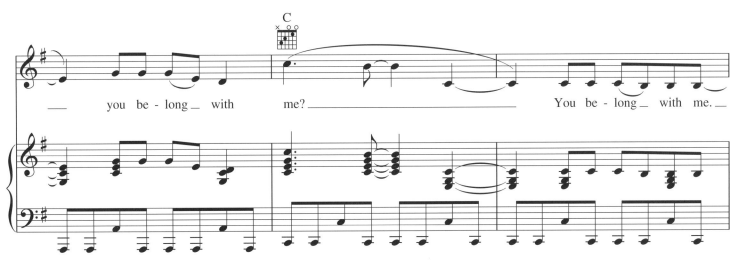

you be-long__ with me?_____ You be-long__ with me.__

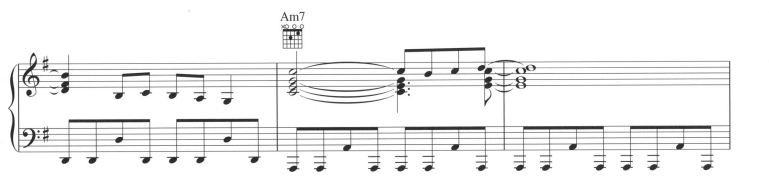

Oh, I re-mem-ber you driv-in' to my house in the

who un-der-stands you? Been here all a - long. So why can't you

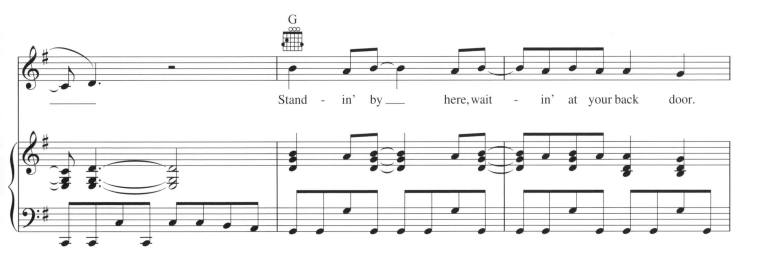

see you be - long with me?

Stand - in' by here, wait - in' at your back door.

All this time how could you not know, ba - by,

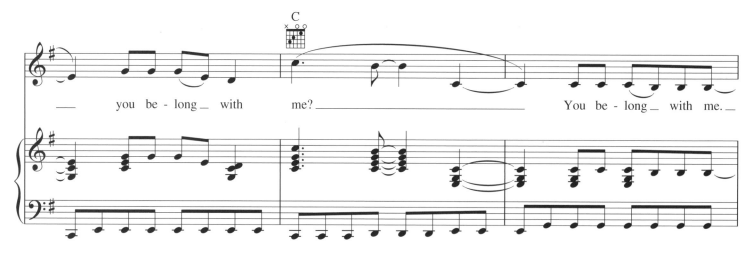

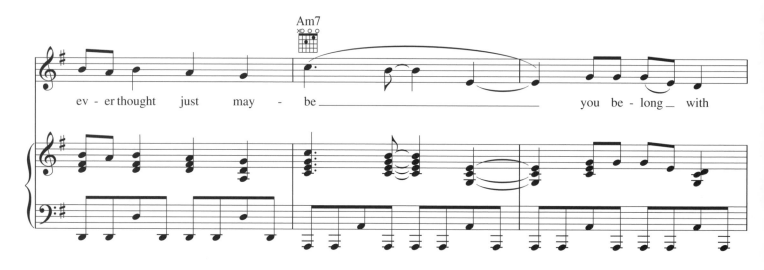

YOU'RE BEAUTIFUL

Words and Music by JAMES BLUNT,
SACHA SKARBEK and AMANDA GHOST

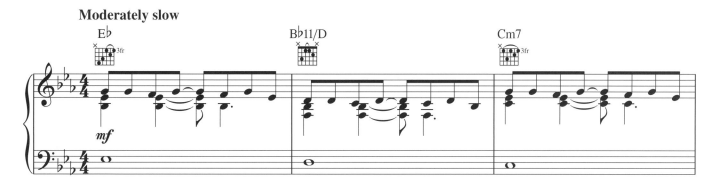

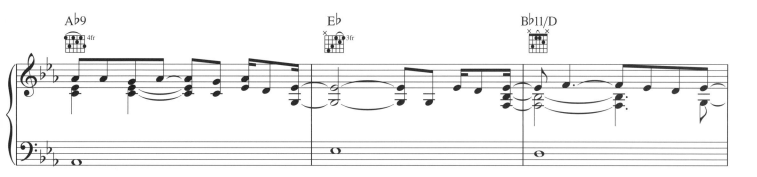

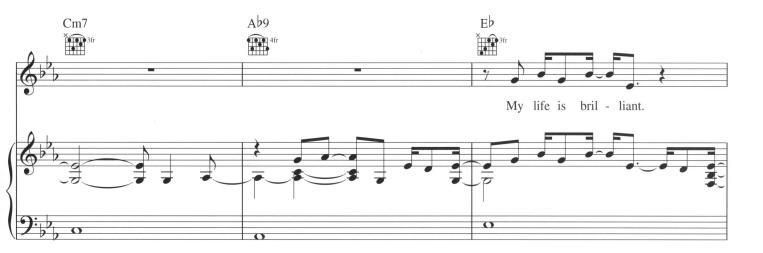

My life is bril - liant.

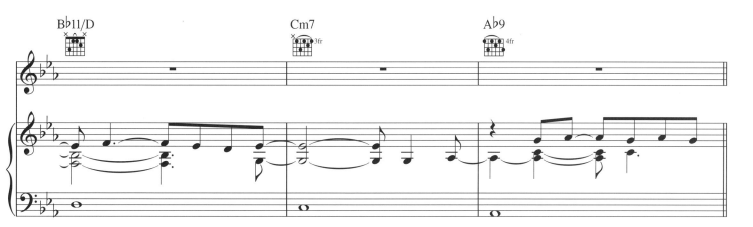

CODA I

La la la la. La la la la.

D.S. al Coda II

La la la la la.

CODA II

thought up that I should be with you.

But it's time to face the truth;

I will nev-er be with you.

YOU'RE NO GOOD

Words and Music by
CLINT BALLARD, JR.

you, don't blame me and I'm go - in' my way; ___ for -

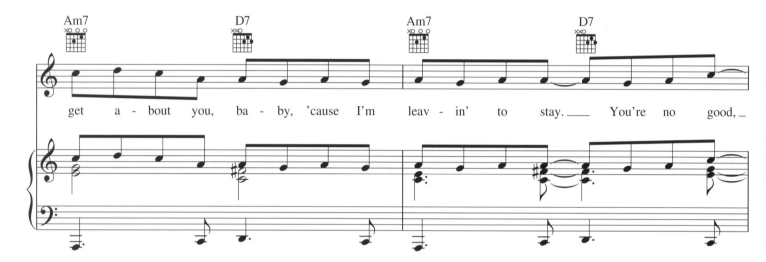

get a - bout you, ba - by, 'cause I'm leav - in' to stay. ___ You're no good, ___

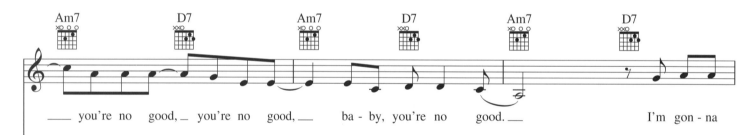

___ you're no good, ___ you're no good, ___ ba - by, you're no good. ___ I'm gon - na

say it a - gain, ___ you're no good, ___ you're no good, ___ you're no good. ___

You've Lost That Lovin' Feelin'

Words and Music by BARRY MANN,
CYNTHIA WEIL and PHIL SPECTOR

You nev - er

close your eyes ___ an - y - more when I kiss your lips. ___
wel - come look ___ in your eyes when I reach for you. ___

___ And there's no ten - der - ness ___ like be - fore in your fin - ger - tips.
___ And, girl, you're start - ing to ___ crit - i - cize lit - tle things ___ I do. ___

gone, gone, gone, whoa oh oh oh.

Now, there's no

Ba-by, ba-by, I'd get down on my knees for you.

If that would make you love me like you used to

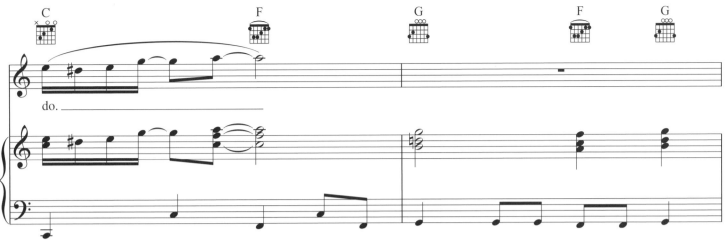

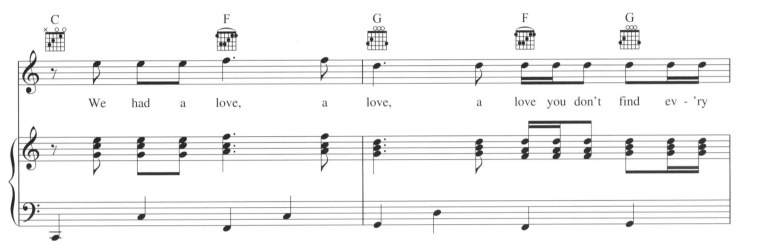

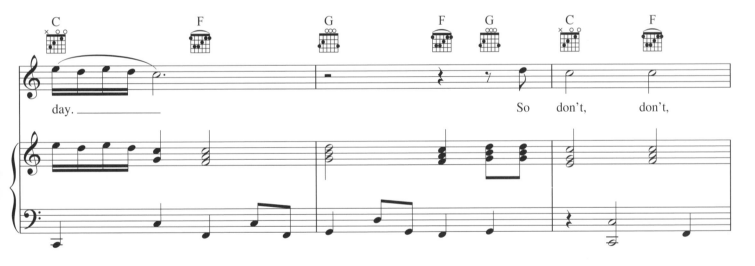

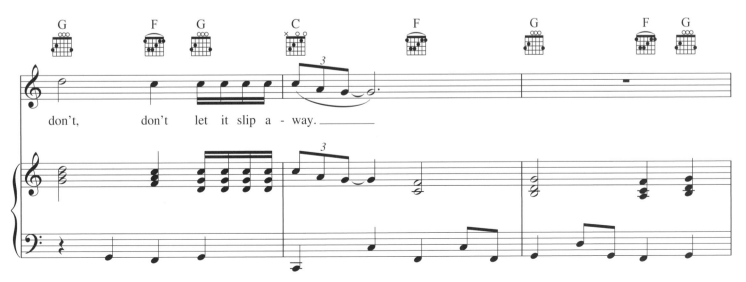

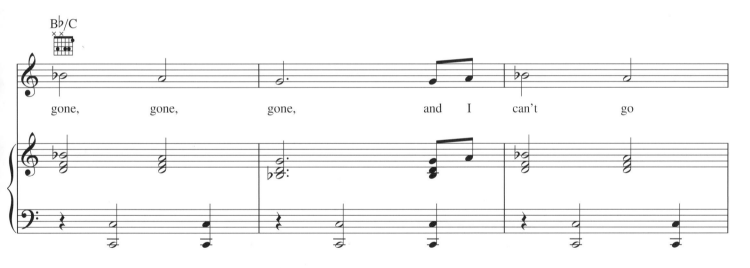

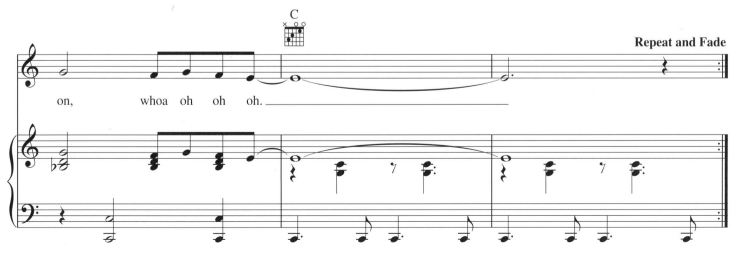

Pro Vocal® Series
Songbook & Sound-Alike CD
Sing 8 Great Songs
with a Professional Band

Whether you're a karaoke singer or an auditioning professional, the Pro Vocal® series is for you! Unlike most karaoke packs, each book in the Pro Vocal Series contains the lyrics, melody, and chord symbols for eight hit songs. The CD contains demos for listening, and separate backing tracks so you can sing along. The CD is playable on any CD player, but it is also enhanced so PC and Mac computer users can adjust the recording to any pitch without changing the tempo! Perfect for home rehearsal, parties, auditions, corporate events, and gigs without a backup band.

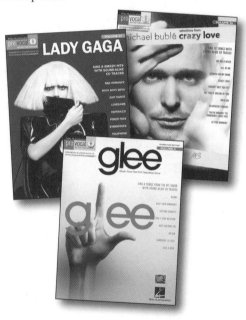

Visit Hal Leonard online at
www.halleonard.com

7777 W. BLUEMOUND RD. P.O. BOX 13819 MILWAUKEE, WI 53213

Prices, contents, & availability subject to change without notice.

0112